CIVIL SOCIETY THROUGH THE LIFECOURSE

Also available in the Civil Society and Social Change series

Civil Society and the Family
By **Esther Muddiman**, **Sally Power** and **Chris Taylor**

HB £75.00 ISBN 9781447355526
208 pages October 2020

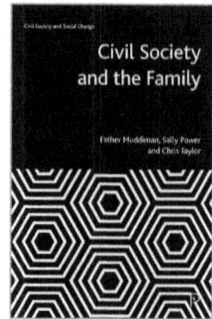

Putting Civil Society in Its Place
Governance, Metagovernance and
Subjectivity
By **Bob Jessop**

HB £75.00 ISBN 9781447354956
248 pages September 2020

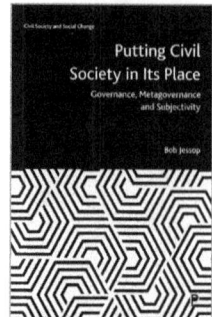

The Foundational Economy and Citizenship
Comparative Perspectives on Civil Repair
Edited by **Filippo Barbera** and
Ian Rees Jones

HB £75.00 ISBN 9781447353355
200 pages September 2020

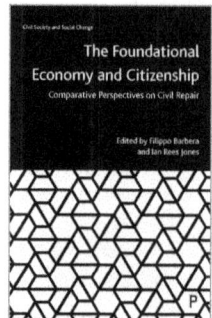

Published with the Wales Institute of Social &
Economic Research, Data & Methods Civil Society
Research Centre

W/SERD

For more information about the series visit

bristoluniversitypress.co.uk/civil-society-and-social-change

CIVIL SOCIETY THROUGH THE LIFECOURSE

Edited by
Sally Power

W/SERD

P

First published in Great Britain in 2022 by

Policy Press, an imprint of
Bristol University Press
University of Bristol
1-9 Old Park Hill
Bristol
BS2 8BB
UK
t: +44 (0)117 374 6645
e: bup-info@bristol.ac.uk

Details of international sales and distribution partners are available at
policy.bristoluniversitypress.co.uk

British Library Cataloguing in Publication Data
A catalogue record for this book is available from the British Library

ISBN 978-1-4473-5483-3 hardcover
ISBN 978-1-4473-5484-0 paperback
ISBN 978-1-4473-5487-1 ePub
ISBN 978-1-4473-5486-4 ePdf

Cover design: Cliff ord Hayes
Front cover image: Black and white geometric pattern ©Freepik.com

Contents

List of tables and figures

Tables

Figures

Notes on contributors

Ceryn Evans is Lecturer in the School of Education at Swansea University. Her research interests include young people's post-16 transitions to further and higher education, training and employment, with particular attention to social class and place and their role in young people's transitions. She is also interested in the relationship between higher education and civil society, with particular interest in higher education's role in graduates' civic participation. She has worked as part of a research team at the Wales Institute of Social & Economic Research & Data (WISERD) at Cardiff University between 2015 and 2017.

Jennifer May Hampton is an early career researcher based at WISERD. She has a background in educational research and statistics, although her research covers a wide range of substantive topics. This includes interdisciplinary work in the areas of education, children's well-being, religion and politics, with the latter examining issues of intergenerational transmission and generational difference. Currently, she is Research Associate in the newly established WISERD Education Data Lab – an ESRC-funded initiative, supporting the Welsh education sector through large-scale and administrative data analysis.

Jesse Heley is Senior Lecturer in the Department of Geography and Earth Sciences at Aberystwyth University. His research focuses on the dynamics of change in the countryside, with a particular focus on the impacts of globalisation on rural communities, rural identity and cultures of volunteering. His work also considers the relationship between rural and urban spaces, rural development strategies and spatial planning.

Martijn J.A. Hogerbrugge worked as a Quantitaive Research Associate at WISERD, before working as a researcher for the Netherlands Civil Service. His PhD was on the bidirectional influence of family relations and negative life events at the ICS Graduate School in the Netherlands. His current research addresses the social participation of older people and the impact of crime and deprivation, while his research interests extend to family sociology, intergenerational and sibling relations, social gerontology, the use of multi-actor data and quantitative research methods.

Laura Jones is a researcher in the Department of Geography and Earth Sciences at Aberystwyth University. She has worked on several research projects focused on aspects of rural communities, land use and change, including the FP7 DERREG project (*Developing Europe's Rural Regions in an Era of Globalization*) and the Wales Rural Observatory.

Esther Muddiman is a postdoctoral researcher based at WISERD. Her role includes working with the series editors to oversee the development and delivery of the Civil Society and Social Change book series. Her research explores the relationship between education, civil society and youth engagement. Building on a background in the sociology of education, her current work considers children's rights and the role of the family in people's accounts of civic, political and environmental engagement.

Rhian Powell is a PhD researcher in the School of Social Sciences at Cardiff University, based in WISERD. Her research explores what inheritance decisions can reveal about relationships to civil society, family and the state. The research aims to provide an insight into how civil society, the family and wealth are regarded and elicit understanding about the long-term sustainability of charities.

Sally Power is Professor in the School of Social Sciences at Cardiff University, and Director of WISERD. She directed the Generations Theme of the ESRC/WISERD Civil Society Research Centre. In addition to her work on civil society, she is also interested in young people's trajectories and the sociology of education policy.

Chris Taylor is Professor of Social Sciences at Cardiff University and is the Academic Director for the Cardiff University Social Science Research Park. He has undertaken a wide range of interdisciplinary research in the fields of education and civil society and has published extensively on issues of participation and inequalities.

Sophie Yarker is Research Fellow working on the Ambition for Ageing Programme led by the Greater Manchester Centre for Voluntary Organisation (GMCVO). Her work considers the themes of belonging, community and urban regeneration, and she has previously worked across two ESRC-funded projects investigating the changing nature of civil society in local communities.

Acknowledgements

This book would not have been possible without the support of the Economic and Social Research Council (ESRC), which funds the WISERD Civil Society Research Centre (Award Numbers ES/L009099/1 and ES/S012435/1). The chapters largely come from the projects within the Centre's *Generations* strand of research which has explored the intergenerational and lifecourse dimensions of civil society.

I would like to thank not only the individual contributors who participated in the projects reported here, but also the wider WISERD community. The ideas in this book were developed through debates and discussions with colleagues at various awaydays and conferences. In addition to the academic input from WISERD colleagues, this book would not have been possible without the technical and administrative support from the WISERD hub team. Particular thanks go to Samuel Jones and Catriona Dickson for their data management skills, to Jane Graves and Chloe McDonnell for organising the events and writing workshops where we shared ideas, and to Alexandra Williams and Tina Woods for their general oversight of WISERD.

Finally, our grateful thanks go to the various research participants who gave up their time to be interviewed, filled in surveys and gave consent for the data to be shared.

Exploring civil society through a lifecourse approach

Sally Power

There has been growing concern over recent decades about the future health of civil society. Robert Putnam (2001) has famously charted the decline in civil society in the US – a decline that he believes has devastating consequences for levels of trust and the future of democracy in America. Here in the UK, there have also been concerns that civil society is in a poor state. For example, there is evidence of an ongoing decline in the number of volunteers (DDCMS 2019), a continuing drop in charitable giving and a steady deterioration in trust in charities, with only a minority now believing that charities are trustworthy (CAF 2019). In terms of political engagement, there also appears to have been a decline in campaigning, even through online petitions (CAF 2019). Membership of trade unions is also at the lowest point in their history (DBEIS 2017).

These various studies not only signal an overall decline in civic engagement, they also reveal generational differences. It is generally the older generations who are more likely to vote, to volunteer and to donate to charities. Young people are the least likely to vote, to volunteer or to donate. In general, and in contrast to their elders, young people are seen to lack a sense of social obligation and civic duty (see, for instance, Stein 2013). There are fears that an already-weakened civil society looks set to enter a phase of terminal decline.

Such predictions do not take into account, though, the possibility that levels of civic and political engagement may wax and wane over the lifecourse. Much of the literature on civil society tends to assume that one can make clear distinctions between those who are active participants and those who are not. This book challenges this assumption and shows how an individual's relationship with civil society changes over time as different lifecourse phases and events both promote and hinder civil society participation. This does not mean that we can ignore broader social trends – or that there is no cause for concern. The trick, as C. Wright Mills argued so many years ago, is to link biography to structure – to explore how the wider socio-historical landscape connects with the 'the inner life and external career' of individuals (1970: 11). The lifecourse approach offers one way of attempting to do this.

The lifecourse approach

A lifecourse perspective is helpful in terms of understanding the relationship between biographies, social change and civil society for a number of reasons. These include the direct correspondence between age and engagement with civil society, the ability to consider the antecedents that shape our later involvement in civil society and how our relationship with civil society changes over time. Elder, one of the principal architects of the lifecourse approach, and his colleagues (Elder et al 2003) outline five 'paradigmatic principles' that will help us to grasp the complexity of linking individual biographies to the wider social structures and social change. These are outlined alongside a commentary on how we relate these principles to the study of civil society in this book.

1. *The principle of lifespan development: human development and ageing are lifelong processes*
   There is often, within sociology and psychology, the often tacit assumption that it is only the developmental years that really count – that when one leaves school, one's life trajectory and overall social orientation is already determined. Of course, these early years are important – however, they are formative rather than determining. Personal life events, such as parenthood, will profoundly change individuals and their capacity to engage with civil society. So too will wider social changes, such as economic restructuring that leads to redundancy, or increasing longevity that leads to 'beanpole households' (Bengtson et al 1990) and 'sandwiched' grandparents (Wellard 2011). All of these changes both increase and decrease an individual's capacity to engage with civil society – as well as shaping their political sensitivities and dispositions to engage.
2. *The principle of agency: individuals construct their own lifecourse through the choices they take within the opportunities and constraints of history and social circumstance*
   Strongly connected to the preceding principle, it is important to bear in mind that while broader structures frame opportunities and constraints, they do not override human agency. The choices that people make *matter* – even if they cannot see all the consequences

of their actions. The massification of higher education, for example, has meant that more and more young people are able to choose to go to university. This has opened up spaces for civic engagement through which young people have the opportunity to develop civic sensibilities and skills. These have important consequences for their subsequent trajectories. Similarly, increased longevity gives older people more opportunity to pursue interests and causes beyond their working life. The extent to which they realise these opportunities will depend on their own choices, although these are framed within parameters defined not only by material resources but by social class, gender, 'race' and ethnicity.

3. *The principle of time and place: the lifecourse of individuals is embedded and shaped by the historical times and places they experience over their lifetime*

Our lives develop in and with communities – communities that are geographically and temporally bounded. These specificities have important implications for how different generations in different places understand and act out social virtues. They reveal changing definitions of 'proper' and 'appropriate' behaviours for men and women, for adults and children. The data that are drawn upon in the book come from individuals who have grown up in the UK, and particularly in Wales. Their experiences, though, span nearly a century. The oldest generation represented in the book would have been alive during, and possibly even fought in, the Second World War. They are likely to understand the nature of civic duty very differently from the youngest generation represented in the book – young people who were born well into this century. Wales is also a context which has seen massive secularisation. From being the most religious country in the UK, it is now the least religious. Again, given the close association between religion and civil society, this will have significant bearing on the continuation or decline of particular forms of civic participation.

4. *The principle of timing: the developmental antecedents and consequences of life transitions, events and behavioural patterns vary according to their timing in a person's life*

There is increasing variation in the timing of transitions and key events in people's lives. For instance, while some young people do leave school at 16, increasing numbers experience extended amounts of further and higher education. The ages at which women become mothers varies widely – from the teenage years up until their 40s and even 50s. There are also increasing disparities in the age at which people retire from paid employment. Some of these transitions are planned, some are unplanned. Some are welcome and some are not. These different timings have consequences for individuals, in terms of their political sensibilities, social networks and resources. And it is of course important to remember that the capacity to control transitions and plan for lifecourse stages will depend on the wealth of social networks and resources that can be drawn upon.

5. *The principle of linked lives: lives are lived interdependently and socio-historical influences are expressed through this network of shared relationships*
   This principle really needs to be emphasised, particularly in relation to civil society where there is a tendency in the literature to bracket out the domestic sphere – or even present the family as being somehow in opposition to civil society (see Power et al 2018). Lives are linked most intimately within the family, and relations between grandparents, parents and children are crucial in understanding how dispositions and civic 'virtues' are fostered. Outside the family, as young people become more independent, the linkages change – new influences come from friendships at university and work, from networks forged through marriage. All of these links shape an individual's awareness and propensity to become engaged in civil society. We know, for instance, that church membership in particular is likely to be an important conduit between the individual and civil society.

It is improbable that any single empirical research project could enact these principles fully. Nevertheless, through combining the insights from a number of different projects, we hope that this book will try to stay faithful to the overall ambition of the lifecourse approach. The chapters all draw from a range of empirical data collected and analysed as part of the ESRC-funded WISERD Civil Society Research Centre,[1] including cross-sectional, longitudinal in-depth interview data to explore how lifecourse transitions and events both promote and inhibit civil society participation. The book examines not only the degree of engagement, but the changing nature and priorities of citizens as they manage the contingencies of career, family and old age within different contexts.

Framing civic and political participation

Civil society is a notoriously slippery concept – one which we could spend most of the book discussing. Many of the debates around the term are about its theoretical positioning (where it sits in relation to the public and private spheres, the state and the market). As we have argued elsewhere (Power et al 2018), while these debates are important, we also badly need greater empirical elucidation of the circumstances, processes and practices that contribute to (or detract from) a vibrant civil society.

Ekman and Amnå (2012), after an extensive review of the literature, conclude that the concepts of both civic engagement and political participation – all of which are seen as key constituents of civil society – are often invoked in ways that are either too broad or too narrow, and with little sense of the relationship between the two. For example, they point out that, in *Bowling Alone*, Putnam (2001) uses the term 'civic engagement' to cover 'just about everything from reading newspapers, political participation, social networks and interpersonal trust to associational involvement' (Ekman and Amnå 2012: 284). Critics have argued that this has stretched what counts as civic engagement to the point that it has potentially become a useless concept – leading to confusion rather than illumination (Berger 2009).

If the concept of civic engagement is too broad, Ekman and Amnå (2012: 286) claim that what counts as political participation tends to be too narrowly defined, focusing only on voting or other forms of participation in formal political processes. In addition, while it is often assumed that civic engagement and political participation are somehow connected, the nature of that connection is often unclear. In order to address these concerns, Ekman and Amnå (2012) have constructed a typology (Table 1.1) that draws attention to the importance of the two different kinds of participation, arguing that civic participation has a latent political function that is related to manifest political participation.

Organisation of the book

Gilleard and Higgs (2016: 302) identify two approaches within lifecourse sociology – one that focuses on the stratification *of* the lifecourse and concentrates on different 'stages' and how these produce particular obligations and opportunities, and another that concentrates on stratification *over* the lifecourse and focuses on how events and institutions shape biographies. These two approaches have methodological implications. Survey and cross-sectional panel data inevitably privilege the examination of stratification *of* the lifecourse, while life-history interview and longitudinal data tend to privilege stratification *over* the lifecourse. We have tried, though, wherever possible, to bring the two dimensions together.

The organisation of the book is largely chronological, beginning with an overview of civil and political participation across the lifecourse,

Table 1.1: A typology of different forms of civic and political participation

	Civic participation (latent-political)		Political participation (manifest)	
	Social involvement (attention)	Civic engagement (action/ practice)	Formal participation	Activism
Individual forms	Taking interest in politics and society Perceiving politics as important	Writing to an editor Giving money to charity Discussing politics and societal issues Reading news about political issues Recycling	Voting in elections or referenda Contacting political representatives or civil servants Running for or holding public office Donating money to political parties or organisations	Boycotting goods/services Signing petitions Supporting campaigns (e.g. wristbands) Handing out political leaflets
Collective forms	Belonging to an association with a societal focus Identifying with a certain ideology and/ or party Lifestyle related involvement, such as veganism.	Volunteering Charity work or faith-based community work Activity within community-based organisations	Membership of a political party or trade union Activity within a party, an organisation or trade union	Involvement in new social movements of forums Demonstrating, participating in strikes, protests and other actions Civil disobedience actions

Source: adapted from Ekman and Amnå (2012: 295).

before considering school students' engagement with civil society and, finally, the priorities and perspectives of older people when thinking about the legacy they will leave after their death.

In Chapter 2, Chris Taylor illustrates how Elder and Giele's (2009) framework for understanding the lifecourse can be readily applied to the study of the relationship between individuals, families and social groups with civil society. The chapter uses longitudinal data from the British Birth Cohort Studies to chart the changing patterns of civic and political participation over the adult lifecourse within the UK. Through setting these data against broader structural changes, the chapter also attempts to identify those aspects that relate to the lifecourse rather than social change. These results are compared against other key international studies in order to compare and contrast our relationship with civil society in different sociopolitical contexts.

Chapter 3 (Sally Power) looks at school students' engagement in civil society – an issue about which very little is really known – despite those negative media portrayals of a self-obsessed and civically disengaged generation. Drawing on survey data from 1,000 14-year-olds, this chapter examines the evidence that may support – or otherwise – some of the commonly held assumptions about young people's self-interestedness. It examines the frequency and nature young people's civic and political participation, including associational membership, volunteering and charitable giving. Although the young people are too young to vote, the chapter discusses their participation in a range of other forms of politically oriented activities, such as participating in online petitions and boycotts. It also examines their attitudes towards the state and civil society – and the implications of these for their future civic and political engagement.

In Chapter 4, Ceryn Evans, Esther Muddiman and Chris Taylor explore the relationship between participation in higher education and the formation of social and political attitudes and civic participation. With the 'massification' of higher education, going to university is an increasingly commonly experienced lifecourse stage. In-depth interviews with UK graduates reveal the role of both pre-university experiences (including parents' social and political attitudes and participation) and university experiences (namely, the degree studied at university and social networks and friendships made while at university) in the formation of social attitudes and civic participation. Thus – while pre-university experiences are hugely important in the development of political views, interest in politics and civic participation – going to university has a distinctive role in amplifying pre-university social attitudes and civic participation. The chapter discusses the significance of the university experience, and particularly the extent to which this experience is shaped by disciplinary specialisms.

In Chapter 5, Esther Muddiman draws on qualitative data from interviews with 20 parents of teenagers to explore how parenthood disrupts, complements and triggers various types of civic engagement. The chapter describes how becoming a parent can limit an individual's ability to maintain their commitment to existing voluntary activities/ associational memberships, disrupting previous ties to civil society. However, it also finds that parenthood provides new opportunities for engagement, especially via educational institutions and parental networks; and that the transition to parenthood itself can lead individuals to reflect on their own relationship to society and the values that they would like to pass on to their children: the desire to model 'good citizenship' within the family home can act as a gateway for participation in civically minded practices.

Volunteering in later life is the focus of Chapter 6 (Martijn J.A. Hogerbrugge). Due to increases in life expectancy and diminishing fertility rates, the age distribution of the population in the UK and other Western countries contains relatively more older persons. While discussions typically highlight the economic and governmental challenges of an ageing population, the higher proportion of older adults also has the potential to bring positive impacts to families and local communities, for instance through volunteering. Thus, given the growing pool of older potential volunteers, it will become evermore important for voluntary sector agencies to get a clearer understanding of what the attitudes and motivations are for older people in terms of volunteering. So far, international research on volunteering by older adults has mostly focused on the determinants affecting the likelihood of an older individual to volunteer. As will be shown in this chapter, distinguishing volunteers from non-volunteers is a far too simplified approach to the study of volunteering as it ignores variations in the number of times and hours people volunteer and the diverse range of motivations they have, as well as how these various aspects relate to each other. Hogerbrugge uses data from the National Survey of Volunteering and Charitable Giving to reveal the complexity of patterns of volunteering undertaken by older people in England.

In Chapter 7, Jennifer May Hampton and Esther Muddiman turn their attention to a lifecourse event that affects older members of the family through focusing on how becoming a grandparent both hinders and fosters civic participation. In an ageing society, older people are more likely to experience becoming a grandparent and to have this role for longer than ever before. The chapter uses multiple sources of data, including large-scale survey data (the UK Household Longitudinal Survey – also known as 'Understanding Society') as well as in-depth interviews with a sample of English and Welsh grandparents, and shows that grandparents play a specific role in providing childcare to their grandchildren and that this investment may simultaneously limit and enable differing forms of civic participation, distinct from their peers without grandchildren.

Another common lifecourse event experienced in later life is retirement. In Chapter 8, Laura Jones, Jesse Heley and Sophie Yarker focus on the lifecourse transition from work to volunteering, and subsequent experiences of civil society participation. Since the 1980s, demographic as well as political and economic changes at the global and national scale have led to increasingly differentiated experiences of the retirement process. For some, this includes retiring in possession of good levels of health, education and disposable incomes, which in turn is shaping different outlooks and expectations regarding this phase of the lifecourse. Drawing on recent work in human geography on the relational geographies of ageing, the chapter finds that the boundaries experienced between work and retirement are increasingly blurred. The decision-making surrounding this transition process is shaped by interrelated factors and motivations including personal preferences, health, finances, family, place, biography, and caring roles and responsibilities. Importantly, the experience of volunteering is frequently made sense of through reference to working lives and the cultures and norms associated with paid employment. However, not all aspects of this latter comparison are desirable and the chapter concludes by reflecting on the extent to which there is an over-professionalisation of volunteering for retirees.

The final empirical chapter (Chapter 9) examines the perspectives and priorities of older people when thinking about the legacy they will leave after their death. Rhian Powell draws on semi-structured interviews with 22 people willing to discuss their ideas about what they would like to do with their assets after they pass away, and particularly whether or not they intend to leave a legacy gift to charity in their will. This research shows that decisions to leave a charitable bequest are complex and require the donor to balance a number of potentially competing obligations – particularly between the family, civil society and the state. When participants think about their inheritance, considerations about these competing institutions are strongly connected and, consequently, how participants think about one will affect their views on the others. For this reason, it is impossible to only discuss participants' attitudes towards civil society without also considering their attitudes towards family and the state.

The final chapter draws the book to a close. After briefly summarising the principal findings of each of the chapters, it identifies emergent themes and reflects on the benefits and drawbacks of using a lifecourse approach to understand changing patterns of engagement with civil society. The chapter concludes with a brief examination of some of the implications of the principal findings for policy makers and other key stakeholders trying to promote greater levels of civic and political engagement.

Notes

[1] The WISERD/Civil Society Research Centre is a £7 million multi-institutional and multidisciplinary collaboration that involved research on 20 focused work-packages over a five-year programme (2014–19).

References

Bengtson, V.L., Rosenthal, C.J. and Burton, L.M. (1990) 'Families and aging: diversity and heterogeneity', in R.H. Binstock and L.K. George (eds) *Handbook of Aging and the Social Sciences* (3rd edn), New York: Academic Press, pp 263–87.

Berger, B. (2009) 'Political theory, political science and the end of civic engagement', *Perspectives on Politics*, 7(2): 335–50.

CAF (Charities Aid Foundation) (2019) *CAF UK Giving 2019: An Overview of Charitable Giving in the UK*, West Malling: Charities Aid Foundation. Available from: https://www.cafonline.org/about-us/publications/2019-publications/uk-giving-2019.

DBEIS (Department for Business, Energy and Industrial Strategy) (2017) Trade union statistics 2016. Available from: www.gov.uk/government/statistics/trade-union-statistics-2016.

DDCMS (Department for Digital, Culture, Media & Sport) (2019) *Community Life Survey*, London: DDCMS. Available from: https://assets.publishing.service.gov.uk/government/uploads/system/uploads/attachment_data/file/820610/Community_Life_Survey_2018-19_report.pdf.

Ekman, J. and Amnå, E. (2012) 'Political participation and civic engagement: towards a new typology', *Human Affairs*, 22(3): 283–300.

Elder, G.H. Jr and Giele, J.Z. (2009) 'Life course studies: an evolving field', in G.H. Elder Jr and J.Z. Giele (eds) *The Craft of Life Course Research*, New York: The Guilford Press, pp 1–24.

Elder, G.H. Jr, Johnson, M.K. and Crosnoe, R. (2003) 'The emergence and development of life course theory', in J.T. Mortimer and M.J. Shanahan (eds) *Handbook of the Life Course*, Boston, MA: Springer, pp 3–19.

Gilleard, C. and Higgs, P. (2016) 'Connecting life span development with the sociology of the life course: a new direction', *Sociology*, 50(2): 301–15.

M & C Saatchi (2017) *Risk, Realism and Ritalin*, London: Saatchi PR. Available from: http://mcsaatchitransform.com/src/assets/pdfs/MCTRANSFORM_RRR.pdf.

Mills, C.W. (1970) *The Sociological Imagination*, Harmondsworth: Pelican.

Power, S., Muddiman, E., Moles, K. and Taylor, C. (2018) 'Civil society: bringing the family back', *Journal of Civil Society*, 14(3): 193–206.

Putnam, R. (2001) *Bowling Alone: The Collapse and Revival of American Community*, New York: Simon & Schuster.

Stein, J. (2013) 'The me me me generation', *Time*, May. Available from: http://time.com/247/millennials-the-me-me-me-generation.

Wellard, S. (2011) *Doing It All? Grandparents, Childcare and Employment: An Analysis of British Social Attitudes Survey Data from 1998 and 2009*, London: Grandparents Plus. Available from: https://www.grandparentsplus.org.uk/report/doing-it-all-grandparents-childcare-and-employment/.

2

Civic participation over the lifecourse

Chris Taylor

Introduction

There is considerable value in exploring our relationship with civil society through the lifecourse for a number of reasons. These include the direct relationship between age and civil society, the ability to consider the antecedents that shape our later involvement in civil society and how our relationship with civil society changes over time. Elder and Giele's (2009) framework for understanding the lifecourse (Figure 2.1) can be readily applied to our study of the relationship between individuals, families and social groups with civil society.

There have only been a few studies that have examined civic participation over the lifecourse using such a perspective. For example, Hogg (2016) used life-history interviews with 26 older-aged volunteers in England in order to examine the nature of their volunteering behaviour over their lifecourse. Using lifecourse maps Hogg investigated Davis Smith and Gay's (2005) categorisation of older volunteers into three main types: constant (volunteering over the lifecourse with the same or similar organisations); serial (volunteering over the lifecourse but intermittently and with different organisations); and trigger (those who begin to volunteer later in life). Using retrospective life-history interviews, Hogg was able to demonstrate how volunteering was often intertwined with other work and non-work roles, so that volunteering 'should be understood as being highly situated within the rhythms and relations of everyday life' (2016: 186). And, clearly, these rhythms and relations change through the lifecourse.

Lindsey and Mohan (2018) also produced similar maps of volunteering trajectories using data from the British Household Panel Survey (BHPS) / Understanding Society (USoc) for more than 2,000 volunteers over 15 years (between 1996 and 2011). Their analysis highlighted the distinction between short-term volunteering (71 per cent of all volunteers) and long-term volunteering (29 per cent

Figure 2.1: Elder and Giele's framework for understanding the lifecourse

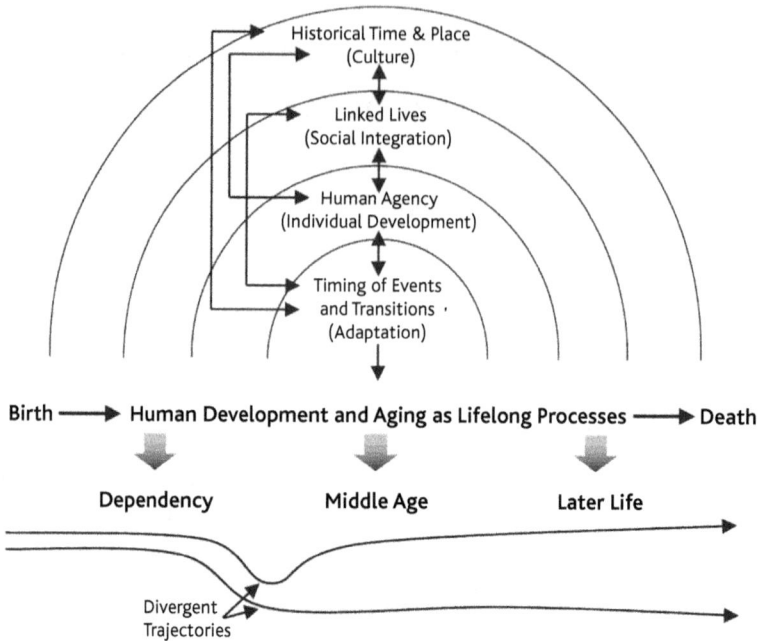

Source: Elder and Giele (2009: 11).

of volunteers). They were also able to demonstrate that over half of all voluntary 'episodes' reported by cohort members were undertaken by less than a third of those that had reported having 'ever' volunteered, what they describe as echoing the notion of a 'civic core' (Mohan and Bulloch 2012). However, in order to consider the interrelationships between volunteering and the lifecourse Lindsey and Mohan had to draw upon qualitative data from a different and smaller dataset, the Mass Observation Project. This was helpful in identifying particular life events as triggers for initiating or ending voluntary activity.

In addition to these UK studies there have also been a small number of other international studies that consider civic participation or volunteering over the lifecourse (Oesterle et al 2004; Rotolo and Wilson 2004; Tang 2006; Broese van Groenou and van Tilburg 2012). Some of these studies use cross-sectional data over time (for example, Tang 2006) or compare individuals of different ages at the same time (such as Rotolo and Wilson 2004). Such studies are useful in comparing the frequency of volunteering at different ages of the lifecourse and identifying how possible predictors of volunteering appear to have different influences at different stages of the lifecourse.

But few studies have been able to consider how an individual's involvement in civil society changes over their lifecourse. Even where this has been possible, most studies are only able to consider this over a limited period of time. For example, Broese van Groenou and van Tilburg (2012) could only track their participants' volunteering activity over a six-year period.

One of the most detailed and longest analyses of volunteering over the lifecourse was that of Lancee and Radl (2014). They used the German Socio-Economic Panel (SOEP) to study longitudinal data on the volunteering trajectories of 42,624 individuals aged between 18 and 80 years across 24 years of their life (from 1985 to 2009). With such a large age-range for cohort members, the authors were able to consider the influence of a wide variety of life events on volunteering, such as going to university, having children, changing employment, retiring and so on. Crucially, although Lancee and Radl observe the greater influence of family transitions on volunteering compared to labour market transitions, they conclude that life events actually have limited influence. Stability of volunteering behaviours (to volunteer or not to volunteer) was found to be a far more important explanation for predicting the occurrence of volunteering during the lifecourse.

The analysis by Lancee and Radl demonstrates the potential of studying volunteering over the entire adult lifecourse. But in the main, most other studies can only offer analysis over relatively short episodes during the lifecourse or are reliant on comparing different groups of individuals at different stages of the lifecourse.

Another feature that all these studies have in common is that they focus almost exclusively on volunteering and, specifically, on reported volunteering. Few studies consider the wider conceptualisation of civic participation, despite known limitations of how volunteering is perceived and reported, particularly in terms of informal volunteering. This is less problematic for more qualitative studies that can explore the concept of volunteering with participants during an interview, for example. However, qualitative studies rarely provide a robust longitudinal perspective, instead relying on a retrospective recall of events. Where longitudinal studies do exist, the nature of the surveys that underpin them does not have the opportunity to explore what is meant by volunteering. As a result, many analyses would seem to under-report the frequency of volunteering activity (Lindsey and Mohan 2018). Considering other forms of civic participation not only might help to mitigate some of the limitations of focusing exclusively on volunteering but could also provide a wider account of how individuals engage with civil society.

The aim of this chapter is to provide much-needed empirical analysis to chart the changing patterns of civic participation over the adult lifecourse within the UK. This analysis uses longitudinal data from the 1958 National Cohort Development Study (NCDS) which has been following the lives of more than 17,000 people born in England, Scotland and Wales during one week in 1958.

The analysis is designed to address some of the main limitations of previous studies in this area. First, unlike the studies already discussed, it compares the frequency of volunteering over the adult lifecourse with two other, frequently occurring, forms of civic participation – voting in UK general elections and trade union membership. Voting is the main way individuals in society exercise their political participation and trade union membership is a useful indicator of social participation, since motivations for membership are often driven by the interplay between individual needs and altruism. And second, by using the NCDS, the analysis examines civic participation over a 39-year period, from when the cohort turned 16 years old (in 1986) to when they were aged 55 years (in 2013) – the most recent collection of data from the cohort. This corresponds to nearly all of participants' working lives.

First, the chapter sets out to present the lifecourse trajectory of civic participation for this cohort of people by examining the frequency of these three forms of civic participation over time. Then, second, the analysis contrasts the lifecourse trajectories in civic participation for different groups of cohort members, based on their gender, education and social class. Since this is a birth cohort study of babies born in Britain during 1958 there is very limited scope to consider ethnicity in this analysis.

Measures of civic participation

This lifecourse analysis is based on one of the UK's major birth cohort studies, the NCDS. This is a longitudinal study of all people born in one week during 1958 across the whole of England, Wales and Scotland. It began with 17,415 babies and has involved 11 sweeps of data collection up to and including 2013 when the cohort were aged 55 years old (University of London, Institute of Education, Centre for Longitudinal Studies 2008a, 2008b, 2008c, 2008d, 2012, 2014, 2015). Over this time period data collection has involved a mixture of face-to-face, telephone and web interviews, self-completion surveys and cognitive and physical assessments. Since the study includes all babies born in the same week the NCDS is considered to be highly representative of the wider population.

There are, of course, numerous ways of conceptualising and measuring civic participation (Putnam 2000; Heitzmann et al 2009; Ekman and Amnå 2012). In this chapter, the analysis focuses upon three key measures of civic participation that reflect the broad spectrum of civic participation. The focus is constrained, inevitably, by what data has been collected from cohort members during the NCDS. And while the cohort study has asked about many different forms of civic participation at various points during the lifecourse, a key condition of this lifecourse perspective is to use measures that have been used repeatedly as the cohort has grown up. Consequently, three sets of measures of civic participation are used (Table 2.1): political participation, membership of a trade union and volunteering activity.

Table 2.1: Measures of civic participation

Age	Year	Political participation	Member of trade union	Formal volunteering activity
16yrs	1974			Undertakes (unpaid) voluntary work often or sometimes (A)
23yrs	1981	Voted in 1979 general election	Currently a member of a trade union	Undertook voluntary work in the past four weeks (A)
33yrs	1991	Voted in 1987 general election	Currently a member of a trade union or staff association	Active participation in at least one voluntary association (B)
42yrs	2000	Voted in 1997 general election	Currently a member of a trade union or staff association	Active participation in at least one voluntary association (B)
44yrs	2002	Biomedical sweep		
46yrs	2004	Voted in 2001 general election		Active participation in at least one voluntary association (B)
50yrs	2008	Voted in 2005 general election	Currently a member of a trade union	Undertakes (unpaid) voluntary work in past year (B) Active participation in at least one voluntary association (A)
55yrs	2013	Voted in 2010 general election		Undertakes (unpaid) voluntary work in past year (A)

Notes:
A = data on whether the cohort member has undertaken any unpaid voluntary work.
B = data on whether cohort members are active participants in at least one voluntary association.

The first measure of political participation is based on whether the cohort members voted in the most recent general election. This question has been asked at every sweep from the fifth sweep (at age 23 years) onwards (cohort members would not have been eligible to vote at earlier sweeps). As a measure this is fairly straightforward, although it is prone to recall bias (Himmelweit et al 1978). Furthermore, the time between the last general election and each sweep varies, for example, from two years (in Sweep 5 when the cohort members were aged 23 years) and four years (in Sweep 6 when the cohort members were aged 33 years). However, the impact of recall bias on the longitudinal analysis of this data is minimised. This is because the analysis considers the same people over time and therefore any systematic bias in recall bias on voting would generally remain constant over time.

The second measure is also relatively straightforward and is based on whether cohort members were members of a trade union at the time they were interviewed. In a couple of sweeps this also included membership of a staff association. However, the number of NCDS cohort members who were only members of a staff association was very small and is unlikely to impact on the subsequent analysis. Membership of a trade union (or staff association) has been asked four times over the cohort members lifecourse. In Sweep 9 (at age 46 years) cohort members were not asked if they were a member but instead asked whether they had taken part in a trade union activity since their last interview (which was two years previously). Being a member of a trade union and taking part in a union activity are clearly very different forms of civic engagement (and was reflected in the data) and so is not included in the subsequent analysis.

The third measure of civic participation considered here is based on the volunteering activity of the cohort members. This is the most complicated measure of the three because of the way cohort members were asked about their volunteering behaviour during the study. In order to provide as much continuous data on volunteering over the lifecourse as possible, the analysis on volunteering activity is based on two main types of question. One set of data is based on questions about whether the cohort member has undertaken any unpaid voluntary work (A), and the other set of data is based on whether cohort members are active participants in at least one voluntary association[1] (B). Both measures indicate some form of active participation, distinct from being a passive member of an association. Each of these two sets of measures have their advantages and disadvantages. The former (A) explicitly cites volunteering in the question, but the latter (B) asks about membership of various 'civic' organisations and is therefore more likely to include forms of civic participation that may not be understood as, and described by participants as, volunteering. A good example of this is being a member of an environmental group, which may include a wide variety of activities and behaviours, ranging from litter-picking and hedging (which may be commonly described as volunteering) to environmental campaigning and bird surveying (civic contributions that may not be typically described as volunteering).

The analysis begins with an overview of the frequency of civic participation over the adult lifecourse, between the age of 16 years in 1974 and age 55 years in 2013. Since this is a longitudinal analysis the results are only based on cohort members who have remained for the duration of the study – totalling 9,136 individuals from across the UK. The relatively high level of attrition during the study means that it would be problematic to generalise to the whole population. But given the nature of the NCDS design, based on everyone in the UK born in the same week, it was not always designed to be generalisable to the wider population. It is still the case that the 9,136 cohort members in the following analysis are very representative of all those born at the same time. Nevertheless, it is helpful to consider in a little detail the impact of attrition on the results. Figures 2.2 and 2.3 show the difference in the incidence of trade union membership and formal volunteering over the lifecourse. The cross-sectional figures are based on everyone in each sweep of the NCDS. The longitudinal figures are based only on those NCDS cohort members who remained in the study between the age of 16 and 55 years. As Figures 2.2 and 2.3 demonstrate, there are little differences in the incidence of trade union membership or formal volunteering between the cross-sectional data and the longitudinal data. Figure 2.2 does show a slight discrepancy in trade union membership in 1981 and 1991 when the participants were 23 and 33 years old. However, it is evident that these differences are only marginal, suggesting that attrition in the NCDS is unlikely to have had a significant impact on observed overall levels and patterns of civic participation.

Therefore, the remainder of the analysis only uses the longitudinal cohort – based on data for the same cohort members who remained in the NCDS between the ages of 16 and 55. It is important to note that the analysis examines the longitudinal nature of civic participation for the whole cohort, not at the individual level. Although the analysis compares the same individuals over time (the cohort members), it does not examine individual trajectories of civic participation, an approach commonly followed in other studies (see, for example, Hogg 2016; Lindsey and Mohan 2018). Instead, the NCDS data provide us with a

Figure 2.2: Trade union membership in the NCDS cohort

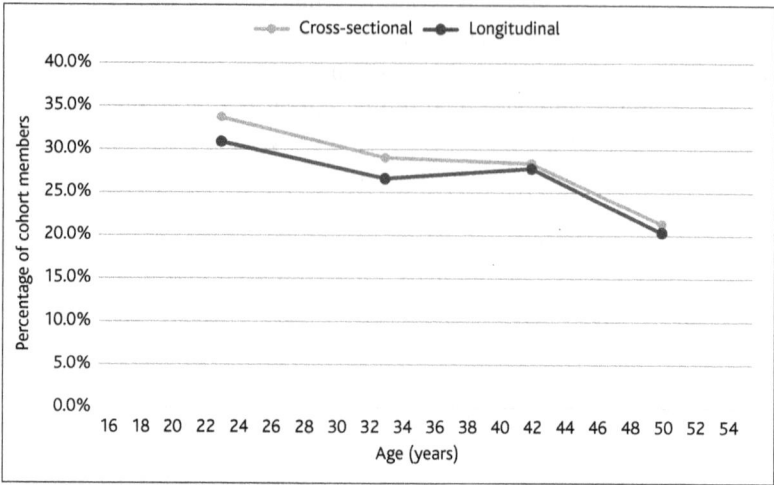

Figure 2.3: Formal volunteering in the NCDS cohort

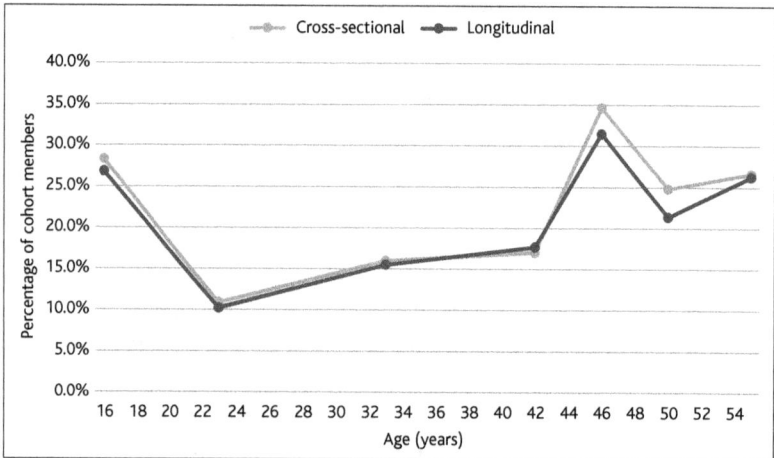

unique opportunity to examine the 'generalised' effect of the lifecourse on civic participation.

Civic participation over the adult lifecourse

Figure 2.4 illustrates the changing incidence of civic participation over the adult lifecourse using the three measures of voting in a recent

Figure 2.4: Civic participation over the lifecourse (voting, trade union membership, formal volunteering)

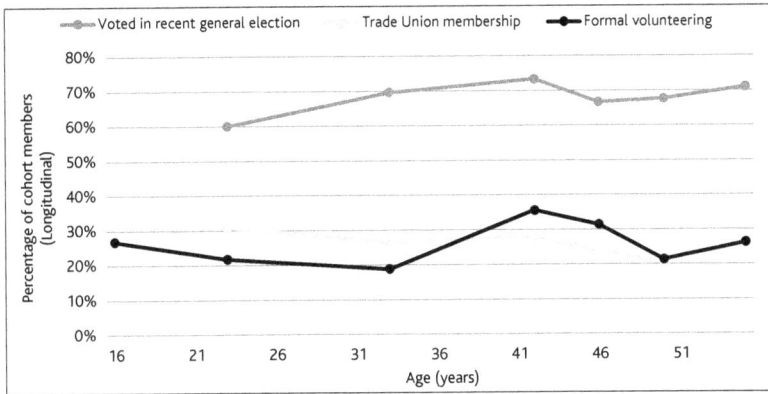

general election, trade union membership and formal volunteering. The first thing that can be seen are that trends in civic participation over the lifecourse vary by the three measures. While levels of voting in a recent general election are much higher than trade union membership and formal volunteering, this is the only measure that shows increasing levels of participation during the first part of adulthood, reaching a peak at age 42 years.[2] In contrast, the relatively lower levels of trade union membership and volunteering generally declined during those first few years of adulthood.

Relatedly, while trends in voting and volunteering rise and fall over the lifecourse, membership of trade unions appears to constantly decline. This suggests this form of civic participation is the least affected by stage in the adult lifecourse, although it does highlight the importance of labour market entry on trade union membership.

The general decline in trade union membership over the lifecourse of the NCDS cohort could reflect wider societal changes in trade union membership over the same time period. For example, trade union membership of all employees declined from 50.4 per cent in 1981, when the cohort were aged 23, to 25.6 per cent in 2013, when the cohort were aged 55. Interestingly, the rate of decline over the lifecourse for the NCDS cohort was lower than overall rate of decline for all workers. However, far fewer of the NCDS cohort members were members of a trade union in 1981 when they were aged 23 (30.9 per cent) than the national figures. This would suggest trade union membership has largely declined because fewer young adults became members or were employed in sectors that were heavily unionised.

Because of these lower levels of entry into trade union membership, overall membership has subsequently declined at a significant rate.

In terms of political participation, levels of voting (in a general election) generally remain relatively stable over the lifecourse. Cohort members were more likely to vote in a general election as they grew older, and that is despite an overall decline in voter turnout in general elections over the same time period. For example, levels of political engagement among adults aged 46 appear to have remained relatively unchanged despite a significant general downward trend in the 2001 general election (67 per cent turnout for cohort members compared to 59 per cent nationally in the same general election). Given this wider decline in voter turnout it is not entirely clear whether the corresponding, albeit smaller, decline in voting among the cohort is related to their age or more widespread political apathy at the time.

It is evident from Figure 2.4 that, of the three measures of civic participation, formal volunteering changes the most by age. Following a period of general decline during early adulthood, formal volunteering then begins to rise again as the adults enter their 40s. This appears to peak at around age 42 before generally declining again during their late 40s. This starts to rise again as the cohort reached the age of 55 years old (in 2013). As noted, these are general trends rather than individual trends. Therefore, it is difficult to assign these changes in volunteering to particular lifecourse events. However, it seems clear that the rise and fall in volunteering activity coincides with particular points in the lifecourse, particularly around child-rearing. The decline in volunteering reaches its lowest level when the NCDS cohort were entered their 30s, at approximately the same time as early family formation and having children. The rise in volunteering as the cohort enters their 40s coincides with the latter half of child-rearing, when their children are likely to have been in secondary school. As other researchers have noted, having children can initially be an obstacle to civic participation (Oesterle et al 2004; Wilson 2012), but then begins to rise again as their children grow up in order to 'build up their stake in community affairs' (Flanagan and Levine 2010: 160).

It is therefore interesting to note that volunteering activity begins to decline again when the cohort were aged 46 and 50 years, likely to reflect the end of child-rearing, that is to say, when their children leave school/home. Volunteering activity does begin to rise again in general as the cohort enters their 50s, possibly reflecting the establishment of new patterns of volunteering activity in their later years. Future data collection of the NCDS cohort will help tell us what happens next to their volunteering activity – will it continue to rise, stabilise or decline again for a third time during their lifecourse?

These trends in formal volunteering among the British NCDS cohort reflect a remarkably similar pattern to that found in Germany (Lancee and Radl 2014). Figure 2.5 shows the results of volunteering activity for men and women using the German SOEP. Although not based on a single cohort, this panel analysis finds a similar pattern of rising and falling levels of volunteering at these various age points, particularly for men (Figure 2.5). The main deviation to that of the NCDS cohort is that the latter rise in volunteering (towards the end of working age) seems to occur later in Germany, when panel members were aged in their 60s compared to the general rise in volunteering activity for NCDS cohort members in their 50s. This could reflect differences in using a longitudinal cohort study (the NCDS) compared to using a panel study (the SOEP). It may also reflect differences in the nature of older people's volunteering activity in the two countries.

What this longitudinal study can show that other panel studies cannot, is how these patterns of volunteering over the lifecourse mask the importance of previous volunteering on later volunteering. As Figure 2.6 illustrates, a large proportion (39.6 per cent) of NCDS cohort members who volunteered during their adult lives volunteered

Figure 2.5: The frequency of volunteering for men and women, by age, in the German Socio-economic Panel (SOEP 1985–2009)

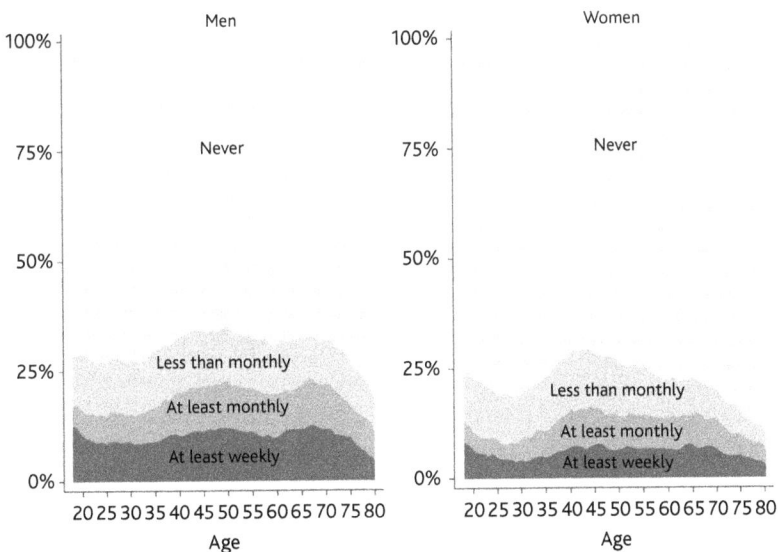

Source: Lancee and Radl (2014: 843).

Figure 2.6: Adult age that NCDS cohort members first reported having volunteered

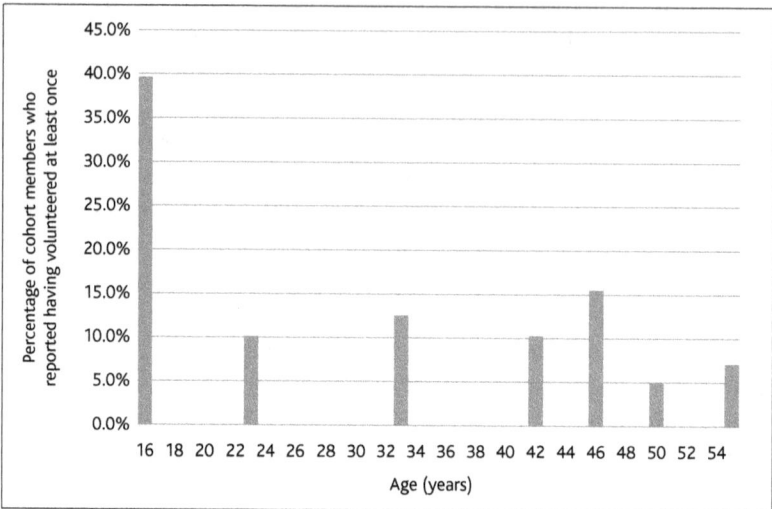

at the age of 16. The percentage of volunteers who volunteered for the first time later in their adult lives mirrors the lifecourse patterns discussed earlier – for example, the peak of volunteering at the age of 46 corresponds to a relatively higher proportion of cohort members who reported that they had volunteered for the first time at the age of 46 years. Similarly, the temporary decline in volunteering as cohort members entered their 50s corresponds to a relatively low proportion of new volunteers at the age of 50. However, these differences by age are overshadowed by the large proportion who first volunteered at age 16. But it is important to note that it does not necessarily mean that volunteering is stable. Conventional theories assumed that civic participation or volunteering (for those that participate in this) remains relatively persistent over the lifecourse (Lancee and Radl 2014). But just under two thirds of volunteers in the NCDS cohort said they had undertaken formal volunteering at only one or two of the seven time points they were asked between the ages of 16 and 55 years. Over 80 per cent of volunteers said they had volunteered at three or fewer time points. Only 2.7 per cent said they had volunteered at six or seven of the time points. So, while volunteering during early adulthood is a strong predictor of later volunteering, it does not mean that early volunteering leads to persistent, stable, volunteering.

Unfortunately, the NCDS does not tell us very much about the nature of volunteering activity, including the amount of time and the form that the activity takes. It is also difficult to disentangle the impact of the lifecourse from temporal factors or wider societal changes in civic participation, as demonstrated by the earlier discussion of declining trade union membership. However, a longitudinal analysis with such a large cohort does allow us to consider how these lifecourse patterns seem to be affected by other key factors. The remainder of this chapter considers these lifecourse patterns by three other known determinants of civic participation: sex, social class and education.

Civic participation over the lifecourse by sex, social class and education

We begin by looking at changes in civic participation over the adult lifecourse by the sex of cohort members. Figure 2.7 shows patterns in trade union membership, voting and formal volunteering for males and females. In the main, the lifecourse patterns are similar for men and women. Males are more likely to have been members of a trade union, but there is a consistent decline in membership over the lifecourse. For females, there is evidence of a resurgence in trade union membership towards the beginning of their 40s. This is likely to reflect a return to work for women who have had children. But it also reaffirms the importance of labour market entry on trade union membership.

There is almost no difference in the patterns of voting behaviour between men and women over the lifecourse, although women are slightly more likely to vote in general elections than men during their 30s.

In terms of formal volunteering the differences between females and males are starker. Women are more likely to be engaged in formal volunteering at an early age than males. And apart from volunteering at age 23, they maintain higher levels of volunteering until they are 55 years old. Interestingly a relatively higher proportion of females are engaged in formal volunteering during their 30s compared to men. This might reflect the association between child-rearing and civic participation. But it is also important to note that there continues to be a peak in formal volunteering for both women and men in their mid-40s. The relatively low levels of formal volunteering for women in their 20s is worth returning to. Given their overall higher levels of participation during the rest of their adulthood, this is quite striking. This might reflect two things. First, that the relationship between formal volunteering and entry to the labour market is different for men and women – perhaps suggesting that it is harder or there are

Figure 2.7: Civic participation by sex

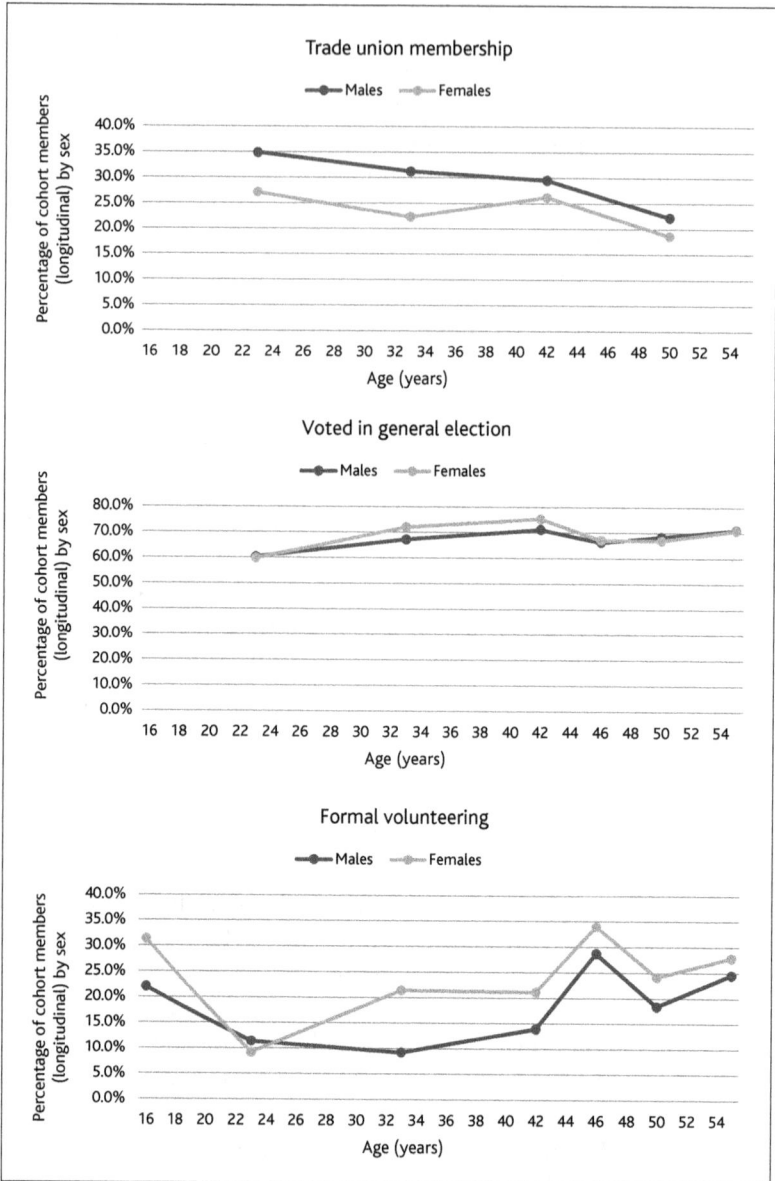

fewer opportunities for women to combine them both. The second conclusion we might draw concerns the relationship between formal volunteering and family formation – suggesting that women have a greater role in family formation, and at the expense of their civic participation.

Next, we consider the relationship between education and civic participation over the adult lifecourse (Figure 2.8). The positive association of university-level education on civic participation has long been established. Some have argued that this simply reflects differing levels of civic participation prior to entering higher education (Egerton

Figure 2.8: Civic participation by education

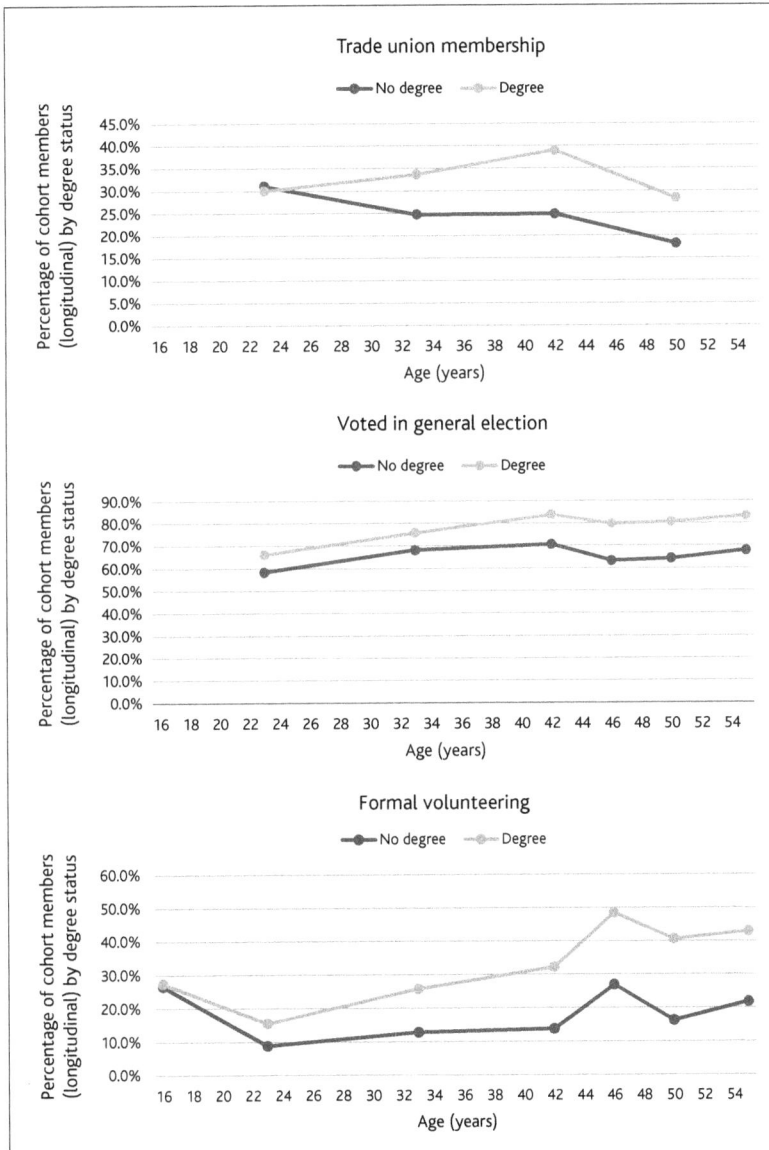

2002). However, there is some evidence that there is still a graduate 'premium' on civic participation (Taylor et al 2019). The lifecourse trends in Figure 2.8 really demonstrate how being a graduate is likely to increase the likelihood for civic participation, in all three forms considered here. Indeed, for this cohort, levels of formal volunteering at age 16, prior to university entry, were very similar for cohort members who did go to university and those that did not. Of course, it is not possible to disentangle the effects of higher education from the preceding post-16 educational experiences, but it is evident from Figure 2.8 that any 'gaps' in civic participation between the graduates and non-graduates continue to grow over the lifecourse. However, it is useful to note that fluctuations in civic participation over the lifecourse for graduates and non-graduates tend to mirror one another, despite the growing gap over time. This would suggest that the impact of the lifecourse and associated lifecourse events, has a similar impact on both groups.

The only exception to this is trade union membership; increasing numbers of graduates became trade union members in their 20s and 30s, despite a decline in union membership for non-graduates at the same time. But interestingly both groups experienced declining levels of trade union membership from their 40s onwards, perhaps reflecting structural changes in union membership at that time (during the early 2000s).

As one might expect, the effect of being a graduate on civic participation is likely to be intertwined with the kind of occupations that graduates enter into. So finally, I consider the impact of social class on civic participation over the adult lifecourse. There are two ways this can be done. The first uses the social class of the cohort members when they were aged 16 (that is, based on the social class of their father – this was the main way social class was measured at the time). The second uses the social class of the cohort members when they reached the age of 55 (that is, based on their own occupations). For comparability, the analysis uses a relatively simple distinction between 'blue-collar' (or working class) and 'white-collar' (or middle class) occupations. Because these social class measures are based on occupations, there are significant proportion of cohort members who remain unclassified for a variety of reasons. Trends in civic participation over the adult lifecourse for the former, termed as the social class origin, are presented in Figure 2.9, and the latter, termed as the social class destination, are presented in Figure 2.10.

There is little difference in levels of trade union membership according to the social class origin of cohort members, although

Figure 2.9: Civic participation by social class (origin)

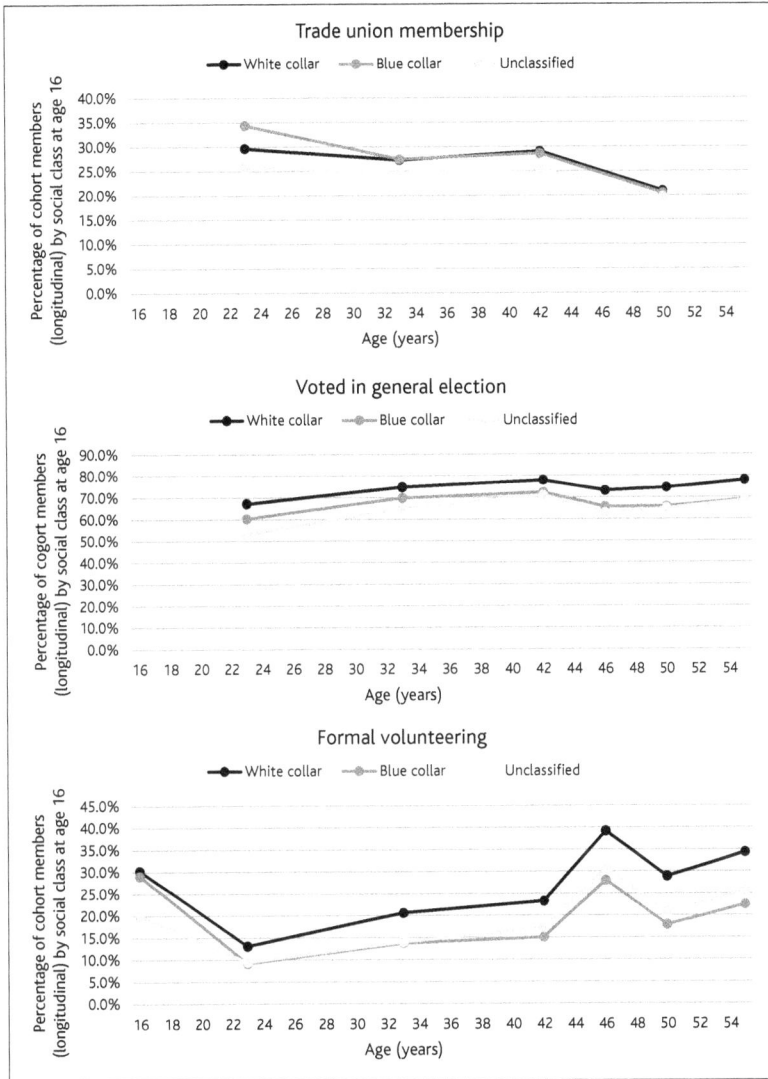

participants from blue-collar backgrounds were slightly more likely to be trade union members in their early 20s (Figure 2.9). In contrast, there are differences in trade union membership based on the cohort's social class destination. This pattern reflects the observation made earlier for graduates and non-graduates. Here white-collar cohort members were more likely to be trade union members, particularly during their 30s. However, by the age of 50 (in 2008) there is little difference in union membership by social class destination. This is different from

Figure 2.10: Civic participation by social class (destination)

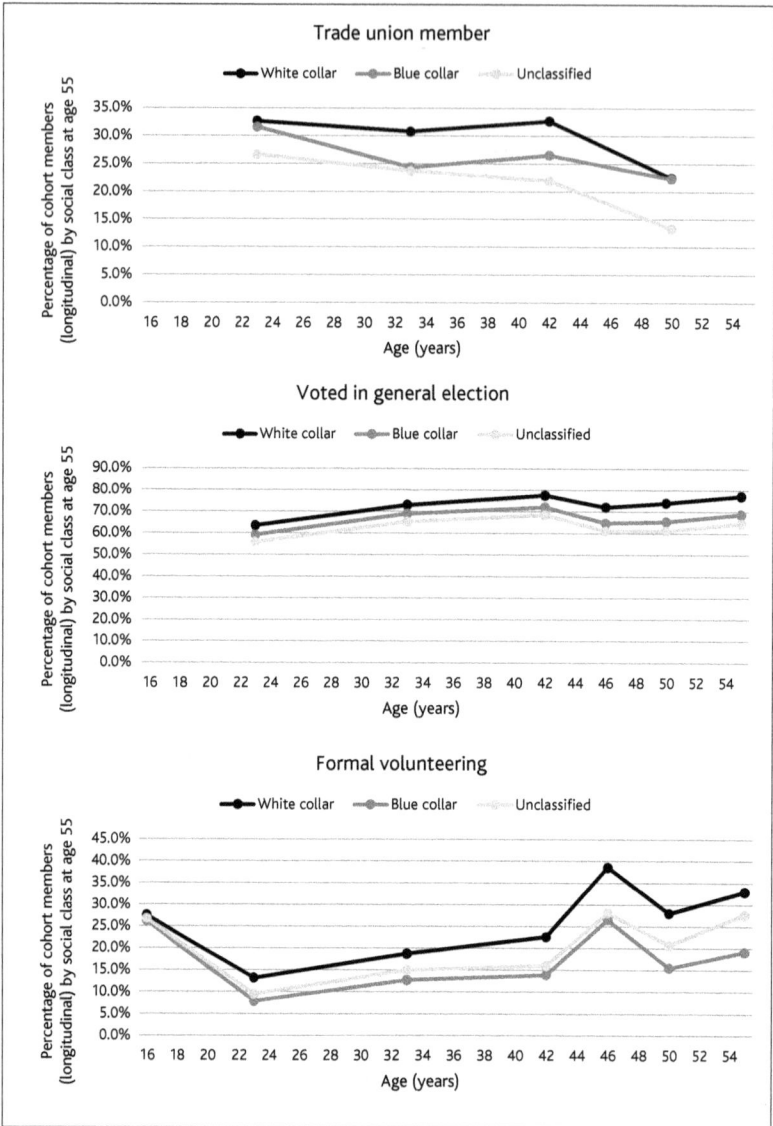

what was observed based on their graduate status, which suggests that graduates were still more likely than non-graduates to be trade union members into their 50s, despite possible differences in their occupations and social class.

For political participation, we observe that white-collar cohort members have been slightly more likely to vote in general elections than their blue-collar counterparts. This difference remains irrespective of whether understood in terms of their social class origins or social class destinations.

Finally, patterns of formal volunteering also appear to be associated with the social class origins and social class destinations of the cohort members. There appears to be very little difference in levels of formal volunteering at age 16 based on their social class background. But as the cohort have grown up, the gap in participation between white-collar and blue-collar cohort members has widened. Importantly, this suggests that the social class background of cohort members has a long-lasting effect on levels of formal volunteering (Figure 2.9), partly because, as noted earlier, early volunteering is a strong predictor of later volunteering. But, in addition, the social class destination of cohort members also appears to be strongly associated with an increasing gap in levels of formal volunteering (Figure 2.10).

Given we can observe differences in levels of civic participation by social class origin and social class destinations this would also suggests that levels of civic participation may be related to social mobility over the lifecourse. Figure 2.11 distinguishes cohort members based on their social class origins and destinations to show the possible relationship between upward and downward social mobility on formal volunteering. This shows a clear social class cleavage in formal volunteering over the lifecourse. Those who are from white-collar backgrounds and remain in white-collar occupations have the highest levels of formal volunteering over their lifecourse. Conversely, those from blue-collar backgrounds and remain in blue-collar occupations have the lowest levels of formal volunteering. Figure 2.11 also shows that the impact of downward social mobility (those from white-collar backgrounds

Figure 2.11: Formal volunteering and social mobility across the adult lifecourse

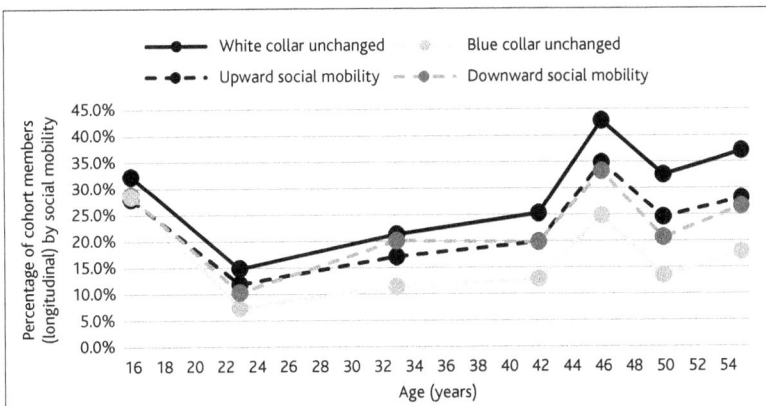

who end up in blue-collar occupations) appears to lead to very similar levels of formal volunteering for those who experience upward social mobility (those from blue-collar backgrounds who end up in white-collar occupations later in life). While this might demonstrate the benefit of upward social mobility on levels of formal volunteering it also suggests that an individual's social class origin has a more important and long-lasting effect on formal volunteering later in life. In turn this could also highlight the importance of intergenerational transmission during childhood, both in terms of participating in formal volunteering at a young age – which is a good predictor of volunteering later in life – and in terms of transmitting the attitudes and values that underpin decisions to volunteer.

As we observed before for graduates and non-graduates, the fluctuations in civic participation at various stages of the lifecourse occur at similar time points and in the same way for each social class. This would suggest again that the influence of the lifecourse on civic participation, and volunteering in particular – the different stages of life or the impact of important life events – appears to be the same for everyone, irrespective of their social class. The same is true for individuals by category of social mobility. Hence, this suggests that coming from a different social class background or the effects of social mobility do not mediate the influence of the lifecourse on civic participation. Changes in the prevalence of formal volunteering over the lifecourse for one group of cohort members appears to mirror the changes for other groups, albeit it at different levels. This would suggest that the lifecourse as an effect on civic participation, particularly in terms of formal volunteering, remains strong, irrespective of wider socio-economic circumstances.

Conclusion

This chapter has examined the relationship between the lifecourse and civic participation. Using three different measures of civic participation over the adult lifecourse it has provided a unique analysis of the changing nature of civic participation for individuals born in the same week in 1958 from when they were 16 years old (in 1974) to when they were 55 years old (in 2013). Using data from a large-scale cohort study, it has tracked the civic participation of more than 9,000 British individuals over a 39-year period, making this one of the longest studies of civic participation ever undertaken. The disadvantage of using a single cohort like this is that it is not possible to separate the effects of the lifecourse from wider structural changes over time – a well-known methodological challenge of any longitudinal study of civic participation, particularly as there have been some major changes in civic participation over recent times. However, by tracking the same individuals over time it is possible to consider the importance of early civic participation on later civic participation. It has also meant that meaningful comparisons between different groups of individuals, based on their gender, education and social class, can be made over their lifecourse.

The three measures of civic participation used here were trade union membership, voting in general elections and participation in formal volunteering – all commonly regarded as representing different forms of civic participation. The relatively simple descriptive analysis has shown that each form of civic participation has its own pattern over the lifecourse, suggesting that each is, to varying degrees, affected by general changes in the adult lifecourse. It has also demonstrated how important prior civic participation is on later civic participation.

In general, we see that entry to the labour market triggers trade union membership, including, it seems, women's later (re)entry to the labour market. But after that, trade union membership seems to steadily decline over the lifecourse. In contrast, political participation, represented here in terms of voting in general elections, tends to increase over the lifecourse. However, both trade union membership and voting appear to be significantly unaffected by particular stages of the lifecourse. We saw a small decline in political participation when the cohort were in their early 40s (in the 2001 UK general election). But voter turnout for the cohort was significantly greater than that of the population overall, suggesting that the positive relationship between voting and older age was mitigating wider political malaise among other voters at that time.

Of the three measures of civic participation considered here, participation in formal volunteering appears to be the most closely related to general stages of the lifecourse. This confirms the findings from other UK small-scale or cross-sectional studies and similar longitudinal analyses in other countries. But we also saw that despite the importance of early adult participation in formal volunteering on later formal volunteering, there is little evidence that formal volunteering is a particularly stable and continuous activity for most participants. There was evidence to suggest that family formation and child-rearing can have negative and positive effects on formal volunteering. Finally, we saw a later-age upturn in formal volunteering as cohort members entered their 50s. It will be interesting to see whether this continues into older age (and as more data is collected from the NCDS cohort).

While there are some distinctions in civic participation by gender – men are more likely to be members of a trade union, women are more likely to undertake formal volunteering and there is little difference in their propensity to vote in general elections – their socio-economic circumstances would appear to have a relatively greater influence on changes in civic participation over the lifecourse. For example, education levels of the cohort members (measured here as having a degree or not) have an important and obvious function in determining levels of civic participation later in adulthood (see Taylor et al 2019). The social class background (or origin) of cohort members also appears to have an important role in determining initial levels of civic participation over the lifecourse, particularly in terms of formal volunteering. Furthermore, while changes to these socio-economic circumstances, such as social mobility, can also contribute to these patterns, there is evidence here that early adult life (or childhood) is more important in shaping later civic participation. The role of education and the intergenerational transmission of civic behaviours and attitudes, particularly during childhood, would seem to be an important component of this.

However, what was also quite striking from this analysis is that none of the socio-economic factors considered here (including changes to those circumstances) appeared to disrupt the impact of various lifecourse transitions or stages on civic participation. For example, the general decline in volunteering during early adulthood appears to affect all groups of adults in pretty much the same way. Similarly, the general rise in volunteering during their 40s and again during their 50s also appears to affect all groups. This would suggest that the lifecourse provides an important context to civic participation, something that policy makers ought to be more mindful of. Understanding the obstacles and motivations to civic participation at different stages of the lifecourse could be very valuable in helping to understand inequalities in civic participation and what Lockwood (1996: 532) terms 'civic stratification'.

Notes

[1] Typically, these include a political party, environmental group, parents' association, residents' group or neighbourhood watch, religious group or church organisation, voluntary services group, other community or civic group, Women's Institute or Townswomen's Guild, or the Scouts and Guides Association.

[2] Levels of voting in a recent general election for the NCDS cohort are fairly commensurate with national levels of voting in these respective general elections. The 1979 general election had a turnout of 76 per cent of all adults in the UK. This compares to 60 per cent of the NCDS cohort, who were aged 21 at the time. Conversely the more recent 2010 general

election had a lower national turnout of 65 per cent, compared to 71 per cent of the NCDS cohort, who were aged 52 years at the time.

References

Broese van Groenou, M. and van Tilburg, T. (2012) 'Six-year follow-up on volunteering in later life: a cohort comparison in the Netherlands', *European Sociological Review*, 28(1): 1–11.

Davis Smith, J. and Gay, P. (2005) *Active Ageing in Active Communities: Volunteering and the Transition to Retirement*, Bristol: Policy Press.

Egerton, M. (2002) 'Higher education and civic engagement', *British Journal of Sociology*, 53(4): 603–20.

Ekman, J. and Amnå, E. (2012) 'Political participation and civic engagement: towards a new typology', *Human Affairs*, 22(3): 283–300.

Elder, G.H. Jr and Giele, J.Z. (2009) 'Life course studies: an evolving field', in G.H. Elder Jr, and J.Z. Giele (eds) *The Craft of Life Course Research*, New York: The Guilford Press, pp 1–24.

Flanagan, C. and Levine, P. (2010) 'Civic engagement and the transition to adulthood', *The Future of Children*, 20(1): 159–79.

Heitzmann, K., Hofbauer, J., Mackerle-Bixa, S. and Strunk, G. (2009) 'Where there's a will, there's a way? Civic participation and social inequality', *Journal of Civil Society*, 5(3): 283–301.

Himmelweit, H.T., Biberian, M.J. and Stockdale, J. (1978) 'Memory for past vote: implications of a study of bias in recall', *British Journal of Political Science*, 8(3): 365–75.

Hogg, E. (2016) 'Constant, serial and trigger volunteers: volunteering across the lifecourse and into older age', *Voluntary Sector Review*, 7(2): 169–90.

Lancee, B. and Radl, J. (2014) 'Volunteering over the life course', *Social Forces*, 93(2): 833–62.

Lindsey, R. and Mohan, J. (2018) *Continuity and Change in Voluntary Action: Patterns, Trends and Understandings*, Bristol: Policy Press.

Lockwood, D. (1996) 'Civic integration and class formation', *British Journal of Sociology*, 47(3): 531–50.

Mohan, J. and Bulloch, S.L. (2012) 'The idea of a "civic core": what are the overlaps between charitable giving, volunteering, and civic participation in England and Wales', Third Sector Research Centre Working Paper No. 73, Birmingham: Third Sector Research Centre. Available from: https://www.birmingham.ac.uk/Documents/college-social-sciences/social-policy/tsrc/working-papers/working-paper-73.pdf.

Oesterle, S., Kirkpatrick Johnson, M. and Mortimer, J.T. (2004) 'Volunteerism during the transition to adulthood: a life course perspective', *Social Forces*, 82(3): 1123–49.

Putnam, R.D. (2000) *Bowling Alone: The Collapse and Revival of American Community*, New York: Simon & Schuster.

Rotolo, T. and Wilson, J. (2004) 'What happened to the "Long Civic Generation"? Explaining cohort differences in volunteerism', *Social Forces*, 82(3): 1091–121.

Tang, F. (2006) 'What resources are needed for volunteerism? A life course perspective', *Journal of Applied Gerontology*, 25(5): 375–90.

Taylor, C., Fox, S., Evans, C. and Rees, G. (2019) 'The "civic premium" of university graduates: the impact of massification on associational membership', *Studies in Higher Education*, ahead of print: https://doi.org/10.1080/03075079.2019.1637837.

University of London, Institute of Education, Centre for Longitudinal Studies (2008a) National Child Development Study: Sweep 4, 1981, and Public Examination Results, 1978, [data collection] (2nd edn), National Children's Bureau [original data producer(s)]. National Children's Bureau. SN: 5566. Available from: http://doi.org/10.5255/UKDA-SN-5566-1.

University of London, Institute of Education, Centre for Longitudinal Studies (2008b) National Child Development Study: Sweep 5, 1991, [data collection] (2nd edn), City University, Social Statistics Research Unit, [original data producer(s)]. City University, Social Statistics Research Unit. SN: 5567. Available from: http://doi.org/10.5255/UKDA-SN-5567-1.

University of London, Institute of Education, Centre for Longitudinal Studies (2008c) National Child Development Study: Sweep 6, 1999–2000, [data collection] (2nd edn), Joint Centre for Longitudinal Research [original data producer(s)]. Joint Centre for Longitudinal Research. SN: 5578. Available from: http://doi.org/10.5255/UKDA-SN-5578-1.

University of London, Institute of Education, Centre for Longitudinal Studies (2008d) National Child Development Study: Sweep 7, 2004–2005, [data collection] (3rd edn), UK Data Service. SN: 5579. Available from: http://doi.org/10.5255/UKDA-SN-5579-1.

University of London, Institute of Education, Centre for Longitudinal Studies (2012) National Child Development Study: Sweep 8, 2008–2009, [data collection] (3rd edn), UK Data Service. SN: 6137. Available from: http://doi.org/10.5255/UKDA-SN-6137-2.

University of London, Institute of Education, Centre for Longitudinal Studies (2014) National Child Development Study: Childhood Data, Sweeps 0–3, 1958–1974, [data collection] (3rd edn), National Birthday Trust Fund, National Children's Bureau [original data producer(s)]. National Birthday Trust Fund. SN: 5565. Available from: http://doi.org/10.5255/UKDA-SN-5565-2.

University of London, Institute of Education, Centre for Longitudinal Studies (2015) National Child Development Study: Sweep 9, 2013, [data collection], UK Data Service. SN: 7669. Available from: http://doi.org/10.5255/UKDA-SN-7669-1.

Wilson, J. (2012) 'Volunteerism research: a review essay', *Nonprofit and Voluntary Sector Quarterly*, 41(2): 176–212.

3

Young people's civic engagement and political participation

Sally Power

In the last chapter, Chris Taylor's analysis of longitudinal data indicated that one of the most significant determinants of civic participation through the lifecourse was early engagement. If this is the case and media representations are to be believed, there are few grounds to be optimistic about future levels of civic participation. Contemporary discourse about young people paints a picture of a generation that is dominated by unfettered consumerism and an obsession with celebrity status and social media. The young people of the 'selfie generation' (Eler 2017) are locked into their mobile phones and preoccupied by the constant stream of social networking and image-making to the extent that they are increasingly isolated and disengaged from the 'real' world. And if 'millennials' are often represented as having a strong sense of their own entitlement – 'the me me me generation' (Stein 2013) – their successors, the 'post-millennials' are allegedly destined to bring 'a new dawn of selfishness' (M & C Saatchi 2017: 25).

In the light of this discourse, it is not surprising that there are fears that the levels of civic and political participation that contribute to a healthy civil society are on the decline. It is widely reported that young people are less likely to vote than older people, they are less likely to volunteer and less likely to give to charities or be involved in other forms of social action (see, for example, CAF 2019).

In this chapter, we try to delve beneath these headlines and explore in more detail the actual extent and nature of young people's civic engagement and political participation through analysis of the responses to a questionnaire survey undertaken by nearly one thousand 14-year-olds from seven schools across South and West Wales. The schools were selected to include diverse communities in that they served in urban (3), rural (2), valley (2), Welsh-speaking (1) and coastal areas (1). The schools were also selected to achieve variation in size, religious affiliation, the presence of sixth form provision, academic profile and percentage of pupils eligible for free school meals (FSM) – the conventional proxy for socio-economic disadvantage. In relation to FSM eligibility, 14.2 per cent of our sample reported that they are eligible, with a further 1.6 per cent selecting 'prefer not to say' and 6.9 per cent indicating that they didn't know. This means that the level of socio-economic disadvantage of our respondents is not too dissimilar from the national level, where 17.8 per cent are eligible for FSM.[1] The analysis indicates of these data a complex picture of both engagement and disengagement, or participation and non-participation. After outlining the current patterns of engagement and participation, we discuss what they imply for the future of civil society.

The complex nature of civic engagement and political participation

As discussed in the introduction, the concepts of both civic engagement and political participation are complex and contested, and the relationship between them is often unclear. In this chapter we draw upon Ekman and Amnå's (2012) typology that draws attention to the importance of the two different kinds of participation (Table 3.1). It indicates the ways in which civic engagement has a latent political function that is related to manifest political participation.

Table 3.1: Types of civic engagement and political participation by young people

	Civic participation (latent-political)		Political participation (manifest)	
	Social involvement (attention)	Civic engagement (action/ practice)	Formal participation	Activism
Individual forms	Taking interest in politics and society Perceiving politics as important	*Giving money to charity Discussing politics and societal issues*	Voting Contacting politicians	*Boycotting goods/services Signing petitions Supporting campaigns (such as wristbands)*
Collective forms	*Belonging to an association with a societal focus* Identifying with a certain ideology	*Volunteering Charity work or fund-raising*	Membership of a political party	*Demonstrating Attending a rally*

Source: adapted from Ekman and Amnå (2012: 295).
Note: Italics indicate the aspects discussed in the text.

In the following section we will examine those aspects of young people's civic and political participation identified by italics in Table 3.1 under the four headings of associational membership, volunteering, charitable giving and political participation. We will not be able to consider all of the examples of participation provided, first, because we do not have data on all of them and, second, because our young people are just too young to be able to participate in formal electoral political processes. However, while Ekman and Amnå's typology is useful in categorising different kinds of activities, the distinction between individual and collective forms of participation is particularly problematic when considering young people. Compulsory attendance at school while living in the family home makes the distinction hard to realise – as most forms of engagement are inevitably undertaken collectively either in the home or in the school. This is something we will return to in our concluding discussion because it has important implications for the sustainability of current levels of civic engagement and social participation.

Associational membership

Following Putnam's argument in *Bowling Alone* (2001) that declining democratic engagement might be related to declining associational activities, there have been a number of studies examining the impact of young people's club membership on social learning. Of particular relevance for us is McFarland and Thomas's (2006) 'Bowling young'. Their analysis of longitudinal data demonstrates that early membership of clubs has a 'nontrivial' impact on political engagement in later life.

Levels of club membership within our sample of young people are relatively high. Across the sample as a whole, over one half (53.6 per cent) are members of school-based clubs and over two thirds (69.5 per cent) are members of non-school-based clubs. As Table 3.2 shows, sport is by far the most common focus for joining of both school- and non-school-based clubs – accounting for 38.2 per cent and 45.4 per cent of our respondents' memberships respectively. 'Other' school-based clubs identified represent a wide range of interests, including Arabic, board and computer games, Christian Union, feminism and gardening. However, in general, aside from sports clubs and youth organisations (such as Scouts and Guides), club membership inside or outside of school appears to be very much a minority pursuit.

If it is the case that joining a club is positively correlated with subsequent future civic and political engagement, it is important

Table 3.2: Young people's club membership (n = 976)

School-based clubs	Sport	38.2%
	Music	10.7%
	School council	3.9%
	Drama	3.3%
	Other	9.5%
Non-school-based clubs	Sport or outdoor activity	45.4%
	Youth organisation	21.5%
	Religious organisation	11.5%
	Cultural organisation	9.1%
	Animal welfare	2.4%
	Environmental	1.9%
	Humanitarian aid / rights organisation	1.2%
	Political organisation / youth parliament	1.0%
	Other	10.9%

to consider the distribution and demographics of membership. It is clear that membership is not evenly distributed across the sample. As Figure 3.1 shows, 46.3 per cent of our respondents are not members of any school-based club and 30.5 per cent are not members of any non-school-based club. Figure 3.1 also indicates a small but significant minority of young people who are members of two or more clubs. There is also a strongly significant relationship between club membership of school and non-school-based clubs – 84.7 per cent of those who joined school clubs are also joiners of non-school-based clubs. It is also possible to identify a small minority of young people who might be called 'super-joiners' – members of three or more clubs either at or out of school (2.4 and 7.6 per cent respectively).

Understanding these different levels of membership is complex and appears to be related to a number of factors. The predominance of sporting activities means that there is a gender imbalance, with boys being disproportionately represented in the 'joining' category. But there is also a school factor in that some schools appear to run more clubs than others.

In terms of socio-economic variables, there does not appear to be a significant relationship between disadvantaged, as measured through FSM eligibility, and school club membership. However, there is a significant relationship between FSM eligibility and non-school-based

Figure 3.1: Number of clubs joined by young people

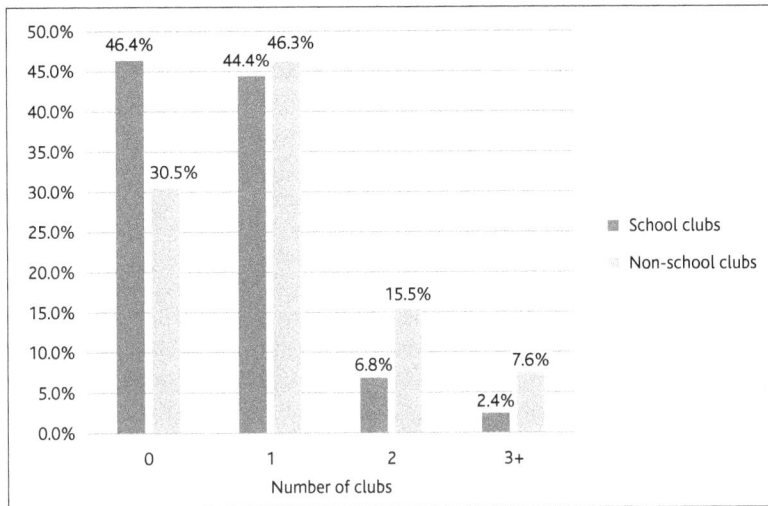

club membership. Whereas nearly three quarters (72.9 per cent) of those above the threshold for FSM eligibility were members of such clubs, this was the case for fewer than two thirds of those who were FSM eligible (63.2 per cent).

As McFarland and Thomas (2006) point out, the voluntary nature of club membership makes it difficult to distinguish the impact of membership from the prior attributes of those disposed to join. Clubs are sorting venues as much as arenas for promoting social learning. The complex relationship between individual attributes and club membership is evident in patterns of religious affiliation, ethnicity and club membership. There is a strong relationship between religious affiliation and club membership (Table 3.3), and particularly notable are the low levels of club membership among our young Muslims. That this is not straightforwardly related to ethnicity is evident in the fact that our black students, who are predominantly Muslim, are also the highest 'joiners' of school clubs – 66.7 per cent of our black students are members of at least one school club, compared to 56.2 per cent of white students and 42.6 per cent of Asian students.

The long-term implications of these patterns of club membership are likely to be complex. Among our sample, being a 'joiner' is positively correlated to aspects of political participation (discussed later). However, this association may not be sustained into later life. While some research (Verba et al 1995) indicates that almost any form of club membership has beneficial effects, McFarland and Thomas's (2006: 412) very detailed analysis of longitudinal data indicates that

Table 3.3: Religious affiliation and club membership

	Non-joiners	Joiners	Super-joiners
Christian (n = 416)	16.6%	56.5%	26.9%
Muslim (n = 175)	34.9%	47.4%	17.7%
Other religion (n = 37)	18.9%	48.6%	32.4%
No religion (n = 292)	21.2%	61.0%	17.8%

Note: $p < .000$.

some clubs are more salient for longer-term political participation than others. They show that membership of sports clubs in general, and of school-based sports clubs in particular, does not lead to long-term political involvement. Given the dominance of sports-related activities in our young people's club membership – and the relatively low levels of membership of more politically salient clubs – one should not necessarily predict that this kind of activity will lead to high levels of political participation in the future.

Volunteering

Volunteering is often considered to be an important indicator – and sometimes the *only* indicator – of civic engagement. Not only is volunteering considered to benefit others, but it is also claimed that it brings benefits to the volunteers themselves. For example, Binder and Freytag (2013) found that respondents' reported levels of life-satisfaction increased in line with the amount of volunteering undertaken. As with civic engagement, definitions of volunteering are problematic and ascertaining levels of volunteering difficult (see, for example, Cnaan et al 1996). One reason for this is that volunteering is the difficulty of distinguishing what is 'voluntary' and whether it is 'formal' or 'informal'. In this analysis, we are defining formal volunteering in terms of whether young people reported 'giving time to help a charity or cause'. Informal volunteering is defined in terms of whether they have been involved in 'supporting other people who aren't friends and relatives'.

It is generally assumed that young people volunteer less than older people. However, there is very little research on the extent to which school students are engaged in volunteering. A survey undertaking by the Charities Aid Foundation (CAF 2019) of those over 16 years old found that only 16 per cent had volunteered for a charity in the past year. This is far less than reported by our young people. The majority

Figure 3.2: Frequency of volunteering of those who volunteer

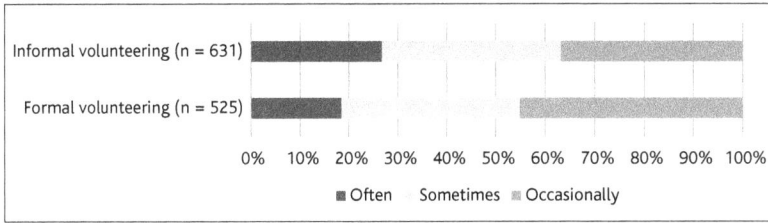

Informal volunteering (n = 631)		
Formal volunteering (n = 525)		

0% 10% 20% 30% 40% 50% 60% 70% 80% 90% 100%

■ Often   Sometimes   ▒ Occasionally

Table 3.4: Relationship between club membership and volunteering

	Non-joiners (n = 190)	Joiners (n = 499)	Super-joiners (n = 197)
Formal volunteering*	52.1%	56.7%	72.6%
Informal volunteering#	62.0%	70.1%	79.2%

Note: * $p < .000$; # $p < .001$.

of our respondents had undertaken some volunteering in the previous year. Nearly 60 per cent had volunteered for a charity or cause, and over 70 per cent had volunteered to provide support to those other than family or friends. Self-reported levels of the frequency of that activity are shown in Figure 3.2, and would indicate the volunteering is undertaken relatively frequently – with well over half volunteering 'often' and 'sometimes'.

As with club membership and political participation, there are strong associations between 'joining' and volunteering (Table 3.4).

However, the nature of the relationships is complex. The gender imbalance works the other way from that found with club membership. As is also evident in most studies on adult volunteering (see, for example, Taniguchi 2006), our female respondents were most likely to have undertaken volunteering than their male classmates – for formal volunteering the difference is 66.1 per cent to 54.5 per cent, for informal volunteering the difference is 74.7 per cent to 67.5 per cent. There is again school-level variation. In some schools, the proportion of students volunteering is over 80 per cent, in others it is less than half. The faith-based schools have higher levels of volunteering than others. This confirms other research on the strong association between religion and volunteering (see, for example, Lim and MacGregor 2012). All our students with a religious affiliation have higher levels of volunteering than those who profess to have no religion. In relation to formal volunteering, 64 per cent of Christians had volunteered in the last 12 months, 63.9 per cent of those of 'other religions', 61.4 per cent of Muslims – all far higher proportions than for those of 'no religion' – of whom only 49.2 per cent had volunteered. Among our respondents, there is no significant relationship between volunteering and ethnicity or eligibility for FSM.

As with club membership, the long-term implications of these high levels of volunteering are unclear. They should certainly not be taken as predictive of future levels of voluntary activity. Despite the high levels of volunteering at school – and at college and university – all the available evidence indicates that there will be a sharp decline in volunteering once our young people become adults. Mohan's (2010) analysis of the profile of adult volunteers reveals what he calls a 'civic core' of white, middle-class, graduates. Dean (2016) argues that the social class biases evident in the paid labour market are also evident in the volunteer market. The drop in levels of volunteering may also result from the way in which volunteering is now being used by schools and educational institutions as a compulsory component of citizenship education – rendering it a form of 'voluntolding' (Kelemen et al 2017: 1234). For example, in Wales, some components of the Welsh Baccalaureate require students to undertake at least ten hours of voluntary work, including clearing litter, cutting grass, painting walls and cleaning footpaths (WJEC 2017). Additionally, volunteering has increasingly become a form of 'hope labour' (Kuehn and Corrigan 2013) in that it holds out for young people a gateway to future employment in the context of an increasingly 'casualised' and precarious labour market.

There must be some concern that these developments are distorting the nature of what volunteering is – in essence a form of voluntary activity. It is possible that this kind of distortion may lead to negative attitudes towards volunteering. There is certainly evidence of deep ambivalence towards volunteering among our young people: 41.2 per cent agreed with the statement that 'volunteering is a way for the government to get people to work for free', while only a minority (15.5 per cent) disagreed with this statement. Such ambivalence must raise issues about the extent to which the apparently very high levels of volunteering undertaken at school will continue as young people leave school are able to 'volunteer' in the true sense of the word.

Charitable giving

There are strong parallels between volunteering and charitable giving. As with volunteering, it is generally thought that younger people are less likely to donate money than older people (see, for example, CAF 2012). Again, our evidence does not support this. The Charities Aid Foundation (CAF 2019) survey mentioned earlier found that 57 per cent of adults reported having given money to a charity in the past 12 months, and 56 per cent reported having given goods. The proportions of donating money and goods are far higher among our young people (Figure 3.3). The overwhelming majority have given money (83.8 per cent) and goods (78.3 per cent) to charities at some point during the last year. Nearly one in five (16.9 per cent and 16.7 per cent) report that they do this often. Perhaps even more noteworthy is the fact that over half (54.9 per cent) have been involved in charitable fundraising during the past year.

While the overall levels of donation of both our male and female respondents are very high, there are gender differences. These findings confirm other research that indicates that females are far more likely to make donations than males. For example, only 7 per cent of our female respondents had donated neither money nor items to charity in the preceding 12 months, compared to 14.3 per cent of boys. Not surprisingly, there is also a statistically significant relationship between socio-economic disadvantage and donating – with those eligible for FSM being less likely to give than others (83.1 per cent compared to 90.4 per cent)

Figure 3.3: Frequency of charitable giving (percentages)

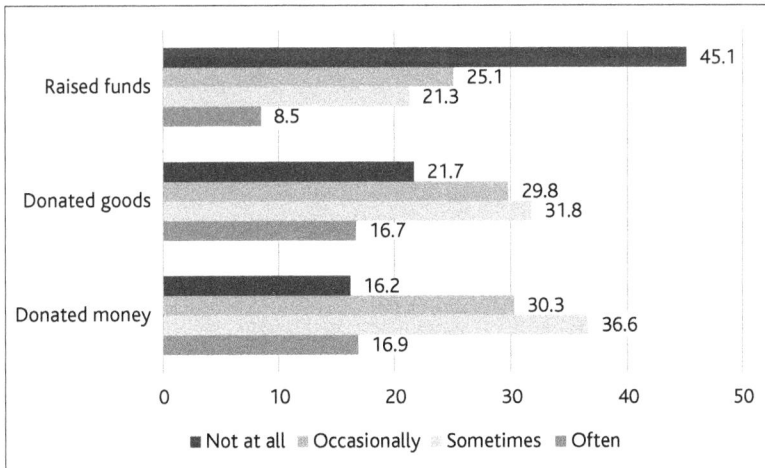

There is no statistically significant relationship between our 'givers' and their ethnicity. There is, however, a strongly significant relationship between giving and having any religious affiliation: 95.7 per cent of Muslims, 92.3 per cent of Christians and 88.9 per cent of those of 'other' religions donated money or items compared with 81 per cent of those of 'no religion'.

In terms of connections between different kinds of civic engagement activities, there is a strong relationship between givers and joiners and between givers and political participation – the majority of givers (59.1 per cent) are politically engaged (discussed later) compared to a minority of non-givers (31.6 per cent). Similarly, our 'joiners' also tended to be 'givers' – so 94.6 per cent of our 'super-joiners' have made donations in the last 12 months, compared to 89.2 per cent of joiners and 83.4 per cent of non-joiners. And again, our volunteers are also more likely to be 'givers', with 98.6 per cent of volunteers having made donations compared to 75.2 per cent of those who haven't volunteered.

As with the high levels of volunteering, we should be cautious about assuming that these overall very high levels of donation – and fundraising – will be sustained once our young people have left school. There has been a widespread 'mainstreaming' of charities into schools (Power and Taylor 2018). Schools often encourage their students to undertake fundraising activities and, in some cases, require them to. Again, with reference to the Welsh Baccalaureate, one of the units stipulates that students must spend ten hours on promotional activities for a selected charity, combined with either 'active fund-raising' or 'active support' (WJEC 2017). Whether making this kind of charitable activity compulsory is beneficial in the long term is questionable. As with volunteering, there is significant ambivalence in our young people's perceptions of charities. As Table 3.5 shows, our students were marginally more likely to agree than disagree with the statement that 'Charities are just big business now'. And they were much likely to see charities as plugging a gap left by government. Nearly half agreed that we would not need charities 'if the government did its job properly', and only a small minority disagreed with this sentiment.

Political participation

As with all the other concepts, what counts as political participation is problematic. Voting in elections is the standard measure of political participation, but clearly that's not applicable to the

Table 3.5: Attitudes towards charities

	Strongly agree/agree	Neither agree not disagree	Disagree/ strongly disagree
Charities are just big businesses now	30.8%	40.2%	29.2%
If the government did its job properly we wouldn't need charities	45.8%	37.3%	16.9%

Table 3.6: Young people's political participation

Worn a campaign badge or wristband	19.8%
Signed a petition	13.7%
Contacted a politician	5.2%
Taken part in a public demonstration	4.9%
Attended a political meeting or rally	4.2%
Boycotted certain products	2.8%

young people in our survey. However, that does not mean that we should discount other forms of participation. Indeed, some argue that alternative modes of engagement, such as consumer boycotts and rallies, will displace traditional modes of representative democratic participation (Loader et al 2014). As we have seen, Ekman and Amnå's (2012) typology distinguishes between formal political participation – from which our young people are largely excluded – and extra-parliamentary participation, which includes a variety of actions listed in Table 3.6.

In general, levels of participation are far lower than the other activities we have discussed in this chapter. They are also far lower than the levels reported in the Charities Aid Foundation survey (CAF 2019), in which 49 per cent of adults had signed a petition and 6 per cent had taken part in a political demonstration. Among our sample, campaign badges and wristbands were selected as the most frequent form of 'political participation', indicative of the growth of what Moore (2008) refers to as the 'ribbon culture'.

After the wearing of badges and wristbands, petition-signing was the second most common form of political action – no doubt facilitated by the ease with which petitions can be initiated and distributed on social media. Of those who identified the subject of the petition, 112 different campaigns were identified which covered wide range of issues (Table 3.7).

Table 3.7: Subject of most recently signed petition (frequency of mentions)

Local cause	22
School-related issue	20
Animal rights	15
Brexit	10
Donald Trump	9
Equality issues (anti-racism, LGBT rights, 'period poverty')	5
Health	4
International causes	4
Anti-poverty	2
Children's rights	2
Miscellaneous	12

Local causes were most frequently mentioned. These included diverse campaigns, such as:

- they wanted to get rid of a pond which was home to an endangered species of newt for a model railway;
- to disallow a rehab centre near my house;
- the council wanted to demolish an old church for flats.

School-related issues were the second most frequent kind of campaign, for example:

- a teacher was going to be sacked because my old school didn't have enough money to keep him;
- to fire a teacher;
- to increase the length of school holidays;
- to get football back onto the girls' curriculum in my school.

As other research (such as CAF 2019) has shown, young people tend to be concerned about animal rights, which formed the third most frequent focus of a petition, for instance:

- to stop dog slaughtering in South–East Asia;
- for bees to stop being extinct/endangered;
- to stop laboratory testing on animals.

Other 'hot issues' related to Brexit and the call for a new referendum and to stop Donald Trump visiting the UK.[2] Then there was a wide range of 'miscellaneous' petitions that were difficult to classify and included two calls for Jeremy Clarkson, a controversial TV presenter, to be reinstated by the BBC, a plea for the 'last Dambuster hero' to be given a knighthood and support for an increase in doctors' pay.

As with club membership, the distribution of participation across the sample is uneven. Nearly half (45.2 per cent) our young people have never undertaken any of the political activities outlined in Table 3.6, while over one quarter (25.9 per cent) had undertaken more than two. One in eight (12.5 per cent) have undertaken three of more. In terms of gender, our female respondents are more likely to participate in political activities than our male respondents. Only just over half (51.7 per cent) of the boys had undertaken any of the activities outlined in Table 3.6, compared to 58.9 per cent of girls. As with almost every other dimension of civic engagement considered in this chapter, being politically engaged is positively correlated with religion. Christians are the 'most' politically engaged (62.3 per cent undertaking at least one of the categories identified in Table 3.6), followed by those of an 'other' religion (56.8 per cent), Muslims (50.9 per cent) and finally, those of no religion (50.7 per cent). There appears to be no significant association political participation and FSM eligibility or ethnicity.

Young people: building a strong civil society for the future?

As we have seen, there are relatively high levels of participation in civic engagement activities, particularly those that relate to club membership, volunteering and charitable giving, that were undertaken by a majority of our young people. Indeed, levels of charitable giving and volunteering are significantly higher than those reported by older people. Levels of political participation are lower, but that may well be associated with their young age. These findings might lead one to be less pessimistic about the future levels of civic engagement among young people – and particularly the post-millennial generation – than contemporary media accounts suggest. However, there are two causes for concern: one is the uneven distribution of participation in civic and politically oriented activities and the second is the issue of sustainability as they our young people leave school.

However, while overall levels are high, there are considerable variations in who gets involved. It would appear that there are some young people who are very involved – whether that is in clubs, volunteering, charity work and/or politically oriented activities – and others who are not involved at all. There is no clear pattern across the sample a whole – although religious affiliation seems to be always associated with higher levels of engagement. Because of the faith dimension of some of the schools in the sample, it is often difficult to disentangle school-sponsored engagement from that associated with religious organisations and the family. Nevertheless, there is a significant amount of research (such as Uslaner 2003) that confirms the significance of religion for civic engagement. With the exception of charitable giving, it is also clear that our young Muslims are less involved clubs, and less involved in volunteering and political activities than young people of other faiths.

However, as we discussed at the beginning of the chapter, the organisational dimension of being a school student may be misleading – indicative of school-sponsored attempts to promote civic engagement rather than strong personal commitments. In this next section we consider the potential sustainability of engagement through examining young people's motivations to get involved, their perceptions of the benefits of their involvement and their thoughts about their own future engagement.

In some of the literature (for instance, Heath 2007), it is claimed that young people's civic engagement, such as volunteering, is driven by instrumental motivations rather than altruism or principles. This is not strongly evident in the reasons given by our respondents (Table 3.8). The possibility of learning skills and gaining qualifications was selected less frequently than other less instrumental reasons. Over 40 per cent reported that they got involved in order to improve things and help people.

Some respondents referred to a personal experience that had motivated them, such as:

• I was bullied all my life and I don't want that to happen to anyone else;
• to raise awareness and help people like my friend.

Table 3.8: Motivations to get involved in charities

To improve things / help people	42.9%
I really enjoy it	28.2%
My friends/family do it	20.6%
To use my skills / learn new ones	14.0%
To meet people / make friends	12.0%
To get a recognised qualification	5.5%

Other motivations included being inspired by particular individuals, for instance:

- I was inspired by someone;
- my youth pastor encouraged me to serve.

The school was cited several times as the principal driver:

- school activity;
- because the whole school was doing it.

While the family appears to be the principal source of involvement (mentioned by 47.8 per cent of respondents), the school is the second most important channel for involvement (mentioned by 36.3 per cent of respondents).

However, while the majority of young people may have been motivated by the desire to make things better or because they enjoyed it, there was significant ambivalence about the benefits of their civic engagement activities both for themselves and for their intended beneficiaries.

As Figure 3.4 shows, while most respondents felt there was some benefit for themselves and others, most thought that there was only 'a little' benefit. Moreover, one fifth felt that they were unsure whether they had benefited personally, and one quarter were unsure that others had benefited.

Figure 3.4: How much has the activity benefited you personally and others?

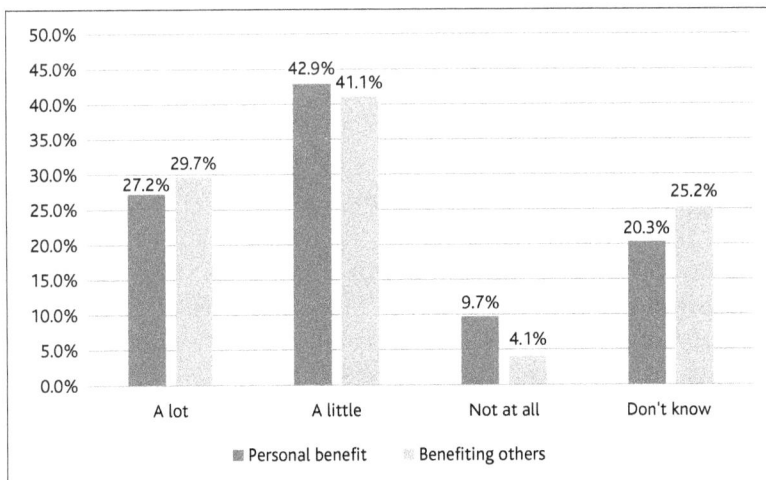

Table 3.9: What might stop you from doing these things in the future?

I don't have enough time	40.7%
I don't feel like I would be able to make a difference	15.3%
My friends aren't doing this type of thing	12.8%
I'm not interested	12.3%
Put off by a previous experience	11.7%
I have a health problem/disability	3.4%
Other	6.9%

There is also a significant level of doubt about the likelihood of future levels of engagement. When asked how likely it is that they would do 'more of these activities in the next 12 months', only just over one fifth (22.8 per cent) said it was 'very likely'. One half (48.4 per cent) would only go so far as to say it was 'possible', while one in eight said it was 'not likely'. The reasons provided for lack of future involvement are largely to do with time (Table 3.9), although there is also evidence of some disillusionment arising from their own experiences and their perceptions of whether the activities are worthwhile.

The role of schools in promoting/enforcing these activities is evident in some of the 'other' responses which reflect a lack of personal knowledge about how to get involved:

- I won't be in school anymore;
- I might not know about it;
- I don't know where to sign up;
- I don't know any help organisations.

Again, their responses suggest that the heavy promotion of volunteering and charitable activities by schools may not lead be sustained in the future.

Conclusion

We began this chapter by referring to the largely negative representations of young people in the media today – and in particular the extent to which they were seen to be selfishly, rather than civically, minded. The data from the young people who participated in our research suggest that these representations are entirely misleading. Using Ekman and Amnå's (2012) typology of civic engagement and political participation we find that our young people are highly engaged – albeit some more than others and in more activities than others. To some extent, the data can be seen as a 'good news, bad news' narrative.

In terms of 'good news', levels of associative activity are relatively high. Levels of charitable activity and volunteering are extraordinarily high – engaged in by the overwhelming majority of young people and far more frequently than by older people. It is difficult to make age-based comparisons in terms of levels of political participation simply because our young people are too young to vote. However, a significant minority had undertaken some kind of politically oriented activity, in particular signing petitions for a wide variety of campaigns. Overall, our young people were motivated to get involved in order to improve things and help people, rather than for more instrumental reasons. These data paint a picture of a post-millennial generation that is actively engaged and civically minded with a strong sense of social responsibility.

On the 'bad news' side of the narrative, there must be doubts about the potential of some forms of engagement for future civic and political participation. For example, in relation to associative activity, the overwhelming majority of club memberships relate to sports – and school sports in particular. Other research indicates that this kind of club membership is the least salient for future levels of political participation. Similarly, while levels of volunteering and charitable activity are high, this high level of engagement can be at least partly explained by school-sponsored activities. The 'mainstreaming' of charities in schools and the requirement that school students participate in volunteering may act as much as a deterrent as an encouragement for future levels of engagement. Our young people were quite ambivalent about the virtues of volunteering and charities – and not entirely convinced that their civic engagement activities were of benefit either to themselves or to others.

Of course, only time will tell whether and how these patterns of engagement carry forward into adult life. It would be unfortunate if school-based promotion of civic engagement were to lead to the diminution rather than the enhancement of civil society in the future.

Notes

[1] See Muddiman et al (2019) for a full description of the project.

[2] This was something of a live issue when the data were being collected as he was due to visit the UK in July 2018.

References

Binder, M. and Freytag, A. (2013) 'Volunteering, subjective well-being and public policy', *Journal of Economic Psychology*, 34: 97–119.

CAF (Charities Aid Foundation) (2012) *Mind the Gap: the growing generational divide in charitable giving: a research paper*, West Malling: Charities Aid Foundation. Available from: https://www.cafonline.org/docs/default-source/about-us-policy-and-campaigns/mind-the-gap-reportddffcb334cae616587efff3200698116.pdf [Accessed 2 July 2020].

CAF (2019) *CAF UK Giving 2019: An Overview of Charitable Giving in the UK*, West Malling: Charities Aid Foundation. Available from: https://www.cafonline.org/about-us/publications/2019-publications/uk-giving-2019.

Cnaan, R.A., Handy, F. and Wadsworth, M. (1996) 'Defining who is a volunteer: conceptual and empirical considerations', *Nonprofit and Voluntary Sector Quarterly*, 25(3): 364–83.

Dean, J. (2016) 'Class diversity and youth volunteering in the United Kingdom: applying Bourdieu's habitus and cultural capital', *Nonprofit and Voluntary Sector Quarterly*, 45(1, Suppl): 95S–113S.

Ekman, J. and Amnå, E. (2012) 'Political participation and civic engagement: towards a new typology', *Human Affairs*, 22(3): 283–300.

Eler, A. (2017) *The Selfie Generation: How Our Self-Images Are Changing Our Notions of Privacy, Sex, Consent, and Culture*, New York: Skyhorse Publishing.

Heath, S. (2007) 'Widening the gap: pre-university gap years and the "economy of experience"', *British Journal of Sociology of Education*, 28(1): 89–103.

Kelemen, M., Mangan, A. and Moffat, S. (2017) 'More than a "little act of kindness"? Towards a typology of volunteering as unpaid work', *Sociology*, 51(6): 1239–56.

Kuehn, K. and Corrigan, T.F. (2013) 'Hope labor: the role of employment prospects in online social production', *The Political Economy of Communication*, 1(1): 9–25.

Lim, C. and MacGregor, C.A. (2012) 'Religion and volunteering in context: disentangling the contextual effects of religion on voluntary behavior', *American Sociological Review*, 77(5): 747–79.

Loader, B.D., Vromen, A. and Xenos, M.A. (2014) 'The networked young citizen: social media, political participation and civic engagement', *Information, Communication and Society*, 17(2): 143–50.

M & C Saatchi (2017) *Risk, Realism and Ritalin*, London: Saatchi PR. Available from: http://mcsaatchitransform.com/src/assets/pdfs/MCTRANSFORM_RRR.pdf.

McFarland, D.A. and Thomas, R.J. (2006) 'Bowling young: how youth voluntary associations influence adult political participation', *American Sociological Review*, 71(3): 401–25.

Mohan, J. (2010) 'Big society threatened by lack of volunteers', *The Guardian*, 24 August. Available from: https://www.theguardian.com/society/joepublic/2010/aug/24/big-society-lack-of-volunteers.

Moore, S.E.H. (2008) *Ribbon Culture: Charity, Compassion, and Public Awareness*, Basingstoke: Palgrave Macmillan.

Muddiman, E., Taylor, C., Power, S. and Moles, K. (2019) 'Young people, family relationships and civic participation', *Journal of Civil Society*, 15(1): 82–98.

Power, S. and Taylor, S. (2018) 'The mainstreaming of charities into schools', *Oxford Review of Education*, 44(6): 702–15.

Putnam, R. (2001) *Bowling Alone: The Collapse and Revival of American Community*, New York: Simon & Schuster.

Stein, J. (2013) 'The me me me generation', *Time*, May. Available from: http://time.com/247/millennials-the-me-me-me-generation.

Taniguchi, H. (2006) 'Men's and women's volunteering: gender differences in the effects of employment and family characteristics', *Nonprofit and Voluntary Sector Quarterly*, 35(1): 83–101.

Uslaner, E.M. (2003) 'Volunteering and social capital: how trust and religion shape civic participation in the United States', in P. Dekker and E. Uslaner (eds) *Social Capital and Participation in Everyday Life*, New York: Routledge, pp 104–17.

Verba, S., Schlozman, K.L. and Brady, H.E. (1995) *Voice and Equality: Civic Voluntarism in American Politics*, Cambridge, MA: Harvard University Press.

WJEC (Welsh Joint Examining Committee) (2017) *Welsh Baccalaureate Key Stage 4 Community Challenge Social Welfare (generic brief)*, Cardiff: WJEC. Available from: https://wjec.co.uk/media/xxmnl4md/ks4-community-challenge-neighbourhood-enhancement-generic_2017.pdf.

4

Graduating into civil society

Ceryn Evans, Esther Muddiman and Chris Taylor

The period between adolescence and adulthood, what Arnett (2004) terms 'emergent adulthood', is a key part of the lifecourse. This is when key socio-economic transitions and growing independence occurs. However, this is not just some 'stage' during the lifecourse, it is a key period when structural factors and exclusion mechanisms can significantly shape future lifecourse trajectories or pathways (Bynner 2005). This can come in many forms – economically, politically, culturally and socially – and can have a significant bearing on individuals' participation in civil society. Indeed, as we have seen earlier, it is a critical period in the lifecourse when levels of volunteering significantly decline before beginning to rise again during mid-adulthood.

For some in society the period of 'emergent adulthood' is dominated by their participation in higher education (HE). In the UK, approximately 45 per cent of school-leavers enter HE by the age of 20 years, although there is significant variation in these figures by region and country of the UK. The opportunities that are provided while at university, educationally and socially, can be transformative for individuals and have long-lasting implications for their later lives. But participation in HE is also a major contributor to divergent trajectories. Consequently, the inequalities that HE confers between graduates and non-graduates has received considerable attention over the years, not least in terms of the socio-economic advantage that HE can afford.

There have been two recent and important developments to these debates. The first is in terms of the impact of increasing levels of HE participation – the consequences of shifting from what Trow (1973) termed an 'elite' era of HE (for the few) to a mass era of HE (for the many). This also recognises the greater heterogeneity in the student body and in the range of universities providing HE. And the second is recognising the social contribution of HE in terms of graduates' contribution to civil society (as distinct from its economic contribution through graduate earnings and employment opportunities). But at the intersection of these two developments is a very simple paradox: how has the massification of HE coincided with a general decline in civic participation? This has been partly addressed by Taylor et al (2019) who have been able to demonstrate that the 'civic premium' of UK university graduates over time has been maintained but has not been able to compensate for a general decline in civic participation. But also, crucially, Taylor et al (2019) suggest that the relationship between graduates and civil society has changed – the graduate 'civic premium' appears to have gone on to benefit some forms of civic participation more than others. Unfortunately, the large-scale dataset that Taylor et al use to generate these findings is unable to say anything about how the graduates' HE experience has contributed or changed their civic participation.

In this chapter we examine how HE contributes to participation in civil society in the UK. In particular, we explore the extent to which citizens 'graduate' into civil society as a result of their educational and social experiences while at university. This chapter draws upon the findings of an ESRC-funded project which involved in-depth interviews with 30 adults aged 30–40 years old who had attended university in the late 1990s and early 2000s. The graduates in the study had been to one of three types of UK university: two 'new' (post-92) universities, three 'old' (pre-92) universities, of which one belonged to the 'Russell Group', and two 'elite' universities (Oxford and Cambridge). Graduates from these diverse types of university were invited to interview because of the universities' distinctive histories, admissions arrangements, student bodies, curricula and social activities. For example, while the 'old' universities and elite universities are 'research intensive' in a way that the post-92 institutions are not, the elite universities adopt particular pedagogical arrangements in which one-to-one teacher–student teaching sessions are commonplace in a way that none of the other universities in this study are able to offer. Including graduates in our study who had studied at different types of university therefore enabled us to explore the extent to which the distinctive features of certain universities (particularly in terms of curriculum, pedagogy and social activities) have any role in the formation of values, attitudes and civic skills necessary for civic participation. Furthermore, the graduates were also selected to represent a range of degree disciplines, including ten social sciences graduates, nine science, technology, engineering or mathematics (STEM) graduates, eight arts and humanities graduates, one business studies graduate and two social and healthcare graduates. This qualitative analysis of qualitative data also builds upon quantitative analysis of large-scale data comparing levels of civic participation among graduates and non-graduates over time (Taylor et al 2019).

Higher education, social attitudes and civic participation

Education has consistently been identified as positively associated with social participation in a variety of national contexts. This includes associational membership, propensity to vote, interest in politics and lack of cynicism about politics (Verba and Nie 1972; Verba et al 1995; Nie et al 1996; Dee 2004; Sondheimer and Green 2010). An individual's level of education is also associated with socially 'liberal' attitudes and views (Nie et al 1996; Easterbrook et al 2016) including tolerance, support for civil liberties, open-mindedness (Nie et al 1996; Egerton 2002; Bynner et al 2003) and freedom from racial prejudice. Indeed, decades of international research has suggested that higher levels of education and greater lengths of time spent in education are positively associated with civic participation and holding liberal social attitudes (Nie et al 1996; Dee 2004; Inglehart and Welzel 2005; Sondheimer and Green 2010; Dalton 2013; Sloam 2014). This relationship has prompted some to argue that education is a key source of civic participation (Denver and Hands 1990; Emler and Frazer 1999) because it generates skills essential for civic engagement such as abstract thought, debate, discussion and rhetorical and organisational skills (Verba et al 1995; Niemi and Junn 2005; Emler and Frazer 1999).

A number of quantitative studies analysing survey data have documented the associations between HE, in particular, with civic participation. Easterbrook et al's (2016) analysis of a range of British and international[1] surveys documented strong associations between higher levels of education, social trust and political interest and argued that most of the beneficial effects of education can be attributed to having a university education. Such findings are supported by Taylor et al (2019), who have shown that the civic premium of going to university exists and remains relatively unchanged over time.

However, other studies, such as Egerton's (2002) analysis of the British Household Panel Survey found that much of the variation in associational membership, a key measure of civic participation, between graduates and non-graduates could be accounted for by variations in associational membership prior to going to university. So, while education is widely accepted as a precursor to civic participation the role and importance of HE is less clear.

Important as these studies are, many of them are unable to adopt a 'pathways' or 'trajectory' perspective, that is, to consider the routes that young people take towards their participation in civil society during emergent adulthood. As Bynner (2005) has argued, it is how these young people shape their lifecourse during this critical period that is important. Critically, this may not necessarily realise itself in certain actions or behaviours but may be important in defining their beliefs and attitudes towards their place and role in civil society.

While it may appear that graduates are no more engaged in civil society than they were prior to going to university this ignores other ways HE could be contributing to their civic participation. For example, the aspiration among school-leavers to go to university and study in HE may be an important determinant of their civic participation prior to leaving compulsory schooling. Similarly, the decision to participate in HE delays their full-time entry into the labour market – a factor commonly associated with a significant and swift decline in civic participation during emergent adulthood. Therefore, it may be the case that graduates' participation in civic society in the years immediately following graduation may also show an equivalent decline, but the effect of delaying this decline and affording young people the additional time to consider their role in civil society may have important consequences, particularly later in their lifecourse.

This broader view about the HE experience on civic participation has prompted some to take a more nuanced view of the relationship between graduates and civil society. Paterson (2009) has suggested that the form of curriculum that graduates experienced is important for imparting skills and knowledge that enable civic participation. Paterson's analysis of the Birth Cohort Study, a cohort of all individuals born in Britain during one week in 1970, revealed that those graduates who had studied on social science, arts and humanities courses were associated with higher levels of civic participation (such as membership of a political party, a charity or school-related organisation) and had greater socially liberal values (including holding anti-racist views, being libertarian, being tolerant of non-traditional families and being concerned with the environment) than graduates who had studied on other courses. Similarly, Hillygus's (2005) research on political participation among college graduates in America, using longitudinal survey data, revealed that those who had been on biology, engineering and chemistry courses were less inclined to participate politically than those from social sciences and humanities courses. Also, in the US, Niemi and Hanmer (2010) found that mathematics, engineering and natural science majors had the lowest voter turnout.

It seems, therefore, that important distinctions may be drawn between graduates studying different kinds of courses while at university. Studying courses in the arts, humanities and social sciences (AHSS) appear to better prepare graduates for future engagement in civil society compared to those pursuing a degree in the STEM disciplines (Nussbaum 2010; Muddiman 2018).

However, the claim that particular disciplines or curricular are associated with socially liberal attitudes and political and civic participation remains contested. Kam and Palmer (2008) argue that after controlling for the effect of pre-adult experiences and influences, the effect of HE on political participation disappears, suggesting that the positive relationship between HE and political participation is accounted for by the way that pre-adult experiences propel individuals to pursue HE and also civic participation. Similarly, Persson (2012) examined the political intention and participation of students on entry to either academic or vocational educational routes and then again after a year of study. He argued that a process of 'self-selection' occurs whereby those who are already politically orientated are more likely to select academic than vocational education, accounting for the higher rate in intention to vote among students following academic pathways. Berinsky and Lenz (2011) also question the view that education has a direct causal effect on political participation, arguing that education operates as a proxy for other factors. These include family background, and the influence of cognitive skill on the propensity both to participate in politics and to continue in education.

This lack of consensus largely reflects the few studies that attempt to understand how graduates perceive their engagement in civil society in relation to their university experience. University can be a time of intense intellectual and social development, but little is known about how both formal and informal aspects of university intersect with a range of pre-university experiences to inform people's social attitudes and civic participation. We cannot fully understand the role of HE in shaping social attitudes and political participation without due consideration of the range of influences and experiences that precede or exist outside of it. These influences may include an individual's social and economic background, childhood experiences of participation and parental social and political attitudes and participation.

In this analysis we therefore draw on graduates' own accounts of their relationship to civil society to explore what role going to university played in the continuing formation of their social and political attitudes and civic participation, and the extent to which these pathways were shaped by their university experience, particularly in terms of their educational and social experiences while at university. Our analysis reveals three sets of university trajectories among our graduates. The first set of university trajectories were those graduates whose relationship with civil society was not affected by their university experience (either the social or pedagogic and curriculum experiences they had at university). This includes graduates who had some involvement in civil society prior to coming to university and those that had little or no involvement in civil society. The attitudes of these graduates towards civil society and their role in civil society did not appear to be affected or altered by their university experience.

The second set of university trajectories were those graduates who suggested that their university experience reinforced their previous views and attitudes towards civil society. This may not have altered their civic attitudes or necessarily increased their civic participation, but these graduates perhaps benefited from having their attitudes towards civil society affirmed, possibly leading to renewed interest to participate in civil society.

The third set of university trajectories were those graduates who found their university experience transformative in terms of their attitudes and behaviours towards civic engagement. Typically, these students referred to the diversity of the student body and the exposure to new perspectives that helped alter or increase their attitudes towards or participation in civil society. Such students appeared to benefit from the opportunities that their university experiences offered.

To be clear, some graduates alluded to the way in which some aspects of their university experiences had helped to reinforce their social and political values or attitudes towards civic participation while other aspects (like the academic course they had studied) had little or no affect (for example, as we will see later in Ryan's case). Nevertheless, graduates' trajectories could be broadly located within one of the three categories that describes how their university experiences played out in their relationships with civil society, documented in Table 4.1.

Crucially, we find that these different university trajectories appeared to be framed by two important characteristics of their university experience:

- the graduates' educational (academic) experiences (the subjects they studied);
- the graduates' social experiences (who they lived with and what extracurricular activities they were involved in).

For the remainder of this chapter we discuss each of these two characteristics to demonstrate how they helped shape the kind of relationship the graduates had with civil society as a result of their university experience. In this discussion we look at a range of ways they reported being engaged with civil society, such as politically and

Table 4.1: Graduate trajectories

Graduate (pseudonym)	HE type	Degree course	Trajectory
Angharad	Russell Group	STEM	Not affected
Nadia	Elite	STEM	Not affected
Mathew	Russell Group	STEM	Not affected
Sarah	Russell Group	STEM	Not affected
Dan	Russell Group	STEM	Not affected
Andy	Russell Group	STEM	Not affected
Ryan	Russell Group	STEM	Reinforced
James	Elite	STEM	Reinforced
Mike	Post-92	STEM	Transformation
Ben	Russell Group	Social science	Reinforced
Dave	Russell Group	Social science	Reinforced
Tanya	Elite	Social science	Reinforced
Caitlyn	Elite	Social science	Reinforced
Martha	Post-92	Social science	Reinforced
Megan	Post-92	Social science	Not affected
Casey	Russell Group	Social science	Transformative
Grace	Post-92	Social science	Transformative
Ellen	Elite	Social science	Transformative
Hannah	Pre-92	Social science	Transformative
Carris	Elite	Arts/humanities	Reinforced
Laura	Elite	Arts/humanities	Reinforced
Chloe	Elite	Arts/humanities	Reinforced
Ffion	Pre-92	Arts/humanities	Reinforced
Maria	Elite	Arts/humanities	Reinforced
Sophie	Russell Group	Arts/humanities	Reinforced
Simon	Elite	Arts/humanities	Reinforced
Joanne	Elite	Arts/humanities	Reinforced
Eleanor	Post-92	Health and social care	Reinforced
Ruth	Post-92	Health and social care	Not affected
Claire	Post-92	Business	Not affected

socially, and we consider their attitudes towards civil society as well as their active participation in it.

Graduates' educational experiences

Political participation during emergent adulthood is difficult to study because in the UK young people are not allowed to vote in a political election until they are 18 years old. And in many cases they may not get to vote for the first time until they are 20 years old due to the timing of certain elections. Crucially, for many graduates the first time they are likely to have had the opportunity to vote is when they were at university. And many studies have demonstrated that the propensity to vote is often dependent upon having previously voted (Shikano and Kittel 2016). Hence the graduates' political engagement is likely to be heavily shaped by their views and political engagement while at university.

The graduates in our study held diverse political opinions, but the vast majority expressed social and political views that would put them on the political 'left'. Two thirds identified as politically 'left-leaning',[2] three graduates identified themselves as Conservative, two were 'floating voters' and had voted for various parties in recent years, and one identified as being in the 'centre ground'. Two graduates did not reveal their political orientations.

Those who had studied an AHSS subject were especially likely to identify as politically 'left-leaning'. This included those who self-identified as strongly left wing (having consistently voted for Labour or having 'socialist' attitudes and values) as well as those who self-identified as having 'centre left' or left-wing orientations and had also voted for other parties such as Green or Plaid. Megan and Martha reflected on their own political preferences:

> 'Certainly as a family now, and now me and the girls can vote, we have always been Labour.' (Megan, social science graduate, post-92 university)

> 'Yeah, I'm a Labour supporter all the way.' (Martha, social science graduate, post-92 university)

Only one AHSS graduate identified as Conservative, while two did not reveal their political orientations. These graduates were also more likely than graduates of STEM/business subjects to be politically active (that is, to vote, to be a member of a party or to take part in demonstrations).

In comparison, the graduates who had studied STEM or business studies were much more heterogenous in terms of their political orientations; four identified as left or centre left, two Conservative, one centre and one Plaid Cymru supporter. Two expressed little sense of affiliation to a political party, having voted for a range of different parties in recent years. Mike, for example, expressed little sense of loyalty to a single political party: "I don't think I've ever voted consistently over the years. It's always been based on that situation there and then kind of thing" (Mike, STEM graduate, post-92 university). STEM graduates were also more likely to express a general lack of interest in politics, were less likely to be a member of a political party and were the least likely to engage in political activities such as voting or taking part in protests or campaigns of a political nature.

As already stated, it is difficult to compare levels of political engagement while at university with prior levels of political engagement. Nevertheless, many AHSS graduates frequently referred to the way in which their choice of subject to study reflected their previous interest in political (and social) issues. However, many discussed how their degree had given them a deeper and broader understanding of political and social issues, helping to confirm or reinforce their interests and engagement in politics.

For example, Caitlyn, an Oxbridge[3] social science graduate, self-identified as strongly left wing and was highly politically engaged: she voted consistently for Labour and had attended various political demonstrations and gatherings in recent years. In the following excerpt, Caitlyn reflects on the role of her degree in the reinforcement and further formation of her social and political views:

> 'I did a module on revolution. There was all kind of things which I was interested in, about kind of like global politics or, you know, political series – a lot of, like, Lenin. I read a lot around Lenin, Marx, and some of it was very theoretical and then some of it was more historical and I really enjoyed it all. I love that stuff … I think it [her degree subject] was hugely influential on me as well – I mean I do – but then it was only confirming things I already felt, I think, in a way. I was always left feeling I always sort of really thought long and hard about social justice. I was quite earnest in my teenage years in that respect, I think, and because of my family background and because of the kind of— I had friends who felt similarly about things I think.' (Caitlyn, social science graduate, Oxbridge university)

Ben, a politically left-wing social science graduate also reflects on where he sees his own social and political views stemming from:

> 'Yeah, I think it's something I'd, I'd hope that I would have thought regardless. But certainly studying something like I said, social sciences does give you an awareness, I think, of social problems and social divides and things like that, and efforts that have been, or could be, made to remedy those in some sort of way. So, yeah, I think the degree probably had a big influence on that sort of thing. But, I'd still like to think that I would hold those sort of views regardless, yeah.'
> (Ben, social science graduate, Russell Group university)

Both Ben and Caitlyn's accounts illuminate the role of the curriculum in reinforcing pre-existing social and political attitudes. As Ben explains, particular aspects of the curriculum, including learning about 'social divides', political systems or social issues provided him with a strong basis for cultivating knowledge of social and political issues. Ben's account is reminiscent of 'liberal education' theory which posits that as an institution for cultivating critical thought, and liberal attitudes, the university, and social science programmes in particular, are especially important spaces for this (Rootes 1980). This chimes with Nussbaum's (1997, 2010) contention that the arts, social sciences and humanities act as discursive spaces that are hugely important for developing the skills essential for social and political engagement: 'the ability to think critically; the ability to transcend local loyalties and to approach the world problems as a 'citizen of the world'; and, finally, 'the ability to imagine sympathetically the predicament of another person' (Nussbaum 2010: 7).

Aspects of social science and humanities curricula typically engage students with political and social issues, providing them with knowledge and understanding needed for later political and civic engagement. According to Nussbaum, these environments cultivate capacities for critical thinking and reflection that are 'crucial in keeping democracies alive and wide awake' (2010: 10). These aspects of disciplinary areas could explain why the social science and humanities graduates were, on the whole, more politically and civically active than the STEM graduates.

In terms of social participation, many graduates took part in multiple civic activities and engaged in them regularly, while others participated in very few or no formally organised activities. Among those who did participate, activities included volunteering for charities, parents' and teachers' associations, school governing boards, Scouts and Guides associations, trade unions[4] and political parties. Others were heavily involved in their communities through informal volunteering and providing help to elderly people locally. For example, Joanne was a highly active member of her local rural community, participating in a range of activities. The following excerpt from her interview illuminates the varied and extensive nature of her participation in community activities:

> 'I am also on the PTA [parent–teacher association] at school so I have a big fundraising role. I am vice chair there, got big events, four or five big events every year and lots of other small things in between. We live in a tiny village … there's no amenities in the village … so a friend, a couple of friends of mine from the village and I were trying to set up some kind of low-level community get-together thing, first Saturday of the month everyone can go and meet somewhere and just hang out and have a chat. I was just going to say for me, things in the community are probably the most important thing to me, so even if it's just little tiny things – like, we've got an old lady who lives a couple of doors down and she's all by herself … when we have time, my daughter goes and reads.' (Joanne, arts/humanities graduate, Oxbridge university)

Again, AHSS graduates were more likely to participate in civic activities than those who studied business or STEM subjects. STEM graduates were the least likely to participate in formally organised clubs, societies and organisations, and where they did participate, they were more likely to be active in sporting rather than cultural or political activities.[5]

For a minority of graduates, however, their educational experiences seemed to 'transform', rather than reinforce their pre-university experiences. This was particularly so for social science graduates. Indeed, a small number of graduates in this study had developed more 'liberal' attitudes as a result of their degree than might have been the case if they'd not gone to university. Some of them were quite different from their parents in both their interest in social and political issues and civic participation. The most pertinent example of this was Casey, who held largely liberal views, was interested in politics and had, until recently, been an active volunteer for a large charity. Although her social and political interests were beginning to emerge before university, they were encouraged and amplified by studying a social science degree: "Oh yeah. It [her degree] just made me aware really, what it can change, what previous governments have done, because although it's sociology it's quite political as well" (Casey, social science graduate, Russell Group university). Casey's excerpt illuminates a subtle but important theme within the accounts of some graduates, whereby going to university and studying a social science had played a very important role in cultivating their own political and social views and social participation in ways quite distinct from their parents. While the seeds of Casey's social and political views and interests had begun to emerge early on in life, it was her degree (and subsequent postgraduate experiences) which played an important role in cultivating and developing these views and interests and may even have developed them in a way that would not have happened if she had not embarked on a university degree. Similar to Casey was Ellen, a social science graduate with left-wing political orientations and a strong interest in political and social issues; she had been a member of the Labour party and was a board member of a national mental health charity. Ellen's interest in social and political issues and her civic participation was much more intense than her parents: "My mum's not political at all so voting generally entails me telling her who she should vote for, my dad is interested but I wouldn't say he was active ..." (Ellen, social science graduate, Oxbridge university). While Ellen emphasised that her political interests had begun to emerge before she went to university, which she attributed to the working-class and strongly Labour geographical location she was bought up in, she nonetheless asserted that her social science degree had played an important part not only in reinforcing her previously held social and political attitudes but also in cultivating her political interests and civic participation: "Yeah, well I guess the content, obviously I studied politics so that has probably made me more informed and more engaged with politics than I would have" (Ellen, social science graduate, Oxbridge university). Thus, while this theme was subtle, it is evident that some forms of curriculum appear to be hugely important in fostering social and political interests and civic participation, particularly among those for whom a habit of civic and political participation was not acquired from their parents.

Like the AHSS graduates, STEM and business studies graduates' social and political views were also informed by their pre-university experiences. Angharad, a Plaid Cymru supporter, reflected on the way in which her parents' social and political views had helped shape her own. When asked to say where she felt her political interests came from, she replied: "Family, and it's probably the area I'm from as well, we've always been … big Plaid members, and I feel sort of … if we didn't have Plaid what would differentiate us from England?" (Angharad, STEM graduate, Russell Group). However, unlike their social science and humanities graduate counterparts, STEM graduates' interviews were devoid of reference to the role of the degree in the formation of their social and political attitudes and civic participation. Present within the STEM graduates' accounts of their degree were many more references to the way their degree had enabled them to develop skills in problem-solving and understanding formulas and equations. Their degree did not engage them so much with debate and discussion, those skills needed for many forms of political and civic participation (Nussbaum 2010). This was evident in Andy's narrative, a computer sciences graduate, when describing his degree:

'Well, a lot of computer science programmes [are] basically problem-solving. That's what you do, so if you haven't got a logical mind you will struggle to create programmes. So for me it was fantastic because I've got a very logical mind. I used to love problem-solving and things like that … I prefer sort of like black or white rather than all those different shades of grey in between. There is a right answer, or a wrong answer kind of thing. I've always preferred that.' (Andy, computer sciences graduate, Russell Group university)

The focus on problem-solving and equations, present in Andy's excerpt, highlights the different educational experiences of the STEM and AHSS graduates. While the STEM graduates emphasised developing problem-solving skills, the AHSS graduates emphasised critical thinking, discussion and debating skills. These differences may help elucidate the relationship between civic participation, political orientation and curriculum encountered in other research (Paterson 2014; Muddiman 2018). If we accept that skills in critical thinking, discussion and debate are particularly important sources of civic participation (Verba et al 1995; Niemi and Junn 2005), then AHSS schools and departments seem to provide important spaces for these skills to develop.

While the STEM and business studies graduates were far less active in associations (except for sporting associations) and were less committed to a particular political ideology compared to the social science graduates, there was some evidence that the greater focus on proof and logic in their degree shaped their approach to political issues. For example, STEM graduates were also more likely to allude to the way in which their voting preferences were driven by considerations around particular policies and agendas and practical issues, resulting in a far more pragmatic view of politics. This is captured in Mike's description of his voting preferences:

> 'There's— I think it's so complicated and the parties don't represent what they used to and I think it ... I just think it's a bit blinkered to just support one party outright because I can find things that I disagree with about all of them. I guess it's just trying to find an intelligent solution to the problems rather than just saying, well, you should do that because it's right or you know— which is, it's a good thing, but yeah, it's tricky because there is no solution to these issues.' (Mike, STEM graduate, post-1992 university)

However, it appears that a more pragmatic approach to political issues was not as conducive for political engagement as having a more ideological view of politics and society, as typically demonstrated by the higher levels of political and social participation among AHSS graduates.

Graduates' social experience

As we have seen, some degree disciplines seem to be more important than others in cultivating the attitudes and skills that encourage civic participation. Consequently, the educational experience of HE, largely divided between AHSS and STEM subjects, leads to an array of civil society trajectories – some (AHSS) leading to high levels of civic participation and others (STEM) leading to low levels of civic participation. This might help explain why there is no clear and unequivocal evidence of HE's impact on civil society. But this still raises an interesting question as to why, on average, most studies find some additional, albeit modest, benefit of going to university on civic participation.

To answer this question, we must look beyond the degree and curriculum that graduates experienced and consider the wider social role of university life, including all the extracurricular activities available to students irrespective of the kind of subject they study.

For the majority of graduates, going to university was an intensely social experience – a time when new friendships were made and social networks developed. For many, these social networks played as much of an important role in the development of their own social and political values as their degree did. As with their educational experiences, these social experiences appeared to help some students reinforce or galvanise their attitudes towards civil society, while for some this had a more transformative effect. And as before, for some graduates their social experience appeared to have had little or no influence on their attitudes and role in civil society.

Clearly, the graduates' educational and social experiences were often intertwined. So, for example, many of the AHSS graduates talked about socialising with 'like-minded' people from their courses. But nevertheless, it was this social experience, as opposed to what was included in their curriculum, that helped continue to shape their attitudes towards civil society. Interestingly, we found that meeting 'like-minded' people did not make any difference to their prior attitudes towards civil society and more often than not led to reinforcing these attitudes. Rarely were these accounts associated with more transformative civil society trajectories. For example, when Ruth was asked about the role of university in the formation of her views she responded:

> 'I think it's hard to, it's hard to pull all of those things apart. I think they were all part of the same time in my life and the way my life was going, on a path that probably was going to go on anyway. I suppose it's difficult to make sweeping statements but, probably, going to university and doing the type of course I did – and had probably put me around like-minded people who probably thought in a similar way to me – and so I don't think that my views on things or my political views or my views on the world have changed but, since going to university, probably I just surrounded myself with people like me really.' (Ruth, health and social care graduate, post-1992 university)

Those graduates who said that their social experience at university was more transformative were more likely to mention the importance of meeting students from diverse backgrounds and with diverse views, perspectives and values: "Yeah and they [her friends at university] were just really interesting people and then you would debate [at dinners], things like religion and politics and … they were just always very engaged, interested in what we thought about things" (Ellen, social science graduate, Oxbridge university). Like Ellen, others also felt that going to university and, in particular, sharing accommodation with people from different backgrounds with wide-ranging views and perspectives, had opened them up to alternative ideas and perspectives. What's more, the social experience of HE also provided an opportunity to directly influence graduates' civic participation. Most student unions in the UK offer a variety of extracurricular clubs, societies and activities covering sports, volunteering, musical, cultural and religious interests to name a few. Ryan, a STEM graduate, reflected on this. For him, while his academic experiences had little role in his attitudes or orientations toward civic participation, the 'social' aspect of university had served to reinforce previously held attitudes towards civic participation. In particular, living with peers in student accommodation meant the discovery of shared interests, which in turn facilitated his participation in activities and taking on a number of important 'civic' responsibilities while at university:

> 'My housemate was in the rambling club, so it ended up that I joined that with him, and then stayed a part of that all the way through uni if I remember rightly; ended up being heavily involved in the committee on that, became president of the rambling club and running stuff, trips to Scotland, Wales, North Wales ... and all around the UK, really, like, organising that, so met— most of my friends now I would say I met through that. And again through another friend I got introduced to the korfball club and joined that and that took over my life for a while and again got properly involved in the committee there. Not so much getting as high as being president of the club, but was treasurer for ages. I got involved with running other clubs outside of university after that and running the Welsh Association in charge of it ... I was secretary on the committee for that, one year ...'
> (Ryan, STEM graduate, Russell Group university)

Similarly, Laura reflected on her involvement in her college's junior common room (JCR) and how she became part of it:

Laura: Oh yeah, I was one of the representatives on the JCR committee which was the junior common room for my college, yeah ... I was JCR secretary, which involved having to sort out the agenda every week, organise the meetings and gather in motions and sort out minutes ...

Interviewer:	And how did you get involved in those roles? Did you sort of nominate yourself or …
Laura:	I think that was because, well I did nominate myself but I was in a group of friends who were also quite keen so one of my friends was the president and another was vice president. Yeah actually there were quite a few of them, there was the rag representative as well. Yeah so these were all my friends, so it was a bit of a friendship group that got voted … voted on, so I think that was probably why I did it because it was part of that group …

(Laura, music graduate, Oxbridge university)

Social networks and friendships formed while at university clearly provide significant opportunities for extracurricular activities, societies and clubs. For graduates like Laura and Ryan, having access to these opportunities reinforced their previously held attitudes and relationships with civil society, but for others, these social experiences transformed them, as we saw previously for graduates like Ellen.

Conclusion

This chapter set out to look beyond 'levels' of education as a determinant of political and social participation to unpick the idea that university students 'graduate' into civil society. Some existing research suggests that HE has a causal effect on individuals' participation in civil society, increasing their likelihood of undertaking voluntary work or engaging with politics (Verba et al 1995). However, other studies have indicated that HE operates as proxy for pre-existing factors which inform both the educational pathways people take and their social and political views (Berinsky and Lenz 2011). Our study reveals that there are a number of interrelated factors influencing the relationship between undergraduate study, the development of social values, and onward involvement in civil society, particularly in terms of students' educational (academic) and social experiences at university. These characteristics appear to then shape the ways young adults continue to develop their attitudes towards civil society and the degree to which they participate in civil society.

Our interviews also highlight the importance of early socialisation during childhood, and how these begin to shape graduates' political and social attitudes. While this process in itself may help determine the kinds of subjects students study at university we find some compelling evidence from some graduates, mainly those studying social science and arts or humanities courses, that their educational experience and the curriculum they studied continued to develop and reinforce these attitudes. In a minority of cases their educational experience was more transformative in terms of heightening their civic attitudes or increasing their civic participation, especially when coupled with their wider social experiences of university and the many new opportunities to engage in civic activities and responsibilities while at university.

However, there were many examples, particularly from STEM and business subjects, where graduates were unable to articulate how their educational experiences had changed their social and political attitudes. While they were able to describe some of the key skills they had acquired through their courses that could be valuable for later civic participation it was often precisely because of their greater attention on logic and reasoning that perhaps hindered them from developing the motivations to participate in civil society in the first place. But when encouraged to participate in social activities, typically through student societies, there were examples where STEM graduates social experiences either served to reinforce previously held attitudes towards civic participation (as it did for Ryan).

Thus, the notion that education straightforwardly leads to the formation of socially liberal attitudes and values, and high levels of political and social participation, is problematic. As we have shown, the curricula or disciplinary culture of certain university departments seems to be more influential in this regard than others. If AHSS degrees are important disciplines for the cultivation of skills and values aligned with civic participation, then schools and universities delivering them are crucial for our democratic landscape. The policy implications of this are substantial; at a time of intense funding cuts to social sciences and arts and humanities departments in universities in the UK and internationally (Prose 2017), the insights provided by this study suggest that investment in these departments is as important for the nation's social landscape, as investment in STEM and business subjects are for the nation's economy. Indeed, as Nussbaum argues, if AHSS subjects are marginalised, nations 'will soon be producing generations of useful machines, rather than complete citizens who can think for themselves, criticise tradition, and understand the significance of another person's sufferings and achievements' (2010: 2).

However, this association between AHSS subjects and the development of an interest in politics and social and political participation cannot be explained by disciplinary knowledge and cultures alone: wider social experiences at university are also important.

The fact that, on the whole, graduates are more likely than non-graduates to be socially and politically active, suggests that the influence of attending university extends beyond formal education and includes informal social experiences. Our study highlights the importance of social networks and friendships developed at university as spaces for fostering social attitudes and cultivating interest in civic activities. This would appear to transcend the disciplinary distinctions identified here, indeed the social mixing facilitated by some forms of student accommodation seems to be important here. The opportunity to meet other young people from a range of backgrounds and studying a variety of subjects was described by many of our participants as an important element of the student experience.

But we have also seen very clearly that the educational and social experiences at university are just part of a continuous process of developing attitudes towards and participation in civil society over the lifecourse. These pathways or trajectories are, for the majority of university participants, being forged prior to entering HE. The extent to which prior experiences are influenced by the aspiration of going to university was outside the remit of this study. Nevertheless, there was also clear evidence that universities can, and do, play an important role in either reinforcing prior attitudes or even helping transform civic attitudes and behaviours. But it is also clear that this period of emergent adulthood can also be quite important in leading to divergent trajectories of civic engagement. Although this study did not involve non-graduates there is evidence from elsewhere to suggest that universities offer a 'civic premium' (see, for example, Taylor et al 2019). But what this study has also shown is that the university experience (including the academic and social experiences) can itself lead to quite divergent trajectories of civic engagement.

Notes

[1] These included the British Social Attitudes Survey, the British Household Panel Survey and The International Social Survey Programme.

[2] This included purely 'left', 'centre left' or 'left-leaning' – indicative of voting for a range of parties, typically the Green Party (an environmentally focused left-leaning party) or Plaid Cymru (a Welsh nationalist socio-democratic party promoting independence for Wales).

[3] For brevity and in order to enhance the anonymity of the data, the term 'Oxbridge' is used to refer to the Universities of Oxford and Cambridge. We do not, however, wish to imply that the Universities of Oxford and Cambridge are the same and we recognise their different structures, systems, locations and student bodies.

⁴ Participation in trade unions typically involved 'membership' with only a minority of participants actively participating in them.

⁵ This might be partially accounted for by gender, as male participants were more active in sporting activities and who dominated the STEM graduates.

References

Arnett, J.J. (2004) *Emerging Adulthood: The Winding Road from Late Teens Through the Twenties*, Oxford: Oxford University Press.

Berinsky, A.J. and Lenz, G.S. (2011) 'Education and political participation: exploring the causal link', *Political Behavior*, 33(3): 357–73.

Bynner, J. (2005) 'Rethinking the youth phase of the life-course: the case for emerging adulthood?', *Journal of Youth Studies*, 8(4): 367–84.

Bynner, J., Schuller, T. and Feinstein, L. (2003) 'Wider benefits of education: skills, higher education and civic engagement', *Zeitschrift für Pädagogik*, 49(3): 341–61.

Dalton, R.J. (2013) *The Apartisan American: Dealignment and Changing Electoral Politics*, Thousand Oaks, CA: CQ Press.

Dee, T.S. (2004) 'Are there civic returns to education?' *Journal of Public Economics*, 88(9/10): 1697–720.

Denver, D. and Hands, G. (1990) 'Does studying politics make a difference? The political knowledge, attitudes and perceptions of school students', *British Journal of Political Science*, 20(2): 263–79.

Easterbrook, M.J., Kuppens, T. and Manstead, A.S.R. (2016) 'The education effect: higher educational qualifications are robustly associated with beneficial personal and sociopolitical outcomes', *Social Indicators Research*, 126(3): 1261–98.

Egerton, M. (2002) 'Higher education and civic engagement', *The British Journal of Sociology*, 53(4): 603–20.

Emler, N. and Frazer, E. (1999) 'Politics: the education effect', *Oxford Review of Education,* 25(1–2): 251–73.

Hillygus, D.S. (2005) 'The missing link: exploring the relationship between higher education and political engagement', *Political Behavior*, 27(1): 25–47.

Inglehart, R. and Welzel, C. (2005) *Modernization, Cultural Change, and Democracy: The Human Development Sequence*, Cambridge: Cambridge University Press.

Kam, C.D. and Palmer, C.L. (2008) 'Reconsidering the effects of education on political participation', *Journal of Politics*, 70(3): 612–31.

Muddiman, E. (2018) 'Degree subject and orientations to civic responsibility: a comparative study of business and sociology students', *Critical Studies in Education*, ahead of print: https://doi.org/10.1080/17508487.2018.1539020.

Nie, N.H., Junn, J. and Stehlik-Barry, K. (1996) *Education and Democratic Citizenship in America*, Chicago: University of Chicago Press.

Niemi, R.G. and Hanmer, M.J. (2010) 'Voter turnout among college students: new data and a rethinking of traditional theories', *Social Science Quarterly*, 91(2): 301–23.

Niemi, R.G. and Junn, J. (2005) *Civic Education: What Makes Students Learn*, New Haven, CT: Yale University Press.

Nussbaum, M. (1997) *Cultivating Humanity: A Classical Defense of Reform in Liberal Education*, London: Harvard University Press.

Nussbaum, M. (2010) *Not for Profit: Why Democracy Needs the Humanities*, Princeton, NJ: Princeton University Press.

Paterson, L. (2009) 'Civic values and the subject matter of educational courses', *Oxford Review of Education*, 35(1): 81–98.

Paterson, L. (2014) 'Education, social attitudes and social participation among adults in Britain', *Sociological Research Online*, 19(1): 187–201.

Persson, M. (2012) 'Does type of education affect political participation? Results from a panel survey of Swedish adolescents', *Scandinavian Political Studies*, 35(3): 198–221.

Prose, F. (2017) 'Humanities teach students to think. Where would we be without them?', *The Guardian*, 12 May. Available from: https://www.theguardian.com/commentisfree/2017/may/12/humanities-students-budget-cuts-university-suny.

Rootes, C.A. (1980) 'Student radicalism: politics of moral protest and legitimation problems of the modern capitalist state', *Theory and Society*, 9(3): 473–502.

Shikano, S. and Kittel, B. (2016) 'Dynamics of voting propensity: experimental tests of adaptive learning models', *Political Research Quarterly*, 69(4): 813–29.

Sloam, J. (2014) 'New voice, less equal the civic and political engagement of young people in the United States and Europe', *Comparative Political Studies*, 47(5): 663–88.

Sondheimer, R.M. and Green, D.P. (2010) 'Using experiments to estimate the effects of education on voter turnout', *American Journal of Political Science*, 54(1): 174–89.

Taylor, C., Fox, S., Evans, C. and Rees, G. (2019) 'The "civic premium" of university graduates: the impact of massification on associational membership', *Studies in Higher Education*, ahead of print: https://srhe.tandfonline.com/doi/full/10.1080/03075079.2019.1637837.

Trow, M. (1973) *Problems in the Transition From Elite to Mass Higher Education*, Berkeley, CA: Carnegie Commission on Higher Education. Available from: https://eric.ed.gov/?id=ED091983.

Verba, S. and Nie, N.H. (1972) *Participation in America: Political Democracy and Social Equality*, New York: Harper and Row.

Verba, S., Schlozman, K.L. and Brady, H.E. (1995) *Voice and Equality: Civic Voluntarism in American Politics*, Cambridge, MA: Harvard University Press.

5

Parenthood and civic engagement

Esther Muddiman

While some research focuses on the effect of age on various types of participation (see, for example, Zukin et al 2006; Quintelier 2007), here we conceptualise lifecourse stages in terms of the roles that an individual assumes during his/her life (Jennings and Niemi 1981; Quaranta 2016). From this perspective, life events such as becoming a parent act as possible 'determinants' of the resources required to participate in civil society (Quaranta 2016). Becoming a parent is a key moment in the lifecourse, with the majority of adults in the UK having at least one child (Graham et al 2017). Little is known about how the dramatic shifts in routines, resources, social networks and priorities associated with parenthood are reflected in patterns of civic engagement. Parents, particularly those of young children, constantly (re)negotiate paid work and other commitments in relation to their changing circumstances, and decisions about voluntary work or political engagement are 'facilitated or constrained by their changing individual and household patterns' (Hogg 2016: 170). Scholars in both Europe (Kroh and Selb 2009; Corbetta et al 2012) and the US (Janoski and Wilson 1995; Jennings 2002; Andolina et al 2003) have underscored the importance of better understanding the articulation between parenthood and civic engagement, both as a lifecourse transition in itself, and as an indicator of the onward supply of engaged citizens. In this chapter we focus on parents with current caring responsibilities for their children and define 'parenting' and 'parenthood' according to the roles, identities and responsibilities adopted by individuals acting as parents, rather than on biological distinctions. Adoptive, and stepparents are therefore included.

Perhaps most obviously, parenthood alters the amount of time and resources available for participating in various civic and political activities such as volunteering, campaigning and providing informal support to neighbours. The 'time budgets' of parents may be further stretched by demographic changes, leading to a rising number of 'beanpole' families (Hagestad 2000) in which those with young children may also be caring for their own parents. In addition to reducing time availability and drawing on household finances, parenthood also increases responsibilities and affects social relationships (Gallagher and Gerstel 2001; Nomaguchi and Milkie 2003). Parents' capacity to engage in civil society activities may therefore be enabled or constrained by a number of different factors including their social networks and wider familial support, the domestic division of labour, other caring responsibilities (for older or unwell relatives, for example), their employment status and financial security, and the health and well-being of the entire household. The impact on the time resources of single parents is likely to be particularly significant, and will be different again for parents who have separated and who share the custody of their children, for whom their parenting responsibilities are concentrated into distinctive periods such as during the week or at weekends.

Notwithstanding the time constraints of caring for children, parenting may provide new opportunities for civic engagement, for example, through helping out at play groups, children's clubs and becoming involved with schools. Parenthood itself may change social and political values, priorities and practices. Indeed, existing research indicates that parents care more about public issues, public services, taxes and education (Elder and Greene 2012). While having children may result in lower propensity to vote (Welch 1977; Wolfinger and Wolfinger 2008), a number of studies in the US have found a positive effect of parenthood on participation – not only engaging in school district politics (Jennings 1979) but also being more attentive to a wider range of political issues (Elder and Greene 2012). Of course, the resources available to parents may be influenced by demographic factors such as socio-economic status and level of education. Parental involvement will also be somewhat dependent on the opportunities presented for participation, which are likely to differ in urban versus rural contexts.

Introducing our data

In this chapter we draw on interview data from the Intergenerational Transmission of Civic Virtues (ITCV) project (for more detail see Muddiman et al 2019) to explore the accounts of parents themselves. We interviewed 18 parents (14 mothers and 4 fathers) of children aged 13–14 years across South Wales over a six-month period in 2017–18 (see Table 5.1). We asked some questions that were specific to this 13–14-year-old child (indicated with an asterisk in Table 5.1), but others encompassed parenting more generally – with there

Table 5.1: Attributes of parent interviewees

Name	Year of birth	Place of birth	Occupation type	Marital status	Voting preference	Religious faith	University degree	Children
Natasha	1971	Wales	Education	Single	Lib Dem/ Remain	Church in Wales	Y	Willow* and Sophie (younger)
Ruth	1974	Wales	Education	Married	Labour/Remain	Roman Catholic	Y	Zain,* Adam, Billy, Erin (all younger)
Miranda	1976	England	Faith based	Married	Conservative/ Remain	Nonconformist	Y	Caleb,* Rachel, Zachary, Ruth (all younger)
Ffion	1967	Wales	Education	Married	Labour/Remain	None	N	Rhys,* Llinos,[a] Sam,[a] Jenny[a] (all older)
Nina	1972	Wales	Education	Married	Labour/Remain	Nonconformist	Y	Tasha* and Suzy (younger)
Bridget	1972	Wales	Third sector	Single	Labour/Remain	Roman Catholic	N	Cian*
Daisy	1968	Wales	Education	Married	Plaid/Remain	Church in Wales	Y	Zina* and Leo (older)
Abby	1977	Wales	Healthcare	Single	Labour/Remain	Nonconformist	N	Russ* and Tanner (older)
Julia	1965	Wales	Civil service	Married	Conservative/ Remain	Church in Wales	N	Bella* and Claire (older)
John	1969	England	Finance	Married	Conservative/ Leave	Church in Wales	N	Stuart* and Jack (younger)
Eve	1966	England	Secretarial	Married	Other/Leave	Nonconformist	N	Theo* and Rose (younger)

(continued)

Table 5.1: Attributes of parent interviewees (continued)

Name	Year of birth	Place of birth	Occupation type	Marital status	Voting preference	Religious faith	University degree	Children
Tara	1979	England	Not available	Not available	UKIP/Leave	Church in Wales	N	Mia*
David	1971	England	Civil service	Married	Labour/Remain	Nonconformist	Y	Alfie* and Bethany (younger)
Nicole	1978	Wales	Finance/ education	Repartnered	Labour/Remain	Roman Catholic	Y	Aleds,* Phoebeª (older), Dewi (younger)
Daniel	1966	England	IT	Married	Labour/Remain	Nonconformist	Y	Natalie* and Toby (older)
Charlotte	1970	England	Education	Married	Labour/Remain	None	Y	Zoe* and Lisa (younger)
Frankie	1978	Wales	Education	Repartnered	Labour/Remain	Roman Catholic	N	Lauren,* Melody (older), Joel and Connor (younger)
Salem	1973	England	Healthcare	Married	Unsure/Leave	Muslim	Y	Abyd,* Rasheed, Sanjay (younger)

Notes:
* indicates the child aged 13–14 at the time of parent interview.
ª indicates adult children who have moved out of the family home.

being a range of older and/or younger siblings in the household or living as young adults elsewhere. Half of those parents interviewed were born in Wales (including two identifying as Welsh/Irish) with the remaining participants having moved to Wales from England. Parents aged ranged from 40 to 52 years old at time of interview. The majority of parents were married, with three single parents and two repartnered parents. Each interview was carried out one-to-one, with the exception of Daisy who wanted her daughter Zina to be included in the process. Almost all of our participants identified as White British and most had a religious faith – although this was far more central in some of their accounts than others. While it is likely that the parents who agreed to be interviewed are more civically or politically engaged than those who did not respond, they are by no means a homogenous group. As we shall see, the type and degree of civil society engagement that parents in the study were engaged with varied over time. This considerable variation in parental accounts allowing us to consider the wide range of processes through which parenthood interacts with civic engagement.

Drawing on the conceptualisations outlined in the introductory chapter of this volume, we take a holistic view of civic participation that includes both formal (constituted) and informal voluntary activity and community work, and both formalised and 'extra-parliamentary' political participation or activism (Ekman and Amnå 2012). In doing so we are alive to the 'attention' and 'identity' aspects of 'latent activism' or civic value formation, including both talk (family conversations and discussions) and practices (family activities). The chapter begins with an exploration of parents' accounts of various factors that foster or inhibit their civic engagement, considering what kinds of opportunities for engagement are afforded by parenthood, and how sustainable these engagement activities might be.

Barriers to parents' engagement

The early years and squeezed time budgets

Existing research indicates that becoming a parent has a dramatic impact on individual time budgets – especially in the initial stages of parenthood, and, in particular, for mothers (Gauthier and Furstenberg 2002; Craig and Mullan 2010; Quaranta and Dotti Sani 2018). Indeed, according to Gauthier and Furstenberg, the transition to parenthood prompts the most significant shift in time use for 18–34-year-olds across nine industrialised countries, when compared to the transition from school to work and the transition to partnership. Time devoted to paid work decreased for women in all nine countries when they became mothers (Gauthier and Furstenberg 2002). Conversely, the transition to parenthood was reflected in increased time spent doing paid work for fathers in Finland, Italy, the Netherlands and the US (Gauthier and Furstenberg 2002). Becoming a parent is associated with an increase of 2.7 hours per day spent on housework for mothers, and an increase of 0.7 hours per day for fathers, and decreased leisure time (Gauthier and Furstenberg 2002). Parenting during the early years is likely to be the most time-intensive: preschool children require more care and attention in ways that may act to divert attention and resources from civic activities and may isolate parents from the public sphere (Quaranta 2016). Indeed, political science scholars have investigating the effect of parenthood on political participation have consistently found that the greatest impact for both mothers and fathers is when children are preschool age, with the influence of parenthood subsequently reducing as children get older (Schlozman et al 1994; Voorstopol and Coffe 2010; Quaranta 2016).

These pressures are evident in the accounts of our interviewees. Although they were all selected because they had teenage children, some parents also had younger, primary-school-aged children. Participants often reflected on their own experiences of the time-intensive early years of parenthood, also drawing on their experiences of caring for nieces and nephews, or on the experiences of relatives and friends who had younger children. For example, Eve spoke of a sister who had been heavily involved in a charity but had become stretched for time with two young children, explaining: "It ebbs and flows anyway, so there's going to be times when you can, and sometimes when you can't." Similarly, Nicole reasons that with "four kids within three years of each other" her sister "hasn't got time to do anything" let alone volunteering.

The impact of parenthood on individual time budgets was expressed by some participants in terms of an 'acceleration' of time, in which intentions and ambitions to volunteer (Ruth), learn a new language (Charlotte), or develop hobbies often fell by the wayside. For example, Ffion reflects on how her life changed when she became a mother: "The years have gone very fast, to be honest, very very fast. It's like a dream, it is. I don't know where the time has gone. It's just bringing up children, I suppose, and they take up all your time, yep" (Ffion, married mother of four).

The importance of support networks

Even with older children, our data suggest that parents are likely to have fewer resources for participation in certain civic and political activities. Ten of the parents we interviewed were working full-time, with four working part-time hours and two out of work. The presence or absence of a support network – either within the family or beyond – is important in parents' accounts of their ability to participate in civic or political activities. For example, Natasha indicated that she would like to get involved with volunteering but didn't feel like she could commit the time, especially since separating from her husband and becoming a single mother while continuing to work full-time. For other parents, having grandparents living close by, or having siblings with similar-aged children who are able to share childcare, eased the time pressure of parenting, potentially making room for civic engagement. Charlotte, mother of two teenage daughters, explained that being a parent limits her ability to travel to visit her own mother (who lives over an hour away) as she needs to be home to take the girls to various clubs and classes over the weekend. Charlotte and her husband Phil both work, and she explains how, with help from her mother, they are able to spread out their annual leave to cover the summer holidays:

> 'It does help with the childcare with not having to take all of the holidays. That means we can take time off together then. I know a lot of my colleagues they have to, they can't have holiday the same time as their partners if they need to cover the school holidays, which isn't particularly good for family life.' (Charlotte, married mother of two)

Sharing of parental responsibilities between mothers and fathers

Parental engagement in civil society may also be shaped by the division of labour within the household (Burns et al 1997; Verba et al 1997; Quaranta 2016). Existing research indicates that, in general, parenthood is far more disruptive and time intensive for mothers than it is for fathers. Despite various legislation and cultural shifts towards equal partnerships and division of domestic labour, parenthood continues to affect men and women differently. Most obviously, women temporarily or permanently exit the labour market during maternity, and their role and orientation to work may shift if or when they return. Conversely, when men become fathers they tend to work more hours and do not spend as much time on housework or childcare as mothers (Anxo et al 2011; Gibb et al 2014). Given that mothers tend to return to work once their children are older (Gauthier and Furstenberg 2002), their participation is affected by parenthood to a greater extent than that of fathers.

This suggests that becoming a parent might impact mothers and fathers differently in terms of their opportunities for civic engagement, and that family responsibilities may be particularly detrimental to women's participation in civil society. Indeed, Quaranta and Dotti Sani (2018) use European Social Survey data to demonstrate that 'family intensive' stages of the lifecourse 'have a stronger negative effect on women's involvement than men's' especially in the areas of 'political interest, party identification and activity' and less so in the areas of voting/demonstrating (2018: 254). Results show that across Europe there is a gender gap in some but not all forms of political engagement, and that 'family dense' life stages 'have a stronger negative effect on women's involvement than on men's' (2018: 256).

Interestingly, this is not straightforwardly the case with our interviewees. In spite of recognising that they had particularly time-intensive family roles (in comparison to their male partners, or due to their role as sole parent), some mothers in this study remarked that it is largely women who engage in voluntary work. For example, Bridget, a single mother to Cian (aged 14), feels that women are more likely to get involved with nurturing causes, compared to men who follow their own personal interests:

> 'It's women that are doing more volunteering despite being a mum, despite working. So, I think that there's something more intrinsic in women to do that stuff than men. There's got to be, it can't just be me as an individual, you know, the data's there really that's saying, well, women tend to be the 'doers'. Whether or not it's the opportunities that are coming up, because the stuff that men will volunteer for is like the football, you know, getting a football team together, so it's something that intrinsically motivates them to volunteer.' (Bridget, single mother of one)

Quaranta suggests that such 'private inequalities' within the family home, with mothers taking on the majority of caregiving responsibilities, may contribute to 'political inequalities': 'family roles and responsibilities can be constraints to participation, especially for women' (Quaranta 2016: 372). While none of the mothers in our study directly identified their parenting responsibilities as a barrier to their participation in politics, a minority of those interviewed did discuss deferring to their husbands or partners during political conversations in the home. Charlotte, for example, explained that her husband is "better informed" on these issues. In the majority of cases, though, mothers were enthusiastic about engaging their children in political discussions, and fathers did not talk about political socialisation as being solely their responsibility. Furthermore, there was little evidence in our data that daughters were being socialised into 'politically passive' roles (Welch 1977).

There was also some evidence of change in relation to the allocation of parenting and household responsibilities between parents – most notably in the case of David and his wife, who both chose to reduce their work to part-time hours so that they could share parenting responsibilities equally. This links to civil society in two important ways. First, it might be argued that David and his wife are 'role modelling' gender equality in the family home and providing an environment in which their children will have a more egalitarian view of maternal and paternal roles. Second, in spreading the time commitments of parenthood and maintaining the household equally, it potentially leaves David's wife with more time to pursue personal interests, social and civic activities.

Tensions between work, community and family commitments

Family commitments and the desire to spend time with children clearly does have an impact on parents' levels of civic engagement. David was involved in a range of voluntary activities but was wary of taking on any more commitments as a working parent:

> 'I've done little bits with, we've got 'Friends' of the local park and things like that. I've done little bits with them, but I've tried not to get too involved. Sometimes with these small local communities, once you sort of do a few things it's hard to get out of. And as you've picked up on, we lead busy lives and so, yeah I'd say it's more of a passing interest at the moment, but down to time.' (David, married father of two)

Similarly, Nina was heavily involved in her local community and described being torn between doing more and wanting to put her own family first: "I'm always being asked to stand as councillor by friends and things like that, but … my family's the most important thing to me at the moment" (Nina, married mother of two). Eve has two young teenagers, works part-time and volunteers for a befriending service despite suffering from a chronic illness herself. Eve describes praying for energy on the drive over to visit Sheila, the elderly lady that she has been spending time with over the last couple of years:

'Yesterday I was praying on my way to go and visit her …
I go after work. I'd had a busy day … Sometimes I'll be
driving home and thinking, gosh, I should be going home,
I shouldn't be going there, but my mind is so full, and, yes,
I was tired yesterday, but I just pray to be able to give to
her.' (Eve, married mother of two)

Eve's account suggests that her commitment to visiting Sheila is very important to her, and that she factors in Sheila's family circumstances and state of mind when trying to balance her time and commitments: "It was really important that I went to see her [this week]. Especially as her daughter [is unwell]. It's even more important at the moment, yeah." This represents a tension for Eve as she tries to balance her desire to support Sheila with her own family responsibilities and the management of her energy levels: "I feel like I can't give more of my time, per se … I have two young children and I need to balance things out. I give what I can." One of the ways Eve managed this tension was to combine the two – involving her children in trips to the garden centre with Sheila and inviting Sheila to family meals in restaurants.

The ongoing negotiation of competing commitments and responsibilities seemed to be felt more acutely among single parents, like Natasha, and older parents, including Eve, who commented, "I was an older parent, and sometimes I think I wish I'd been like 20, do you know what I mean? I'm just knackered half the time." It was very common for parents to look ahead to a time in the future when their working or familial commitments had lessened. David, for example, talked about his desire to be more involved in civic activities in his retirement: "I'd love to do the sort of thing my dad did. He was, every Wednesday, every week without fail, going out and doing stuff like that." Similarly, John suggests that if less of his time was committed to other things he would have more time to engage with volunteering to support his sons' extracurricular activities: "Yeah, if I was retired I'd probably do more."

Overcoming barriers? Civic engagement as a family activity

Our data also suggest that it is also possible for parents' pre-existing voluntary activities to intertwine with family time, and in some cases, can bring families closer together. For example. David explained how his wife's keen running interest had led to him and his son joining her on a weekly 'parkrun'[1] with David's son "following the footsteps" of his father and regularly volunteering as a marshal for the event. All three would travel to the event on a Saturday morning and would take it in turns to marshal while the other two ran the course: "He'll do the same as us with the parkrun, he'll volunteer as well as run. He volunteers a fair bit for that." In fact, David's son Alfie (aged 14 at the time of interview) was also volunteering as a Cub Group leader in addition to being a Scout and had become the "driving force" getting his parents involved with helping out there. David explains that the combined voluntary commitments of his two children, his wife and himself sometimes impact on family time, admitting "we could be better at spending time together". Although volunteering and helping others seems to be a key part of David's family identity, bringing them closer together as a family unit, he describes how they also try to "slow down" and carve out quality time together either around the dinner table or arranging trips to the cinema together, away from their various voluntary commitments.

Interestingly, some charities and non-governmental organisations (NGOs) are beginning to mobilise ideas of family to promote involvement. In her scoping review of families and volunteering, Jochum (2015, 2019) identifies various 'family volunteering' opportunities offered by local branches of social and healthcare charities. For example, for the 2015 'volunteers week', Doncaster NCT (National Childbirth Trust) used the slogan 'Volunteering for NCT can be a family affair!' and included photos of parents with young children in their promotional campaign on social media.

New opportunities for involvement

While parenthood can restrict some forms of civic engagement, our discussions with parents suggest that it can foster others. In this section we examine participant accounts of parenthood prompting new interests or shifting perspectives and triggering involvement in networks. A number of studies in the US have found a positive effect of parenthood on political participation – not only engaging in school district politics (Jennings 1979) but also being more attentive to a wider range of political issues (Elder and Greene 2012). In extending social networks (Janoski and Wilson 1995; Wilson and Musick 1997; Elder and Greene 2012; Quaranta 2016), parenthood may provide new or different opportunities for involvement in civil society. Parenting school-age children (as opposed preschool children) is likely to present new opportunities for involvement in civil society (McGlenn 1980; Sundeen 1990; Schlozman et al 1994; Smith 1994; Rotolo 2000; Oesterle et al 2004; Nesbit 2012). New social networks may also enhance some of the traits such as confidence and sociability that aid further or diversifying involvement.

Children's clubs and groups

In our parents' accounts, it was common for parents to get involved with children's clubs and activities as their own children joined these various groups. This included uniformed groups like the Guides and Scouts, and children's clubs linked to religious organisations. Charlotte got involved with helping out with her local Beavers, Cubs and Scouts groups when her daughters joined. At the height of her involvement she was on the executive committee, helping to organise fetes and supervising parties and sleepovers. Since her own daughters have left the Scouts she has scaled back her involvement but continues to help:

> 'Both girls used to do Scouts, so I did used to go and help at that but then Zoe got too old and Lisa left … I will still be helping with the Scout Post again this year … Lisa will still be doing that with me, so we'll pick up the letters and deliver those around here, we've done that for the past three or four years.' (Charlotte, married mother of two)

During the interview Charlotte wondered whether she would become more involved again in the future: "I mean part of me thinks maybe I'd go back and help with the Scouts when the girls get a bit older and need me a bit less", but she conceded that she might prefer to spend time on other interests that she enjoys instead. John, on the other hand, became involved as a swimming coach after taking and collecting his son from lessons and witnessing the shortage of volunteers:

> 'With Jack and his swimming, I would go there, drop him off, and then I'd probably just sit there and watch him. And then, I could see that the coaches or teachers were

struggling. Well I'm just sitting there, I may as well try and help them out … so then I was there all the time, whenever I took him I was coaching as well. Not him … but the lane next to him or something.' (John, married father of two)

While his son's interest in swimming maps on to (and was possibly influenced by) John's own love of the sport, John frames his participation in terms of wanting to help out to keep the swimming club going, rather than in terms of his own personal gratification: "Most organisations, football clubs, rugby clubs, swimming clubs, whatever, there's usually about ten people that ever volunteer to do something. So I will try and help out a bit, so that's how I got involved, because I will try and do some stuff otherwise things won't work out." John now wakes at 5 am most weekdays to take his son Jack to swimming practice; John's parents then pick Jack up from school and take him to his second practice each afternoon. John also helps out at swimming competitions in a time-keeping and coaching role. The whole family is involved in Jack's swimming schedule and this means that the children see their grandparents more often than they might otherwise. John's account suggests that sharing his interests with his sons and supporting their efforts makes him happy and helps him to bond with them. Interestingly, Jack's previous interest in chess had also prompted John's involvement: "I used to help out with doing, organising things for chess teams, like on committees, picking teams and stuff." John's involvement dwindled as Jack's interests have shifted: "I'm not doing as much of that as I used to because Jack's moved more into swimming than chess", endorsing the fact that John's participation is linked to his son's interests.

School involvement

Many of the parents interviewed reported getting involved with school activities through their children. Nicole described being "recruited" as a school governor and explained that this had "snowballed" into other types of engagement "because you've stuck your head above the crowd". Ffion reflects on her involvement with her children's junior school PTA (parent–teacher association) as her only experience of voluntary work:

'Helping out at events and things … just helped out serving cakes and raffles and things like that, at school, general things we used to do like that. Christmas time, or discos, some things like that, I used to help out. So that's all really in general, yeah. But nothing else, I haven't done any other voluntary work, no.' (Ffion, married mother of four)

Ffion describes how things changed when her children moved up to secondary school and she didn't feel the same connection as she had with the junior school when her children were younger: "when they go to comp, it's just away from that and, you know, it's not the same anymore then", adding "they've got a connection when they're younger, but with the comp now it's not". Unlike Ffion, both Nicole and David could be described as 'constant volunteers' (Hogg 2016), both having prior experience of volunteering before becoming parents but seizing the opportunity to become more involved in their children's education as a mutually beneficial activity:

'I do volunteer work anyway and it just is important to do the volunteer work. They asked me to do it at a time when I'd just finished doing some volunteer work for something else. So yes, and with the benefits of that it meant that [the school] has been oversubscribed I was able to get a strong statement and reference.' (Nicole, repartnered mother of three)

'If I'm being honest, probably what got me started on it was something that we did in church where we talked about not being insular, and not just doing stuff within the church, and going out into the wider community. And so when this parent governor slot came up, I thought that's the sort of thing that I should be doing, so that's what motivated me to do it in the first place.' (David, married father of two)

While most parents curtail their school involvement once their children move on, David made the decision to remain, describing being motivated by enjoying the challenge, a sense of reciprocity and being active in his local community:

'I enjoy it, it's a challenge, a different challenge than the challenge I get in work, and it's, yeah, the kids' education. I've seen what the school has done for my children and I'd like to continue for the children coming up as well … It's good to be involved in the local community. I mix with local business people and other people within the local area where I live as well, so that's good.' (David)

There are signs in both David's and Nicole's accounts that their involvement in education extends beyond their own children's welfare and expands to a wider concern for the public good. All of the parents interviewed were also very positive about the volunteering opportunities provided at school and encouraged their own children to participate. Salem, for example, is pleased that his son Abyd is doing "certain volunteering tasks" for his Duke of Edinburgh Award as something that has "come from the school".

Parenthood and shifting values/motivations

In this section we examine whether or not parenthood encourages individuals to think differently about social and political issues. Research in the US has identified a number of differences between the political values and practices of mothers and non-mothers, including level of involvement, knowledge, efficacy and trust (McGlenn 1980; Jennings and Niemi 1981; Schlozman et al 1994). While many parents in this study were reluctant to say that parenthood had prompted a big shift in their values or beliefs, it was common for them to talk about feeling more responsible and viewing social issues through a different lens:

> 'I think becoming a parent you realise that … we're very quick to judge how people parent, how people are, what you do with your children, what you say … I feel we put so much pressure on various sectors of society – it's like, life's hard enough. I suppose with becoming a parent I hope it made me tolerant, more accepting and less judgemental generally of people, you know?' (Eve, married mother of two)

> 'For me, with Cian, I want him to have everything and to have all of those experiences. So you've got a different thing then, I suppose, that drives you.' (Bridget, single mother of one)

Environmental consciousness

A key theme coming out of the interviews was an increased concern with issues of sustainability and environmentalism in light of introducing new life into the world. This chimes with existing research into climate change (Graham et al 2017) suggesting that ideas about the world your children and grandchildren will grow up in profoundly change your own perceptions of environmental sustainability. For some parents, this was wrapped up in thinking about their children's own lifespan, while for others the link was more directly linked to perceptions of the increased environmental footprint of having a family. Participants in our study tried to find new ways to be environmentally friendly when they became parents. Nicole, for example, used "real" washable nappies to avoid landfill. However, for other parents in the study, trying to be environmentally responsible with young children was especially difficult. For example, Ruth, a married mother of four, said "I remember with Billy trying to do nappies that I could wash and whatever, and it lasted a little while, until I couldn't cope with the other children, doing it all." Miranda, also married and with four children, echoed this sentiment, saying "I couldn't cope with washing the nappies."

Living 'environmentally' sometimes aligned with a general desire to cut the costs associated with running a household. For example, Miranda spoke of trying not to waste food due to being "on a limited budget" and needing to plan meals carefully. When being more ethical or environmental entailed an additional cost, she described trying her best when she could, saying "if I can buy something that's British instead of flown in from Mozambique then I will". For Miranda, her ethical or environmental values had to be realised within certain "parameters" and was enacted through "small" choices like buying Fairtrade coffee and wine, instead of making bigger shifts: "We looked at getting an electric car, we looked at doing it on finance ... but it couldn't get us far enough ... and we were like, well, if we go and see his family, we'd have to stop for six hours in the middle to charge the car" (Miranda, married mother of four).

This tension between living ethically or environmentally and living cost-effectively was also present in Nicole's account. She explained that "as much as you want to make these conscious decisions", cost "unfortunately is quite a big driver at the moment, it's not enabling us to make the right decisions". She gives the examples of the cost of public transport and the higher cost of "ethical" or environmentally friendly goods:

> 'It should never be more expensive to go on a train than for you to drive yourself. So, as much as you want to make these conscious decisions, and we're always saying, you know, it's not good for the environment constantly getting

on the plane, or constantly driving everywhere, but who can afford to do that? Everything is more expensive if you want to buy it correctly. If you want to by local produce, you know, in season … that's more expensive, so you can only do so much can't you?' (Nicole, repartnered mother of three)

Of course, you don't have to be a parent to tussle with environmental tensions around transport and consumer choices, but the impact (both environmental and financial) of these decisions are multiplied when applied to a family setting. It may also be the case that parents feel their household budgets are more stretched compared to those without children with a similar income or, conversely, that they feel more pressure to make more environmental choices in support of their children's wishes.

Some parents' attention was drawn to environmental issues at a later stage via their children's education at school. For example, Charlotte learned new things about how to live sustainably from her two daughters:

'I think the children have both sort of had green issues, not forced on them, but they have been discussed and they know a lot about it from school. They get a lot of that sort of environmental education passed on from school, so they know the right things to do.' (Charlotte, married mother of two)

Ffion described how her oldest son, Sam, explains "global warming and all the rest of it" to her because he "knows all the facts". As a result of these discussions, Ffion said she had begun to notice when she is walking her dog along the coast "all the rubbish that's washed up" and to be more aware of environmental issues. Similarly, Nicole told me about the things she learned when her son Dewi did a school project on the Swansea tidal lagoon, and Bridget explained that the environmental knowledge that her son Cian has picked up at school "has kind of reinforced that at home". She contrasts this with recollections of her own childhood, when less was known about issues of sustainability:

'Well, I suppose the education around it wasn't, you know? It's kind of been the last 15, 20 years hasn't it? There's been a massive push on recycling and the environment and the carbon footprint. It wasn't something that was massively on the agenda when I was growing up. Certainly, now I think it's the kids that are educating— you know, that two-way learning. Because I can remember Cian coming home from school and saying "if it's not dirty wash at thirty", and I'd never heard of that, but it's something that kind of gets in your head and you remember. So, yes, I think that the education is coming from the bottom up now.' (Bridget, single mother of one)

In fact, it was very common for parents to juxtapose the environmental consciousness of their children with their own childhood experiences:

'I'm forty now, so I am just not sure that we were aware what an impact, maybe somebody was, but I'm not sure we were aware quite of the impact that we were having ... I can't remember when the outcry about the ozone layer was, but it happened when I was a child, at some point.' (Miranda, married mother of four)

'I don't think there was that much awareness when I was growing up. There certainly wasn't recycling was there? I don't remember doing recycling apart from putting back the milk bottles or your pop bottles, that's about the only recycling we did.' (Nicole, repartnered mother of three)

These points highlight the different social and cultural contexts experienced by those growing up in different decades, but indicate that having children may be one way for parents to connect with emerging social, ecological or political issues that they may not otherwise come into contact with.

Politicising family food decisions

Parents described how their own eating habits and family practices had changed as a result of their children's ethical or environmental values. For example, Nina's younger daughter wanted to follow a vegan diet because "ethics are quite important to her, with animals and stuff". Nina found it "really hard being a mum for a twelve-year-old vegan", especially during family trips or special occasions. She has agreed a compromise with her daughter Suzy where Suzy eats a vegetarian diet and the whole family have adapted to eating "as organically, and as free range" as they can. Natasha's daughter

Sophie is enthusiastic about Fairtrade after experiencing 'Fairtrade Fortnight' at school. Natasha says she is happy to support this in a moderate way – "I wouldn't look for it, but we are quite happy … when it's got the little symbol." Daniel was also prompted to consider the ethical and environmental dimensions of his food choices by his daughter's desire to become a vegetarian after having a lesson on chicken farming at school:

> 'Mel and I have been thinking about this for ages and we kind of know, if I'm honest, that you should be a vegetarian or something if you're going to be living as lightly on the land as possible. We were on our way up to some friends … and Natalie turned to us halfway up and went "Oh, Mum and Dad, I've decided to be a vegetarian" and we were like "Okay". Now, actually six meals out of seven are vegetarian because our daughter … has kind of forced us into it. In a sense … our children are making us do things. It's not just the generations coming down, it's the generations coming up that push as well.' (Daniel, married father of two)

These types of family food negotiations combine a number of different elements, including financial cost, time effectiveness and ease of preparation, taste preferences, ethics and environmental considerations. Our data indicate that parents, and, in particular, mothers, will often strive to harmonise family eating patterns to maintain a sense of togetherness experienced during shared family meals. Buying, preparing and serving different options for different family members entails both practical and financial costs that these parents would rather avoid.

Family spaces for mutual civic learning

The examples in the previous two subsections point towards the negotiation of environmental and ethical values in relation to family life and the running of the household. We also encountered accounts of **synergistic** learning interactions (Jessel et al 2004) in which both generations learn from each other. Daniel gives a particularly enthusiastic account of his family experience of "living below the line" when prompted by his son Toby:

> '[T]he best thing we've ever done in our family was, a few years ago, my son Toby … read about something on

the internet called "live below the line" ... You have to live for five days ... it works out a £1 per person per day. That is the poverty line. We did it as a family ... so we got £20 and went shopping and bought the things. It was quite transformational for us as a family. It was an incredible thing. What we found is, we'd start thinking about where our food came from, about waste, a lot more than we had. In our house, we say grace before a meal and it usually lasts about ten seconds, four seconds sometimes, really short. And were becoming more thankful all of sudden we started to say really long graces.' (Daniel, married father of two)

Daniel emphasised the importance of Toby initially suggesting the challenge, as something that the whole family learned from and as something that brought them closer to one another. It also highlighted an often taken-for-granted aspect of daily practice, leading him to reflect: "I think actually the small decisions we make about the practicalities of our lives are, in many ways, the expression of ... what our world view truly is."

Discussion: civic learning in the family home

Are parents more likely to be civically engaged?

It is widely recognised that parenthood significantly alters not only the time available to individuals, but also their (emotional and cognitive) capacity, to engage with current affairs or political issues beyond the family home – especially in the initial stages of caring for very young children. Many existing studies detail the strained time budgets of parents, and the limitations of familial responsibilities on types of participation that require high levels of commitment, antisocial hours or frequent travel. However, in this chapter we have detailed how certain types of civic engagement might be maintained or adapted to accommodate family life, and how parenthood itself might even trigger new forms of civic engagement. So while parenthood might limit some forms of civic engagement, it sparks or prompts others. This has implications for how we conceptualise altruism and selfishness within the family, and underscores the importance of parenthood as a significant moment in the lifecourse for our understandings of civic engagement.

Parenthood: activating or modifying civic engagement?

Existing research indicates that while, for some people, civic engagement is a core part of their identity and remains constant throughout their life, for others, engagement is episodic and triggered or halted by particular stages or events in the lifecourse (Hogg 2016). Indeed, two broad types of orientation to civic engagement emerged among the parents in our study: some parents (such as David, Nicole and Daniel), gave accounts of long-standing involvement with various civic activities and political movements throughout their youth and prior to becoming a parent. Other parents (such as Ffion and John), however, described having no prior involvement in voluntary or civically oriented work before having children. The accounts of these parents chime with research in Italy suggesting that parents extend their social networks, become more aware of community issues, and get involved in local activities concerning their children's welfare (Quaranta and Dotti Sani 2018). These parents were more likely to describe episodic child-centred engagement based in the interests and activities of their offspring. We explore the character of both types of involvement in the following subsections.

What kinds of engagement are parents most likely to be involved with?

In this chapter we have considered the differential impact of parenthood on mothers and fathers, shedding light on the 'heavier burden' carried by women, whose participation may be more heavily impacted by the transition to parenthood (Quaranta 2016: 389). In many cases, becoming a parent is more disruptive to the rhythms and routines of daily life for mothers than it is fathers. Pregnancy often signals a break in, or indeed the end of, paid employment, and a dislocation from existing social networks. The early responsibilities of parenthood tend to fall more heavily on women, and, especially in those families where fathers work full-time in a role outside of the home, motherhood can be isolating. Consequently, mothers in our study were much more likely than fathers to be engaged in voluntary work centring around caring for, playing with and helping to teach young children. Helping out at a play group, for example, seemed to provide the mothers in our study with an opportunity to develop new networks and to adjust to their new role as a parent.

Interestingly, while mothers were more likely to describe taking on caring roles closely linked to their pre-existing parenting responsibilities (and traditional expectations of the maternal role) – supervising discos and sleepovers, baking cakes and making cups of tea – fathers were more likely to discuss voluntary roles linked to particular skills or interests. This may indicate that men, as fathers, are more likely to feel as though they have something to offer if it is rooted in a particular skillset that they know they possess. These more specialised roles may help fathers to recognise the tangible impact of their involvement, enabling them to feel useful.

How sustainable are various types of parental civic engagement?

Those in our core committed group (described by Hogg (2016) as 'constant volunteers') described modifying or renegotiating pre-existing civic roles to fit in with family life on becoming a parent. Their ideological commitment to, and orientation towards, particular causes or values was not altered, but the time they were able to allocate to particular activities was affected to a greater or lesser degree. For those in this group, parenting responsibilities added another element to their existing negotiations of balancing civic engagement with paid employment and other caring and household responsibilities. These parents spoke about how they were able to integrate their voluntary or political activities into their family life, and spoke enthusiastically about having more time to pursue these interests once their parenting responsibilities had diminished or if they were able to retire or reduce their hours at work. On the other hand, among those whose involvement had been triggered by parenthood, many described the time-limited nature of their involvement with various groups as their own children grew out of them, and as their capacity for engagement ebbed and flowed. In this sense, it could be argued that the types of civic engagement prompted or facilitated by parenthood are also those that were most likely to be abandoned once they outgrow their personal resonance.

Those in the 'constant' group were much more likely to indicate that they had already, or would seek to continue with any 'child-centred' forms of civic engagement that they had taken on as a parent, beyond the bounds of their own children's involvement. This was clear in David's account of his transition from parent governor to school governor. However, it would not be fair or right to imply that episodically involved parents are in any way less committed or less 'virtuous' than constant volunteers. Many factors may influence an individual's capacity to take on additional or 'non-essential' responsibilities beyond the home, and parental responsibilities weigh particularly heavily on those with little family or wider support. The parents in our study each grappled with complex and competing demands on their time, and there is little to suggest that degree of civic involvement straightforwardly reflects levels of civic concern.

Instead, we suggest that the prior significance of, and familiarity with, civic engagement can help individuals to integrate certain practices and values into their family life as parents, forming part of a shared identity. Almost all of the parents in our study spoke about a tension between their voluntary commitments and the desire to spend time with their family. These tensions were heightened by work pressures and the absence of support networks. It seems that this pressure can be alleviated by reframing civic activities as family activities. This was visible in Eve's account of involving her husband and children in her befriending of Sheila, therefore sharing both some of the responsibilities associated with her role, and combining two potentially conflicting calls on her time. It was also echoed in David's account of attending and volunteering at parkruns as a family activity. Similarly, while some parents described being unable to keep up with current affairs and political issues, others made links between their own politics and their child-rearing practices. Nicole, for example, positioned learning about and discussing political issues as a family activity, and took her children along to the polling station whenever she voted. In this sense, her political engagement was not separate from, but incorporated into, her role as a mother. It might be the case, then, that for parents with a history of civic or political engagement prior to parenthood, that their continued involvement, as part of their core identity and a habit formed over years, is prioritised in a way that might not come naturally to those whose participation has been triggered by parenthood. It may also be the case that a desire to pass on certain 'civic virtues' to their own children propels these kinds of activity to the forefront of the family home.

However, we do not wish to write-off any form of civic engagement triggered by parenthood completely. Following Shudson (1998) we recognise the potentially latent or monitorial dimensions of civic attention, and argue that positive experiences and the social networks developed during even the most transient or episodic periods of engagement might lead to greater attentiveness to social issues and further participation – perhaps of a different type – in the future. Indeed, many of the parents in our study described a dynamic process of shifting perspectives and renegotiating values as their children developed their own thoughts and ideas.

Parenthood, shifting values and temporal extension of influence

Another key discovery in our exploration of the relationship between parenthood and civic engagement is the shift in mindset prompted by bringing new life into the world. The parents in our study spoke about experiencing a greater sense of responsibility and described how their attention was drawn to environmental issues, in particular. Graham et al (2017) describe this reframing as a shift towards biographical or intergenerational time, in which an individual's concern for their own well-being and that of those around them extends to encapsulate their children, and even their grandchildren. This 'temporal extension' of concern might be an important means of distilling the urgency of environmental action, underlining the personal or familial ramifications (see Robinson 2018). This could motivate individuals, as family members, to engage with more environmentally friendly practices.

Shifting their attitudes and practices towards environmental issues was not the only change in mindset described by parents. They also discussed becoming more aware of numerous political and social issues through discussion and debate with their children during the teenage years and beyond. In numerous instances, parents described learning from their children, prompting them to expand their understandings, re-evaluate tacitly held beliefs and reflect on the social changes that had taken place since their own childhoods. These episodes of synergistic learning might help to bridge generational divides in a way that helps both parents and children to contextualise contemporary issues and to think creatively about how to move towards a more socially responsible and inclusive organisation of society.

What does child-centred civic engagement tell us about our understandings of selfishness and altruism?

As we have seen, the types of civic participation most likely to be triggered by parenthood are those linked to the well-being, personal development and education of a parent's children. The parents in our study described getting involved with various children's groups and clubs, and playing an active role in their children's education at school. For some parents, this allowed them to demonstrate or build on a skill or interest that they already have (for example John was able to employ his own interest in swimming and chess to support his son's activities). It could be argued that this type of involvement is largely self-interested: it is based around activities and events that the parent volunteer is likely to find enjoyable, and it is motivated, in part, by wanting to provide a positive experience for their own child or children, with benefits to other children perhaps being more peripheral. However, there are a number of important points to consider before drawing the conclusion that child-centred volunteering is solely self- or family-oriented.

First, we know that the likelihood of a person to volunteer their time is strongly linked to their sense of self-confidence and whether or not they think that their skills will be useful or valued by others. It takes a certain degree of courage to approach an already established group, and offering your skills requires a degree of confidence in your own self-efficacy. However, if a parent is already dropping their child off at a sports practice or dance lesson, then they are able to become familiar with how these group activities are managed and the range of roles that are required. In this very practical sense, parenthood may encourage the participation of individuals who may not otherwise have the confidence, familiarity or motivation to join a voluntary group. More specialised or skill-based involvement might also help parents (particularly fathers) to pinpoint the contribution that they are making. It may therefore be the case that interest- or skills-based engagement may be more about 'having something to offer' than 'something to gain'.

And, second, it is widely recognised that civic engagement is at its most effective and sustainable when participants feel there is both a personal benefit to taking part, and a wider benefit to a cause, group, local community or society more generally. Civic engagement triggered by the desire to provide for your children is likely to feel fulfilling on a personal level and, once in place, if a parent feels they are making a positive difference to other children (or to the environment or the community, for example), then this is likely to galvanise the sense of well-being from their participation.

Note

[1] See http://www.parkrun.org.uk/aboutus/.

References

Andolina, M.W., Jenkins, K., Zukin, C. and Keeter, S. (2003) 'Habits from home, lessons from school: influences on youth civic engagement', *PS: Political Science & Politics*, 36(2): 275–80.

Anxo, D., Mencarini, L., Pailhé, A., Solaz, A., Tanturri, M.L. and Flood, L. (2011) 'Gender differences in time use over the life course in France, Italy, Sweden, and the US', *Feminist Economics*, 17(3): 159–195.

Burns, K., Lehman Schlozman, K.L. and Verba, S. (1997) 'The public consequences of private inequality: family life and citizen participation', *The American Political Science Review*, 91(2): 373–89.

Corbetta, P., Tuorto, D. and Cavazza, N. (2012) 'Genitori e figli 35 anni dopo: la politica non abita più qui' ['Parents and children 35 years later: politics does not live here anymore'], *Rivista Italiana di Scienza Politica*, 42: 3–28.

Craig, L. and Mullan, K. (2010) 'Parenthood, gender and work-family time in the United States, Australia, Italy, France, and Denmark', *Journal of Marriage and Family*, 72(5): 1344–61.

Ekman, J. and Amnå, E. (2012) 'Political participation and civic engagement: towards a new typology', *Human Affairs*, 22(3): 283–300.

Elder, L. and Greene, S. (2012) *The Politics of Parenthood: Causes and Consequences of the Politicization of the American Family*, Albany, NY: State University of New York Press.

Gallagher, S.K. and Gerstel, N. (2001) 'Connections and constraints: the effects of children on caregiving', *Journal of Marriage and Family*, 63(1): 265–75.

Gauthier, A.H. and Furstenberg, F.F. Jr (2002) 'The transition to adulthood: a time use perspective', *Annals of the American Academy of Political and Social Science*, 580(1): 153–71.

Gibb, S.J., Fergusson, D.M., Horwood, I.J. and Boden, J.M. (2014) 'The effects of parenthood on workforce participation and income for men and women', *Journal of Family and Economic Issues*, DOI: 10.1007/s10834-013-9353-4.

Graham, H.M., Bland, J.M., Cookson, R.A., Kanaan, M. and White, P.C.L. (2017) 'Do people favour policies that protect future generations? Evidence from a British survey of adults', *Journal of Social Policy*, 43(3): 423–45.

Hagestad, G.O. (2000) *Adult intergenerational relationships. Generations and Gender Programme: exploring future research and data collection options*, New York and Geneva: United Nations.

Hogg, E. (2016) 'Constant, serial and trigger volunteers: volunteering across the lifecourse and into older age', *Voluntary Sector Review*, 7(2): 169–90.

Janoski, T. and Wilson, J. (1995) 'Pathways to voluntarism: family socialization and status transmission models', *Social Forces*, 74(1): 271–92.

Jennings, M.K. (1979) 'Another look at the life cycle and political participation', *American Journal of Political Science*, 23(4): 755–71.

Jennings, M.K. (2002) 'Generation units and the student protest movement in the United States: an intra- and intergenerational analysis', *Political Psychology*, 23(2): 303–24.

Jennings M.K. and Niemi, R.G. (1981) *Generations and Politics: A Panel Study of Young Adults and Their Parents*, Princeton: Princeton University Press.

Jessel, J., Gregory, E., Tahera, A., Kenner, C. and Mahera, R. (2004) 'Children and their grandaprents at home: a mutually supportive context for learning and linguistic development', *English Quarterly*, 36(4): 16–23.

Jochum, V. (2015) 'Volunteering: a family affair?' *NCVO Blog*, 5 June, National Council for Voluntary Organisations. Available from: https://blogs.ncvo.org.uk/2015/06/05/volunteering-a-family-affair/.

Jochum, V. (2019) 'Exploring the links between family and volunteering', *NCVO Blog*, 3 July, National Council for Voluntary Organisations. Available from: https://blogs.ncvo.org.uk/2019/07/03/exploring-the-links-between-family-and-volunteering/.

Kroh, M. and Selb, P. (2009) 'Inheritance and the dynamics of party identification', *Political Behavior*, 31(4): 559–74.

McGlen, N.E. (1980) 'The impact of parenthood on political participation', *Western Political Quarterly*, 33(3): 297–313.

Muddiman, E., Taylor, C., Power, S. and Moles, K. (2019) 'Young people, family relationships and civic participation', *Journal of Civil Society*, 15(1): 82–98.

Nesbit, R. (2012) 'The influence of major life cycle events on volunteering', *Nonprofit and Voluntary Sector Quarterly*, 41(6): 1153–74.

Nomaguchi, K.M. and Milkie, M.A. (2003) 'Costs and rewards of children: the effects of becoming a parent on adults' lives', *Journal of Marriage and Family*, 65(2): 356–74.

Oesterle, S., Johnson, M.K. and Mortimer, J.T. (2004) 'Volunteerism during the transition to adulthood: a life course perspective', *Social Forces*, 82(3): 1123–49.

Quaranta, M. (2016) 'Leaving home, finding a partner and having kids: gender differences in political participation across the life course in Italy', *Acta Politica*, 51(3): 372–97.

Quaranta, M. and Dotti Sani, G. (2018) 'Left behind? Gender gaps in political engagement over the life course in twenty-seven European countries', *Social Politics*, 25(2): 254–86.

Quintelier, E. (2007) 'Differences in political participation between young and old people', *Contemporary Politics*, 51(4): 355–70.

Robinson, M. (2018) *Climate Justice: Hope, Resilience and the Fight for a Sustainable Future*, London: Bloomsbury.

Rotolo, T. (2000) 'A time to join, a time to quit: the influence of life cycle transitions on voluntary association membership', *Social Forces*, 78(3): 1133–61.

Schlozman, K.L., Burns, N. and Verba, S. (1994) 'Gender and the pathways to participation: the role of resources', *Journal of Politics*, 56(4): 963–90.

Schudson, M. (1998) *The Good Citizen*, New York: Free Press.

Smith, D.H. (1994) 'Determinants of voluntary association participation and volunteering: a literature review', *Nonprofit and Voluntary Sector Quarterly*, 23(3): 243–63.

Sundeen, R.A. (1990) 'Family life course status and volunteer behavior: implications for the single parent', *Sociological Perspectives*, 33(4): 483–500.

Verba, S., Burns, N. and Schlozman, K.L. (1997) 'Knowing and caring about politics: gender and political engagement', *Journal of Politics*, 59(4): 1051–72.

Voorpostel, M. and Coffé, H. (2010) 'Transitions in partnership and parental status, gender, and political and civic participation', *European Sociological Review*, 28(1): 28–42.

Welch, S. (1977) 'Women as Political Animals? A Test of Some Explanations for Male-Female Political Participation Differences', *American Journal of Political Science*, 21(November): 711–31.

Wilson, J. and Musick, M. (1997) 'Who cares? Toward an integrated theory of volunteer work', *American Sociological Review*, 62(5): 694–713.

Wolfinger, N.H. and Wolfinger, R.E. (2008) 'Family structure and voter turnout', *Social Forces*, 86(4): 1513–28.

Zukin, C., Keeter, S., Andolina, M., Jenkins, K. and Delli Carpini, M.X. (2006) *A New Engagement?: Political Participation, Civic Life and the Changing American Citizen*, Oxford: Oxford University Press.

6

Volunteering in later life

Martijn J.A. Hogerbrugge

Due to increases in life expectancy and diminishing fertility rates, the age distribution of the population in the UK and other Western countries is coming gradually to contain relatively more older persons. Projections produced by the UK's Office for National Statistics (ONS) show that in a space of 50 years, there are likely to be an additional 8.6 million people aged 65 and over living in the UK, with the share of older people similarly increasing by 8.5 percentage points from 18 per cent in 2016 to 26.5 per cent in 2066 (ONS 2017). Moreover, the proportion of very old persons living in the UK (those aged 85 and over) will treble from 1.6 million people in 2016 to 5.1 million in 2066.

While discussions typically highlight the economic and governmental challenges an ageing population impede on society (see, for example, Harper 2014; Bloom et al 2015), the higher proportion of older adults also has the potential to bring positive impulses to families and local communities (Healy 2004). By providing childcare, financial, practical and emotional support, older generations often play a central role within their families, whereas (early) retirement and the transition to an empty nest offer older adults the time to contribute to their community, for instance through volunteering. Thus, given the growing pool of older potential volunteers, it will become ever more relevant for voluntary sector agencies to get a clearer understanding of what the current attitudes and motivations are for older people in terms of volunteering.

So far, international research on volunteering by older adults has mostly focused on the determinants affecting the likelihood of an older individual to volunteer, paying special attention to changes in the employment and family spheres (for an overview, see Morrow-Howell 2010). As will be shown in this chapter, distinguishing volunteers from non-volunteers is a far too simplified approach to the study of volunteering as it ignores variations in the number of times and hours people volunteer and the diverse range of motivations they have, as well as how these various aspects relate to each other. Likewise, when describing these volunteering activities and motivations, differences and similarities between the various age groups will be highlighted, challenging the conception that volunteers aged 50 and over form a homogenous group.

To describe the various aspects of volunteering among older adults, data from 'Helping Out', a study on volunteering and charitable giving conducted in late 2006 and early 2007 is used in this chapter (Department for Communities and Local Government 2008). The study built on three earlier national surveys of volunteering conducted in 1981, 1991 and 1997, and ran as a follow-up study to the 2005 Citizenship Survey. The sample for the 'Helping Out' study was drawn from those members of both the main sample (general population) and the boost sample (minority ethnic) of the Citizenship Survey who provided consent to be recontacted for future research and who lived in England. A total of 4,514 respondents were recontacted of whom 2,705 were successfully interviewed using Computer Assisted Personal Interviewing (CAPI), resulting in a final response rate of 60 per cent. Of this final sample, 420 respondents (or 15.5 per cent) originated from the boost sample. Additional details on the sampling procedure and field work of the 'Helping Out' study can be found in the technical report (Low and Butt 2007). For the present chapter, only respondents who were 50 years or older are used, resulting in an analytical sample of 1,200 respondents.[1]

Volunteering: proportions, frequencies and hours

Traditionally, research on volunteering has mainly looked at the differences between volunteers and non-volunteers. While this simple distinction does give an indication of the incidence of volunteering and how it varies by age, Figure 6.1 shows that it tells only part of the story. As indicated by the solid black line, the proportion of volunteers fluctuates around 60 per cent for individuals aged 50 and over, with a peak around the age of 60 and a sharp decline to around 41.7 per cent for those aged 80 and over, mirroring previous studies on volunteering in old age. But if one looks at the bars in Figure 6.1, which represent the average number of hours individuals of a particular age group volunteer, a sharp peak in hours volunteered can be seen for those aged 65–69 years. Moreover, as illustrated by the solid grey line, the number of times this group volunteers in a given year is lower than for the preceding and succeeding age groups. It thus seems that, while a relatively smaller proportion of individuals aged 65–69 years volunteer

Figure 6.1: Proportion of volunteers, frequency and hours of volunteering

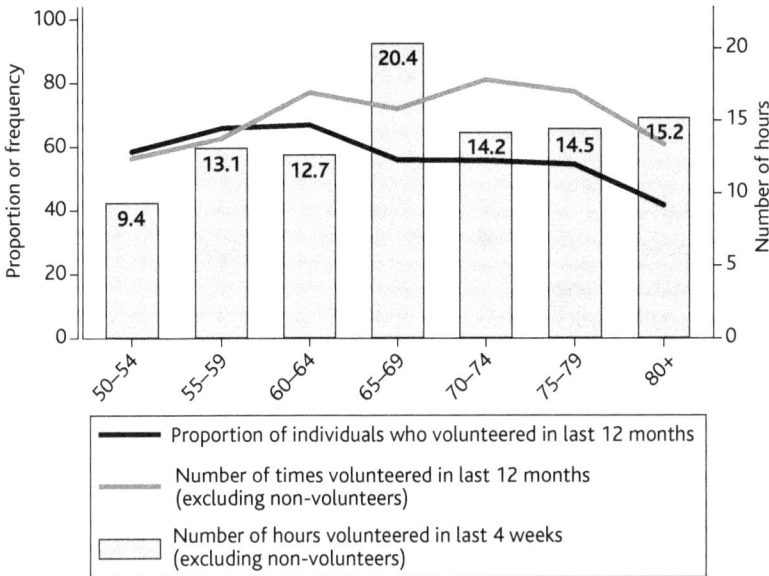

and this smaller group volunteers less frequently, they actually volunteer on average for the most hours.

There are many possible reasons for this peak in volunteering activity among the 65–69-year-olds. The most obvious one, which has already been shown to be of major influence in previous empirical studies on volunteering activity (for instance, Van den Bogaard et al 2014; Tang 2015), is the retirement of previously employed individuals. As retirees no longer need to work for pay, they simply have more time available to volunteer (Mutchler et al 2003). Moreover, retirees might start investing more hours in the role of volunteer to compensate for the loss of social roles, networks and resources, and to protect themselves from possible social exclusion and loneliness following retirement (Moen et al 2000). These compensation and protection mechanisms are also likely to be at play for those individuals who have been recently widowed – a life event one typically experiences later in life.

To explore the impact of such events, as well as to illustrate the differences between various groups in the sample and how the use of different metrics in research on volunteering can affect its conclusions, logistic and Poisson regression models on the likelihood to volunteer, the frequency of volunteering and the number of hours volunteered were estimated. Table 6.1 summarises the results from these models. Comparing the impact of the background characteristics on the

Table 6.1: Impact of background characteristics on levels of volunteering

	Volunteer	Frequency	Hours
	Marginal effect	Unstd coeff.	Unstd coeff.
Gender (reference category = male)			
Female	0.072*	0.054**	0.060**
Age (centred)	−0.002	0.005**	0.022**
Age^2 (centred)	−0.001*	−0.001**	0.001
Marital status (reference category = married)			
Civil partnership or cohabiting	−0.115	0.316**	−0.054
Divorced	0.027	0.105**	−0.066*
Widowed	−0.047	−0.065**	−0.367**
Single	0.029	0.130**	0.033
Educational degree (reference category = no qualifications)			
GCSE grade D–G	−0.035	−0.372**	−0.435**
GCSE grade A–C	0.132*	0.122**	−0.368**
Trade apprenticeships	−0.093	0.252**	0.071
A/AS levels	0.149*	0.040†	−0.367**
Higher degree / postgraduate qualifications	0.322**	0.247**	0.172**
Other qualification, including overseas	0.113†	0.187**	0.167**
No information (respondent over 70 years old)	0.170*	0.207**	−0.468**
Main activity (reference category = employed)			
Unemployed	−0.047	0.530**	−0.014
Home keeper	0.100	0.477**	1.339**
Temporary or long-term injury or illness	−0.021	−0.429**	−0.423**
Retired	0.050	0.137**	0.524**
Other	−0.072	0.567**	1.342**
Income level (reference category = < £5,000)			
£5,000–£9,999	−0.002	0.119**	0.068†
£10,000–£14,999	0.017	0.135**	0.303**
£15,000–£19,999	0.060	0.111**	0.153**

(continued)

Table **6.**1: Impact of background characteristics on levels of volunteering (continued)

	Volunteer	Frequency	Hours
	Marginal effect	Unstd coeff.	Unstd coeff.
£20,000–£29,999	0.065	0.117**	0.405**
£30,000–£49,999	0.082	−0.093**	−0.059
£50,000 or more	0.072	0.075*	0.400**
Don't know or refused	0.059	0.279**	0.439**
Religion (reference category = no religion)			
Christian	0.153*	0.230**	0.411**
Hindu	−0.043	−0.391**	−0.088
Muslim	−0.171	−0.152**	0.246*
Buddhist, Jewish or other	0.103	−0.115**	0.605**
Religious, but not actively practising	0.038	−0.071**	0.186**
Disabled (reference category = not disabled)			
Disabled, but no limitation in daily activity	−0.004	0.251**	0.258**
Disabled, experiences limitations	−0.244**	0.050**	0.013
Constant		3.793**	1.817**
Probability	0.613		
N	1,193	710	710

Notes: † = *p* < .10, * = *p* < .05, ** = *p* < .0.

various dependent variables, it becomes apparent that the likelihood to volunteer is less strongly determined by the characteristics of an individual than either the number of times or hours one volunteered. The only characteristics to significantly affect the likelihood to volunteer in the analytical sample are gender, educational qualification and disability, with women, the higher educated and the non–disabled having higher proportions of volunteers. The number of times and hours one volunteers, on the other hand, is found to be affected not only by gender, educational qualification and level of disability, but also by one's age, marital and employment statuses, income level and religious background. While the impact of the background characteristics of respondents is generally in line with previous research (Smith 1994; Wilson and Musick 1997; Wilson 2000), it is noteworthy that the impact of some characteristics, like marital status, education and religious background, differ for the number of times and hours spent volunteering. This further highlights that the individuals who volunteer most frequently are not necessarily the ones who also volunteer for the most hours. It is clearly important, therefore, that future research on volunteering includes information on both aspects of volunteering activity.

Type of organisations and activities

Besides questions on the hours and frequency of volunteering, the survey for the 'Helping Out' study contained detailed questions on the type of organisations respondents volunteered for, as well as the type of volunteering activities they undertook in the 12 months prior to the study. Starting with the type of organisations, Table 6.2 provides an overview of the proportion of volunteers in the study doing unpaid work for each type of organisation, split out over different age groups. Respondents were allowed to give multiple responses (hence, the proportions add up to over 100 per cent), while non-volunteers were omitted from the calculation of the various proportions.

While the average number of types of organisations respondents volunteer for hardly varies over the age groups – standing at around two, with about half of the volunteers working for just one type of organisation, about a quarter working for two different types, and the remaining quarter working for three or more types – examining the distribution of the various types of organisations does reveal some interesting patterns. As can be expected with the transition from having children at home to 'empty nesting', the percentage of volunteers working for schools, colleges or universities, as well as organisations aimed at children or young people, drops significantly by age. Likewise, the percentage of volunteers working for trade unions reduces from 8.5 per cent among the 50–54-year-olds, to almost none after the typical retirement age of 65. And while the percentage of volunteers working for sports- and exercise-related organisations drops sharply among those aged 75 and over, this decrease is actually preceded by a strong increase from 13.5 per cent among the 50–54-year-olds to 20.5 per cent among those aged 70–74 years.

Unsurprisingly, the proportion of volunteers working for organisations aimed at the elderly is highest among the two oldest age groups. Moreover, when these proportions are compared to the proportion of volunteers working for the other type of organisations, it becomes apparent that volunteers aged 75 and over are mainly volunteering for organisation types aimed at the elderly. The only exception to this observation would be the proportion of volunteers working for religious organisations; starting from age 60, each successive age group

Table 6.2: Type of organisations volunteered for in the last 12 months – proportions per age group

	50–54	55–59	60–64	65–69	70–74	75–79	80+	All
Schools, colleges, or universities	27.7	13.3	15.0	12.8	14.1	10.2	3.3	15.6
Children or young people	13.5	12.1	9.0	11.9	10.3	6.1	6.7	10.9
The elderly	14.2	13.9	16.5	18.3	14.1	22.4	26.7	16.3
Hobbies/ recreation/social clubs	11.3	15.6	17.3	18.3	14.1	16.3	16.7	15.4
Sports/exercise	13.5	17.3	17.3	17.4	20.5	4.1	0.0	15.3
Religion	23.4	22.5	24.1	27.5	28.2	30.6	53.3	26.2
Justice and human rights	6.4	2.3	4.5	2.8	2.5	4.1	3.3	3.8
Conservation, environment, heritage	8.5	8.1	12.8	13.8	11.5	2.0	6.7	9.8
The arts and museums	7.1	4.6	6.8	11.9	7.7	10.2	6.7	7.4
Animal welfare	7.1	9.2	12.8	7.3	6.4	6.1	3.3	8.4
Social welfare	5.7	6.4	6.0	8.3	6.4	4.1	10.0	6.5
Overseas aid / disaster relief	9.9	8.1	12.8	3.7	7.7	12.2	6.7	8.8
Health and disability	20.6	20.2	20.3	22.0	23.1	20.4	20.0	20.9
Safety, first aid	5.0	2.9	1.5	3.7	3.8	4.1	3.3	3.4
Local community or citizens' groups	19.1	24.3	24.1	21.1	28.2	14.3	16.7	22.2
Politics	9.2	2.9	6.0	5.5	9.0	6.1	10.0	6.3
Trade union activity	8.5	4.6	3.8	1.8	0.0	2.0	0.0	3.9
Other	8.5	6.9	8.3	10.1	10.3	6.1	6.7	8.3
Average total number of organisations	2.2	2.0	2.2	2.2	2.2	1.8	2.0	2.1
N	141	173	133	109	78	49	30	713

is more likely to have a larger proportion of volunteers working for this type of organisation. Most likely this is due to the fact that older people are more religious (Crockett and Voas 2006). Whether this is due to a cohort or age effect cannot be determined with these cross-sectional data, but it seems plausible that both effects are at work here, with older generations (cohorts) being more religious than younger generations and individuals becoming more religious as they get older and reach an age that is increasingly closer to death (Crockett and Voas 2006).

Another phenomenon associated with old age that can be observed in the data is that of generativity, a developmental stage first coined by Erikson (1950) to describe middle-aged adults' increasing interest in establishing and guiding the next generation by investing in what one will leave behind (Slater 2003). Compared to the youngest and oldest age groups, volunteers aged 55–75 years are proportionally more active in organisations associated with conservation, the environment, heritage, the arts, museums and animal welfare – all causes concerned with preserving those aspects of life an individual might deem important for future generations. Similarly, while not as strongly linked to concerns of generativity, the proportion of volunteers working for citizens' groups or local community organisations is highest among the 55–75-year-olds.

Finally, about half of the organisation types listed in Table 6.2 either show little variation in the proportion of volunteers working in each age group, or the changes between age groups show no clear trend. For instance, the proportion of volunteers working for organisations associated with health and disability is about 20 per cent at each age group, while the proportion of volunteers for political organisations increases and decreases continuously over the consecutive age groups. Other organisation types that fall in either category are organisations related to hobbies, recreation, social clubs, justice and human rights, social welfare, overseas aid, disaster relief, and safety and first aid.

Turning to the types of activities volunteers undertook in the 12 months prior to the survey (Table 6.3), it can be observed that the average total number of activities a volunteer takes on declines with each successive age group. This is in contrast to the earlier observation that the average number of organisations older people volunteer for remains virtually the same. It thus seems that volunteers remain active within the same number of organisation types, but their level of activity in terms of the variety of tasks they carry out reduces over age.

Looking at the various activities separately, one can see that the decline is especially noticeable among the activities related to befriending, mentoring or educating/teaching/coaching people, and giving advice, information or providing counselling, as well as for activities in which

Table 6.3: Type of volunteering activities done in the last 12 months – proportions per age group

	50–54	55–59	60–64	65–69	70–74	75–79	80+	All
Raising money	66.0	61.8	60.9	68.8	59.0	51.0	63.3	62.6
Leading group/ committee	31.2	30.6	36.8	43.1	35.9	32.7	20.0	34.1
Organising or helping at event	51.8	39.9	51.1	39.4	48.7	38.8	43.3	45.3
Visiting people	18.4	18.5	27.1	24.8	30.8	34.7	26.7	23.8
Befriending or mentoring people	17.0	19.7	21.1	14.7	11.5	24.5	16.7	18.0
Educating/ teaching/ coaching	24.1	19.7	24.1	13.8	9.0	12.2	6.7	18.2
Giving advice/ information/ counselling	22.7	19.7	23.3	21.1	19.2	16.3	6.7	20.3
Secretarial, admin, or clerical work	28.4	22.5	27.8	27.5	21.8	24.5	6.7	24.8
Providing transport / driving	15.6	16.8	19.5	22.0	20.5	24.5	16.7	18.8
Representing	21.3	22.0	25.6	22.0	17.9	14.3	3.3	20.8
Campaigning	21.3	22.0	16.5	14.7	10.3	14.3	10.0	17.4
Other practical help	26.2	28.9	35.6	32.1	26.9	38.8	26.7	30.3
Any other help	14.2	11.0	25.6	18.3	17.9	14.3	23.3	17.0
Average total number of activities	3.6	3.3	3.9	3.6	3.3	3.4	2.7	3.5
N	141	173	133	109	78	49	30	713

the volunteer represents or campaigns for a voluntary organisation. The exception to this general decline is the sudden increase of volunteers involved in befriending, mentoring, educating/teaching/coaching or campaigning activities among the 75–79-year-olds. At the same time, volunteers in this age group are found to be less likely to raise money or help organise an event – two types of activities that have the highest proportions of volunteers among the other age groups. To what extent this anomaly is due to specific changes in the life circumstances of the 75–79-year-olds, or whether it could be attributed to the small number of volunteers observed among the very old requires further study, preferably using longitudinal panel data. This would also help answer the question as to what extent the sharp decline of volunteers doing secretarial, administrative or clerical work among those aged 80 and over is an artefact of the small sample size, or whether this actually reflects a decline of persons in this age group who are still fit to take on this more mentally demanding type of activity.

Despite the low number of observations among the oldest age groups, there is one clear trend to be observed in the data: several types of activities have about the same proportion of volunteers doing them irrespective of age, namely raising money, organising or helping at an event, providing transport and other (practical) help. Moreover, of these, raising money and organising or helping at an event are the two types of activities that are done by at least, or nearly, half of all volunteers at each age group. This might not be surprising, given the quite likely incidental character of these type of volunteering activities. Other activities that are less often carried out by volunteers, such as befriending, mentoring or educating people, are likely to require more continuous involvement over longer periods of time, thus making it less likely a person will take on this type of activity.

Table 6.4 shows what type of activities older individuals performed when they volunteered for a certain type of organisations (rows), as well as in what organisation the various type of activities are most commonly carried out (columns), with proportions that are higher than the total proportion of volunteers doing this type of activity for any type of organisation (see last column of Table 6.3). The last column (number 14) also shows the average number of activities a volunteer performs when he or she is active within that type of organisation. Starting with the latter, it becomes apparent that religious organisations are not only the type of organisations older people volunteer most often for (26.2 per cent of all volunteers; see last column of Table 6.2), it is also the type of organisation volunteers undertake the highest number of types of activities for. And more than for any other type of organisation,

Table 6.4: Type of volunteering activities done in the last 12 months – proportions by organisation type

Type of organisation	1	2	3	4	5	6	7	8	9	10	11	12	13	14	N
Schools, colleges, or universities	43.4	26.6	39.8	3.5	6.2	23.9	15.9	9.7	7.1	10.6	7.1	19.5	6.2	2.5	113
Children or young people	52.6	21.8	44.9	5.1	14.1	19.2	10.3	23.1	20.5	11.5	10.3	21.8	7.7	2.9	78
The elderly	33.6	8.6	15.5	28.5	12.9	2.6	8.6	6.0	17.2	3.5	1.7	37.1	8.6	2.1	116
Hobbies/recreation/social clubs	40.9	33.6	37.3	10.0	10.0	9.1	3.6	20.0	12.7	16.4	2.7	17.3	13.6	2.5	110
Sports/exercise	45.9	33.0	45.0	7.3	12.8	19.3	10.1	25.7	19.3	17.4	10.1	19.3	3.7	2.9	109
Religion	55.6	28.9	44.4	39.6	15.0	15.5	14.4	18.2	20.9	12.3	9.6	27.3	11.2	3.3	187
Justice and human rights	25.9	25.9	22.2	11.1	25.9	18.5	25.9	14.8	11.1	25.9	37.0	7.4	7.4	2.8	27
Conservation, environment, heritage	41.4	15.7	18.6	1.4	2.9	7.1	4.3	17.1	2.9	11.4	14.3	21.4	22.9	2.1	70
The arts and museums	39.6	34.0	30.2	3.8	3.8	5.7	17.0	22.6	11.3	13.2	9.4	18.9	11.3	2.5	53
Animal welfare	73.3	8.3	10.0	5.0	6.7	8.3	11.7	8.3	6.7	8.3	6.7	15.0	13.3	2.0	60
Social welfare	63.0	19.6	23.9	13.0	13.0	10.9	23.9	4.4	4.4	15.2	6.5	0.0	6.5	2.2	46
Overseas aid / disaster relief	71.4	9.5	17.5	7.9	7.9	9.5	7.9	12.7	4.8	9.5	12.7	12.7	11.1	2.2	63
Health and disability	57.7	11.4	15.4	12.8	10.7	4.7	13.4	8.7	8.1	6.7	5.4	14.8	12.1	1.9	149
Safety, first aid	70.8	4.2	16.7	0.0	0.0	8.3	0.0	8.3	4.2	16.7	4.2	12.5	4.2	1.8	24

(continued)

Table 6.4: Type of volunteering activities done in the last 12 months – proportions by organisation type (continued)

	1	2	3	4	5	6	7	8	9	10	11	12	13	14	N
Local community or citizens' groups	42.4	33.5	35.4	13.3	7.0	6.3	15.2	20.3	4.4	20.3	17.1	16.5	11.4	2.7	158
Politics	40.0	**35.6**	15.6	13.3	8.9	0.0	17.8	13.3	2.2	**26.7**	**60.0**	11.1	2.2	2.9	45
Trade union activity	21.4	21.4	10.7	7.1	14.3	3.6	**28.6**	21.4	0.0	**39.3**	**39.3**	10.7	3.6	2.2	28
Other	50.9	18.6	37.3	13.6	6.8	6.8	13.6	23.7	6.8	11.9	6.8	18.6	13.6	2.6	59

Notes:

(1) raising money; (2) leading group/committee; (3) organising or helping at event; (4) visiting people; (5) befriending or mentoring people; (6) educating/teaching/coaching; (7) giving advice/information/counselling; (8) secretarial, admin or clerical work; (9) providing transport / driving; (10) representing; (11) campaigning; (12) other practical help; (13) any other help; (14) average number of activities done for organisation by volunteer.

Proportions higher than the total proportion of volunteers doing a type of activity for any type of organisation (see last column of Table 6.3) are in bold.

the volunteering work includes visiting people, as 39.6 per cent of all volunteers in religious organisations undertake this activity, whereas the average is just 23.8 per cent (see last column of Table 6.3). On the other end, it can be seen that older individuals who volunteer for organisations related to health and disability or safety and first aid are undertaking, on average, the least number of types of activities (1.9 and 1.8 per cent respectively).

While there are several activities that are more frequently performed in certain types of organisations, the biggest differences can be found among the fundraising, representing and campaigning activities: volunteers who are active in organisations related to animal welfare, social welfare, overseas aid and disaster relief or safety and first aid are far more frequently involved in fundraising activities (column 1), whereas volunteers for justice and human rights, or for political or trade union organisations are most frequently doing representing or campaigning activities for these type of organisations (columns 10 and 11). On the other hand, fundraising activities are done least often by volunteers who are active for organisations related to the elderly, justice and human rights, or trade unions, whereas representing and campaigning activities are done least often by those active in organisations related to animal welfare, overseas aid and disaster relief, health and disability, or safety and first aid, as well as the elderly.

Motivations

The type of organisations for which older volunteers are active, and the type of activities they undertake, will probably be related to the motivations they have to volunteer. The 'Helping Out' study contained a section in which respondents who had volunteered in the 12 months prior to the interview were asked to indicate what motivated them to volunteer. The list of motivations they could choose from is given in Table 6.5, and includes options such as 'wanting to improve things', 'to meet new people', 'to learn new skills', or because of one's 'religious beliefs or philosophy of life'.

As can be seen in the first column of Table 6.5, older respondents most commonly indicated that they chose to volunteer because they wanted to improve things or help people (51.4 per cent), because they had spare time to do so (47.7 per cent), or because they felt the cause was important (46.2 per cent). Motivations related to one's career or qualifications were least often chosen (2.3 and 1.9 per cent respectively), as were motivations related to reciprocity (had received help or support before) or other, unspecified reasons. Other

Table 6.5: Motivations to volunteer – types of volunteers and related characteristics (n = 702)

Motivations	All	Family	Altruist	Career	Manifold	Other
Wanted to improve things / help people	51.4	0.28	**0.73**	0.46	**0.87**	0.08
Wanted to meet new people / make friends	34.6	0.20	0.16	**0.64**	**0.70**	0.00
The cause was really important	46.2	0.32	**0.59**	0.28	**0.90**	0.18
My friends/family did it	18.7	**0.27**	0.07	0.06	0.38	0.00
Connected with the needs of my family/friends	19.8	**0.27**	0.12	0.07	0.36	0.00
Felt there was a need in my community	34.0	0.13	0.38	0.38	**0.77**	0.16
Had received voluntary help/support before	4.3	0.03	0.03	0.00	0.16	0.00
Would give a chance to learn new skills	12.5	0.03	0.00	0.29	0.37	0.00
Would give a chance to use existing skills	30.6	0.09	0.23	**0.55**	**0.70**	0.00
Help getting on in career	2.3	0.01	0.00	**0.05**	0.06	0.00
Part of religious belief to help people	22.2	0.07	**0.37**	0.04	0.59	0.16
Part of philosophy of life to help people	33.2	0.15	**0.42**	0.23	**0.84**	0.00
Would give a chance to get qualifications	1.9	0.00	0.00	**0.05**	0.05	0.00
Had spare time to do it	47.7	**0.49**	0.26	**0.60**	**0.72**	0.10
Felt there was no one else to do it	14.5	0.10	0.15	0.18	0.23	0.00
Other reasons	5.1	0.00	0.02	0.07	0.05	**0.99**

(continued)

Table 6.5: Motivations to volunteer – types of volunteers and related characteristics (n = 702) (continued)

Characteristics	All	Family	Altruist	Career	Manifold	Other
Age	62.4	62.1	62.0	63.0	62.8	64.7
Gender (% female)	52.6	51.4	56.0	51.2	57.0	**26.3**
Number of organisations volunteered for	2.1	**1.8**	**2.5**	2.1	**2.4**	1.7
Number of times volunteered past 12 months	67.8	**53.3**	75.5	**78.4**	**82.6**	74.4
Hours volunteered past 4 weeks	13.5	**9.8**	14.8	14.7	**19.4**	20.1
Distribution of types		37.1	25.5	20.0	14.9	2.5

Note: significant differences (*p* < .05) from the average probabilities are in bold.

motivations were named by at least one out of ten older volunteers (learning new skills), or by one out of three at most (wanting to meet new people).

It is important to note that respondents were allowed to name multiple motivations, with just 15 per cent of the volunteering respondents naming a single motivation, and an additional 70 per cent naming two to six motivations. Consequently, instead of focusing on each motivation separately, it would be more insightful to examine which combinations of motivations are frequently mentioned together by respondents. To determine which subgroups of respondents can be distinguished in the data, a latent class analysis was conducted (for an introduction to this method, please see Lanza et al 2013). After comparing model fit indices, parsimony and interpretability across seven models with varying numbers of latent classes (subgroups), it was decided that a five-class solution described the various types of responses found in the data best. On the right-hand side of Table 6.5, the item-response probabilities for each motivation within each class of this five-class model are listed. To facilitate interpretation, probabilities greater than the average likelihood a response or motivation is observed in the overall sample in bold.

Starting with the most 'extreme' types in the 'Other' and 'Manifold' columns, these are volunteers who are likely to either list a large number of motivations, or to list a motivation that is not included in any of the predetermined type of motivations. When assigning the various response patterns to respondents, the former type of respondent, whom could be labelled as having 'manifold' motivations, is observed in about 15 per cent of the cases. This percentage matches the proportion of respondents who had selected seven or more motivations to volunteer. The latter type of respondent, who will be labelled simply as having 'other' motivations, is only observed among 2.5 per cent of the respondents, which is about half of all respondents who answered to have, or to also have, other motivations than the one listed in the questionnaire.

The previous statistics were for the complete sample of 50-year-olds and over. When splitting out the various motivations over the various age groups, interesting differences can be observed in the data, as can be seen in Figure 6.2. While the majority of motivations are not clearly mentioned more or less often the older a respondent is, it is clear that older respondents are less likely to volunteer because they wanted to improve things. On the other hand, older respondents are more likely to report to volunteer because of religious beliefs, because they wanted to meet new people, because they had time to spare, or

Figure 6.2: Motivations by age group

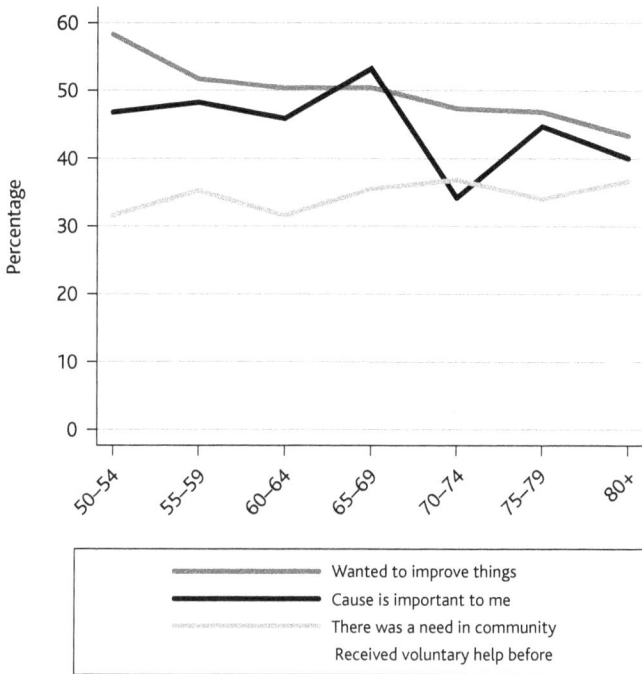

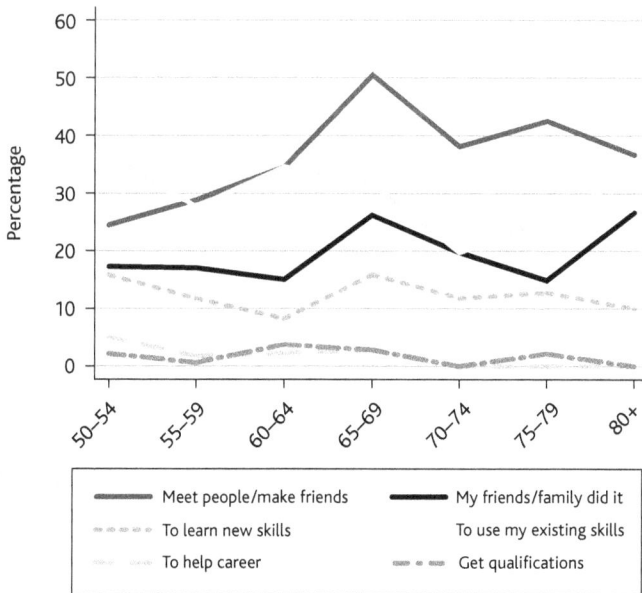

(continued)

Figure 6.2: Motivations by age group (continued)

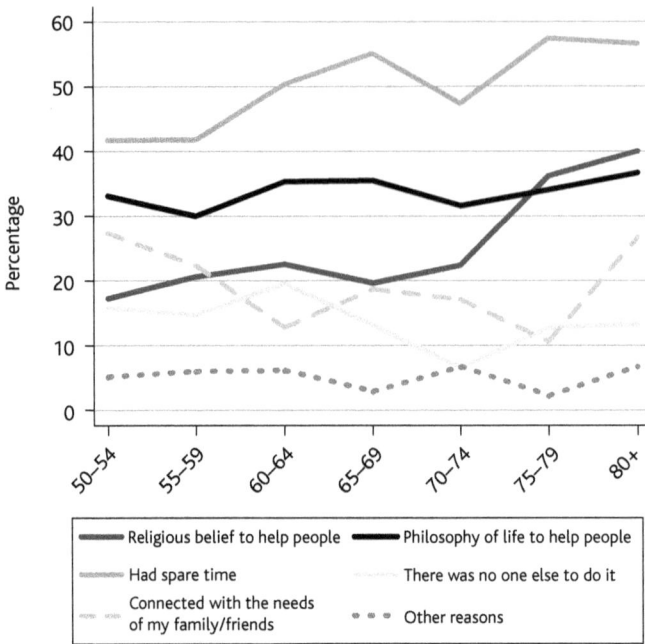

because of reasons of reciprocity ('have been helped before'). What is also apparent in the three boxes with line plots, is that for the majority of motivations, a spike can be seen in the number of 65–69-year-old volunteers mentioning it.

The more interesting response patterns are listed in the first three columns of the five-class typology. Looking at the item-response probabilities listed in the first, it can be seen that respondents falling in this class are about 40 per cent more likely to indicate they volunteered because their friends or family did it, or because the volunteering activity was connected with the needs of their family. They are also slightly more likely to volunteer because they had spare time. But because the difference in probability with the overall sample is only minor, it seems appropriate to label respondents falling in this class as being motivated to volunteer because of 'family and/or friends'. Over one third of all respondents show responses similar to this pattern. The second most commonly observed response pattern is characterised by higher probabilities for motivations related to a respondent's wish to improve things and either because the cause is important to them, and/or because of religious or philosophical reasons. As they are all motivations that are not related to personal development, but rather to improve the well-being of others, respondents who fall into this class can be labelled as having 'altruistic' motivations. About one out of every four respondents show responses that are similar to this group of motivations. Finally, the middle column shows a response pattern in which motivations related to learning new skills, using and maintaining old skills, receiving qualifications, and progressing one's career are more likely to be mentioned. One out of five respondents are likely to have such a response pattern and can be seen to have motivations that are related to progress one's career.

After assigning respondents to the latent class for which the probability was highest, more can be said about differences between each type of respondent. As can be seen in the lower part of Table 6.5, there are no significant differences in the average age or gender composition of the respondent types – with the exception of an over-representation of men among respondents who are likely to fall in the 'other' motivation type. More interesting differences can be seen when looking at variations in the number of organisations respondents volunteered for, as well the frequency and time they spent volunteering. Of the five types, the ones who volunteer because of reasons related to family and friends were found to volunteer for the least number of organisations, the least number of times and the least number of hours. On the other hand, volunteers who were highly likely to list a large and diverse number of motivations (those labelled 'manifold') were found to volunteer for a larger number of organisations than average and to volunteer the greatest number of times, as well as to volunteer the largest number of hours. Respondents who volunteered because of altruistic reasons are significantly more likely to be active in a larger number of organisations (but did not differ significantly from other volunteers when it came to the number of times or hours spent volunteering), while respondents who volunteered to help their career did so significantly more times per year than the sample average.

Turning to the various types of organisations and activities volunteers were active in, the previous observation on levels of engagement are mirrored in Table 6.6. That is, respondents who volunteered because of reasons connected to family and friends were in general less likely to be active in an organisation when the difference with the sample average was significant (the exception being organisations related to health and disability), as well as less likely to do most volunteering activities. Respondents whose motivations to volunteer could be labelled 'manifold', on the other hand, were significantly more likely to be active in religious or political organisations and organisations related to children or young people, in addition to being more likely to undertake almost all volunteering activity types. As could be

Table 6.6: Types of volunteers – distribution over organisation and activity types (n= 702)

	All	Family	Altruist	Career	Manifold	Other
Type of organisation						
Schools, colleges or universities	15.8	15.2	20.5	13.4	14.0	10.5
Children or young people	11.0	8.6	11.5	7.9	20.0	15.8
The elderly	15.5	16.2	14.5	15.8	17.0	5.3
Hobbies/recreation/social clubs	15.5	12.4	15.1	22.1	17.0	15.8
Sports/exercise	15.4	15.5	11.5	23.6	12.0	10.5
Religion	26.5	14.5	44.6	11.8	50.0	26.3
Justice and human rights	3.9	3.1	7.8	1.6	3.0	0.0
Conservation, environment, heritage	9.7	7.3	9.6	14.2	12.0	5.3
The arts and museums	7.4	5.2	9.0	11.0	8.0	0.0
Animal welfare	8.4	11.0	6.6	8.7	5.0	0.0
Social welfare	6.6	4.1	8.4	7.9	8.0	10.5
Overseas aid / disaster relief	8.8	5.5	15.1	4.7	11.0	21.1
Health and disability	21.1	25.5	19.3	14.2	21.0	15.8
Safety, first aid	3.4	3.5	3.6	3.9	3.0	0.0
Local community or citizens' groups	22.5	18.6	23.5	28.4	27.0	10.5
Politics	6.4	2.1	12.1	5.5	10.0	10.5
Trade union activity	4.0	3.5	8.4	2.4	1.0	0.0

(continued)

Table 6.6: Types of volunteers – distribution over organisation and activity types (n= 702) (continued)

	All	Family	Altruist	Career	Manifold	Other
Other	8.1	8.3	8.4	10.3	3.0	15.8
Type of activity						
Raising money	62.6	61.4	63.9	59.8	71.0	68.4
Leading group/committee	34.1	**22.1**	**46.4**	38.6	**48.0**	15.8
Organising or helping at event	45.3	**36.9**	50.6	51.2	**57.0**	42.1
Visiting people	23.8	**17.2**	**34.9**	**15.0**	**33.0**	21.1
Befriending or mentoring people	18.0	**7.6**	**25.3**	20.5	**29.0**	21.1
Educating/teaching/coaching	18.2	**9.7**	**25.3**	22.8	**27.0**	10.5
Giving advice/information/counselling	20.3	**10.3**	**32.5**	18.1	**32.0**	21.1
Secretarial, admin or clerical work	24.8	**17.6**	29.5	28.4	**34.0**	26.3
Providing transport / driving	18.8	**13.8**	16.3	**24.4**	27.0	26.3
Representing	20.8	**11.4**	**31.9**	23.6	30.0	10.5
Campaigning	17.4	10.7	**26.5**	17.3	24.0	10.5
Other practical help	30.3	**24.1**	34.9	29.9	**40.0**	15.8
Any other help	17.0	15.1	18.7	16.5	19.0	15.8

Note: significant differences (*p* < .05) from the average probability are in bold.

expected, respondents who volunteered because of altruistic reasons were significantly more likely to volunteer for religious organisations, or organisations involved with overseas aid or disaster relief, while they were also (unexpectedly) more likely to be active within political organisations. The latter finding could be explained by their higher than average likelihood of performing representation and campaigning activities – two kinds of volunteering activities that were previously shown to be most often done within political organisations (see Table 6.4). Other activities that are significantly more likely to be undertaken by respondents who volunteer because of altruistic reasons are leading a group or committee and visiting, befriending, mentoring, educating, teaching, coaching or advising/counselling people. Career orientated volunteers, finally, were significantly more likely to be active within hobby, recreational, social or sports clubs and provide transport to others, while being significantly less likely to be active within religious organisations or organisations related to health and disabilities and less likely to visit people.

Perceived barriers among non-volunteers

Thus far, this chapter has looked at differences between non-volunteers and volunteers, and the variation in activities and motivations among the latter group. While the determinants affecting the likelihood to volunteer has been explored in the analyses presented in Table 6.1, the 'Helping Out' study also enquired what barriers respondents experienced that prevented them to volunteer. Table 6.7 provides an overview of these barriers as indicated by the 487 older respondents who did not volunteer, split out by age groups.

Most frequently, non-volunteers mention a lack of time, health issues or old age as barriers to do volunteering work. Note, however, that time constraints are most frequently mentioned by the two youngest age groups, and are gradually mentioned less and less as the age of the respondent increases. Health issues and old age, on the other hand, are, unsurprisingly, increasingly mentioned as barriers the older a non-volunteer is – although the increase in health issues levels off after the age of 70. What also becomes apparent when glancing over Table 6.7 is that – apart from health issues and old age – all barriers are mentioned more frequently by respondents who are in age groups below 70 years of age. This can also be observed by the average number of barriers mentioned in each age group: this is persistently close to four for the four younger age groups, whereas this is around three among the three oldest age groups. It seems that when health issues and old age are not much of a factor for the younger respondents, they will list more frequently other barriers. It is as if they want to provide enough reasons to defend their choice not to volunteer.

Among the 50–70-year-olds, besides a lack of spare time, the second or third most commonly mentioned barrier is the perceived bureaucracy within volunteering organisations. This suggests that these respondents did volunteer in the past, but that their experience was not entirely positive and they stopped volunteering subsequently. As this is one of the most frequently mentioned barriers, there seems to be room for improvement among volunteering organisations to

Table 6.7: Barriers mentioned by non-volunteers – proportions per age group

	50–54	55–59	60–64	65–69	70–74	75–79	80+	All
Not enough spare time	64.0	75.6	56.1	45.3	22.6	14.6	14.3	48.0
Don't have the right skills	28.0	33.3	28.8	26.7	17.7	24.4	9.5	25.7
Worried about not fitting in socially	22.0	16.7	18.2	12.8	9.7	26.8	9.5	16.6
Worried about potential costs	20.0	16.7	15.1	12.8	12.9	12.2	11.9	15.2
Feels too old	19.0	18.9	28.8	33.7	51.6	63.4	69.0	35.1
Worried about losing benefits	3.0	5.6	4.5	5.8	1.6	12.2	0.0	4.5
Family/partner does not approve	16.0	15.6	16.7	16.3	14.5	9.8	7.1	14.6
Wouldn't be able to stop once involved	35.0	35.6	28.8	14.0	11.3	22.0	16.7	24.8
Put off by all bureaucracy	51.0	38.9	48.5	34.9	17.7	29.3	14.3	36.3
Worried about personal safety	28.0	23.3	24.2	24.4	16.1	17.1	16.7	22.6
Worried about liability	39.0	31.1	39.4	27.9	16.1	29.3	9.5	29.4
Don't know how to get information	26.0	26.7	30.3	20.9	8.1	14.6	9.5	21.1
Can't because of illness or disability	33.0	40.0	37.9	51.2	58.1	58.5	57.1	45.6
Other barriers	7.0	4.4	12.1	14.0	16.1	17.1	14.3	11.1
Average number of barriers mentioned	3.9	3.8	4.0	3.6	2.8	3.5	2.6	3.5
N	100	90	66	86	62	41	42	487

reduce bureaucracy levels and help maintain volunteers within their organisations more. Likewise, worries about personal safety and liability are frequently mentioned by the 50–70-year-olds as well – two perceived barriers of volunteering work that are either misconceptions, and can thus be reduced by ways of communication, or which are aspects of volunteering work that volunteering organisations can reduce to make volunteering work more attractive – especially when there is a need for more (older) volunteers.

With respect to the three oldest age groups, the 75–80-year-olds differ from the two other older age groups in some interesting ways. First of all, they mention on average a higher number of barriers – an average that is actually quite similar to the averages of the younger age groups. Second, for some reason, they list worries about liability, as well as perceived levels of bureaucracy, more often as barriers to volunteer than the two other older age groups. And third, more than any other age group, their concerns about not fitting in socially and worries about losing benefits are mentioned as barriers. What the reasons for these deviations from the other older age groups are remains to be explored in future studies. However, it is worth noting that among the respondents who did volunteer, similar unexpected variations from the other older age groups could be seen when it came to type of volunteering activities they had done in the past 12 months (as seen in Table 6.3). This provides further evidence that apparently there is something happening (or has happened when it is a cohort effect) among the 75–79-year-old age group that caused them to differ so much from those that are slightly younger or slightly older. What this exactly is remains to be answered in future research, which should also focus on establishing whether the observed differences are due to changes in the life circumstances of 75–79-year-olds (age effects), or due to particular events and experiences shared by all 75–79-year-olds (cohort effects).

Conclusion

Using survey data from 'Helping Out', a study on volunteering and charitable giving in England, this chapter has shown that older volunteers (aged 50 and over) are far from a homogenous group when it comes to their level of involvement (both in terms of frequency and hours), the types of volunteering activities they undertake and the reasons they give for their decision to volunteer. Likewise, non-volunteers were shown to vary greatly in the reasons they gave either not to volunteer at all, or to cease volunteering, and these reasons were found to vary widely by age. These findings underline the importance for future studies to stop employing the far too simple distinction between volunteers and non-volunteers in their analyses, and start incorporating more elaborate measures to differentiate between the various types of volunteers and non-volunteers that can be observed within the population at any age.

While the data have helped to highlight the heterogeneity of the older population when it comes to volunteering activities, some caveats need to be addressed. First of all, the data are cross-sectional, making any inferences on causality, as well as the distinction between age and cohort effects, impossible. Ideally, future studies that collect data on volunteering activities will adopt a panel design, so that the same individuals are surveyed several times over a longer time period. This will make it possible to assess what impact changes in the life circumstances of individuals have on their volunteering activities, but also what impact their volunteering activities will have on their life in terms of well-being and health. Second, while sufficient for describing patterns of volunteering activities, the sample size was relatively small – especially among the very old. Ideally, a future panel study should oversample old and very old individuals to assure that enough respondents will be present in the various waves of data collection. Finally, one needs to keep in mind that the data were collected in England only. As previous research has shown that volunteering levels vary greatly by country (Plagnol and Huppert 2010), one needs to be careful generalising the conclusions from this study to other contexts.

Despite these shortcomings, the data presented in this chapter have helped to inform us what older volunteers look like in terms of their background characteristics, what impact these characteristics have on their level of involvement, what kind of volunteering activities they perform and in what type of organisations.

Notes

[1] Please refer to the Appendix for an overview of the background characteristics of the analytical sample.

References

Bloom, D.E., Canning, D. and Lubet, A. (2015) 'Global population aging: facts, challenges, solutions & perspectives', *Daedalus*, 144(2): 80–92.

Crockett, A. and Voas, D. (2006) 'Generations of Decline: Religious Change in 20th-Century Britain', *Journal for the Scientific Study of Religion*, 45: 567–584.

Department for Communities and Local Government, National Centre for Social Research, Institute for Volunteering Research (2008) *National Survey of Volunteering and Charitable Giving, 2006-2007* [data collection], UK Data Service. SN: 5793. Available from: http://doi.org/10.5255/UKDA-SN-5793-1.

Erikson, E.H. (1950) 'Eight ages of man', in E.H. Erikson (ed) *Childhood and Society*, New York: W.W. Norton, pp 247–74.

Harper, S. (2014) 'Economic and social implications of aging societies', *Science*, 346(6209): 587–91.

Healy, J. (2004) 'The benefits of an ageing population', Discussion Paper No. 63, Sydney: Australian Institute.

Lanza, S.T., Bray, B.C. and Collins, L.M. (2013) 'An introduction to latent class and latent transition analysis', in J.A. Schinka and W.F. Velicer (eds) *Handbook of Psychology, Volume 2: Research Methods in Psychology*, Hoboken, NJ: Wiley, pp 691–716.

Low, N. and Butt, S. (2007) 'Helping out: a national survey of volunteering and charitable giving', technical report, London: National Centre for Social Research.

Moen, P., Fields, V., Quick, H.E. and Hofmeister, H. (2000) 'A life course approach to retirement and social integration', in K. Pillemer, P. Moen, E. Wethington and N. Glasgow (eds) *Social Integration in the Second Half of Life*, Baltimore, MD: Johns Hopkins University Press, pp 75–107.

Morrow-Howell, N. (2010) 'Volunteering in later life: research frontiers', *The Journals of Gerontology: Series B*, 65B(4): 461–9.

Mutchler, J.E., Burr, J.A. and Caro, F.G. (2003) 'From paid worker to volunteer: leaving the paid workforce and volunteering in later life', *Social Forces*, 81(4): 1267–93.

ONS (Office for National Statistics) (2017) 'Principal projection – UK summary: 2016-based national population projections', [data file]. Available from: https://www.ons.gov.uk/peoplepopulationandcommunity/populationandmigration/populationprojections/datasets/tablea11principalprojectionuksummary.

Plagnol, A.C. and Huppert, F.A. (2010) 'Happy to help? Exploring the factors associated with variations in rates of volunteering across Europe', *Social Indicators Research*, 97(2): 157–76.

Slater, C.L. (2003) 'Generativity versus stagnation: an elaboration of Erikson's adult stage of human development', *Journal of Adult Development*, 10(1): 53–65.

Smith, D.H. (1994) 'Determinants of voluntary association participation and volunteering: a literature review', *Nonprofit and Volunteering Sector Quarterly*, 23(3): 243–63.

Tang, F. (2015) 'Retirement patterns and their relationship to volunteering', *Nonprofit and Volunteering Sector Quarterly*, 45(5): 910–30.

Van den Bogaard, L., Henkens, K. and Kalmijn, M. (2014) 'So now what? Effects of retirement on civic engagement', *Ageing & Society*, 34(7): 1170–92.

Wilson, J. (2000) 'Volunteering', *Annual Review of Sociology*, 26: 215–40.

Wilson, J. and Musick, M. (1997) 'Who cares? Towards an integrated theory of volunteer work', *American Sociological Review*, 62(5): 694–713.

Appendix

Background characteristics of analytical sample (n = 1,200)

	Percentage
Gender	
Male	50.17
Female	49.83
Age groups	
50–54 years old	20.08
55–59 years old	21.92
60–64 years old	16.58
65–69 years old	16.25
70–74 years old	11.67
75–79 years old	7.50
80+ years old	6.00
Marital status	
Married	58.72
Civil partnership or cohabiting	2.42
Divorced	14.85
Widowed	16.35
Single	7.67
Highest educational degree	
No qualifications	20.13
GCSE grade D–G	2.17
GCSE grade A–C	7.52
Trade apprenticeships	3.43

(continued)

Appendix (continued)

	Percentage
A/AS levels	7.10
Higher degree / postgraduate qualifications	26.15
Other qualification, including overseas	8.19
No information (respondent over 70 years old)	25.31
Main activity	
Employed	36.33
Unemployed	1.00
Home keeper	2.00
Temporary or long-term injury or illness	8.17
Retired	50.92
Other	1.58
Income level	
< £5,000	18.00
£5,000–£9,999	23.25
£10,000–£14,999	14.17
£15,000–£19,999	10.00
£20,000–£29,999	12.08
£30,000–£49,999	8.58
£50,000 or more	2.83
Don't know or refused	11.08
Religious denomination and activity	
Christian	36.95
Hindu	2.34
Muslim	2.84
Buddhist, Jewish or other	2.42
Religious, but not actively practising	47.37
No religion	8.09
Disabled	
Not disabled	56.69
Disabled, but no limitation in daily activity	9.62
Disabled and experiences limitations in daily activity	33.70

7

Grandparenting and participation in civil society

Jennifer May Hampton and Esther Muddiman

This chapter explores an often-overlooked lifecourse transition in relation to civil society: that of becoming a grandparent. Most existing lifecourse studies on the impact of family obligations on civic engagement focus on the impact of becoming a parent – and as we have seen in the previous chapter, parenthood can have a significant impact on an individual's relationship with civil society. This chapter extends this analysis and, through acknowledging the significance of the grandparent–grandchild relationship (Smith 2005), explores the types of civic engagement that might be triggered or halted by grandparenthood.

Television and children's books tend to portray grandparents as old, frail, fussy, infirm and sedentary (Janelli and Sorge 2002; Smith 2005). As part of the older population, grandparents are generally perceived to be the beneficiaries of care rather than as actively contributing to civil society through, for example, voluntary work, political participation or associational membership. Indeed, a persistent focus on an individual's economic contribution throughout their working life and rising concerns about the public health burden of ageing populations work together to position older individuals as a worrisome responsibility for their descendants. This does not give the full picture of grandparenthood, however: the average age of becoming a grandparent in Britain is actually 55 (Leopold and Skopek 2015), meaning that many grandparents are relatively young, active, in paid employment and engaged in their communities.

Despite grandparenthood being a central aspect of later life (Margolis 2016), which most adults will experience, the area remains under-researched (Smith 2005), particularly from the point of view of the grandparent. Little of the existing research focuses on the experiences of grandparents themselves and the effect that having grandchildren can have on their day-to-day lives. This chapter addresses this gap in the literature. We begin with a comparison of grandparents and non-grandparents drawing on nationally representative cross-sectional survey data, and then draw on in-depth interviews with grandparents themselves. We explore the activities and practices associated with 'grandparenting' as a trigger for, or barrier to, active engagement in civil society, taking a particular interest in how the role of grandparent interacts with individuals' participation in civil society and ask how being a grandparent shapes their patterns of interest and participation.

Introducing our data

The UK Household Longitudinal Survey (UKHLS) – also known as 'Understanding Society' – (University of Essex 2018), has been collecting interview data from a nationally representative sample of approximately 40,000 households every year since 2008. It covers a range of different topics, including family structure, family relationships, membership of various clubs and groups, and participation in non-work activities such as volunteering. We focus on data collected between 2013 and 2016. In order to be confident in our comparison of those with grandchildren to those without, the data was constrained to those over the age of 40 who were also retired (N = 10,446). Within this group, 71 per cent had grandchildren and, of these, 3 per cent were co-resident with their grandchildren. Through our analysis of the UKHLS, some clear patterns of participation between grandparents and non-grandparents emerge.

We build our understanding further with reference to qualitative data drawn from in-depth interviews with grandparents in England and Wales conducted as part of the ITCV project – which sought to deepen our understanding of civic engagement according to intergenerational bonds (see Muddiman et al 2019). Interviews with grandparents formed part of the second phase of this study, after a survey administered to 1,000 children aged 13–14 across schools in South and West Wales. Pupils involved with the project took home surveys and invitations for their parents and grandparents to participate in the study, resulting in interviews with 16 grandmothers and 4 grandfathers during 2017 (see Table 7.1). Interviews with grandparents covered issues related to both their own civic engagement (including involvement with volunteering, religious beliefs and practices, political and other perspectives) and their family life and relationships with their children and grandchildren. Table 7.1 provides some information about the grandparents interviewed. These participants were all grandparent to teenage grandchildren and had a mean age of 74. The oldest grandparent, Winnie, was

Table 7.1: Grandparents interviewed as part of the ITCV project

Name	Year of Birth	Nationality	Retired	Occupation type	Marital status	Other family members interviewed as parents
1. Winnie[a]	1931	English	Y	Health/social care	Widowed	Daniel (son)
2. Muriel[b]	1934	Welsh	Y	Secretarial	Widowed	Daisy (daughter)
3. Roger	1937	English	Y	Engineering	Repartnered	Eve (daughter)
4. Maria	-	English	Y	Health/social care		-
5. Ray[b]	1937	Welsh	Y	Self-employed	Widowed	Julia (daughter)
6. Carol	1941	English	Y	Secretarial	Married	Natasha (daughter)
7. Bonnie	1941	Welsh	Y	-	Married	-
8. Veronica[a]	1942	English	Y	Health/social care	Widowed	David (son)
9. Annie[b]	1943	English	Y	Health/social care	Separated	-
10. Colleen[b]	1943	Welsh/Irish	Y	Secretarial	Married	Ruth (daughter)
11. Rita[a]	1945	English	Y	Health/social care	Married	John (son)
12. Gwen	1946	Welsh	Y	Secretarial	Widowed	Ffion (daughter)
13. Moira[b]	1946	Welsh/Irish	Y	Health/social care	Widowed	Bridget (daughter)
14. Ian[b]	1948	English	Y	Managerial	Married	Nina (daughter)
15. Beryl[b]	-	Welsh	Y	Scientist	Married	Nina (daughter)
16. Victor[b]	1949	Welsh	Y	Skilled manual	Married	Nicole (daughter)
17. Shelly[b]	1955	Welsh	?	-	?	Tara (daughter)
18. Penny	1959	Welsh	N	Health/social care	Repartnered	Abby (daughter)
19. Gillian[b]	-	English	N	Education	Married	Miranda (daughter)
20. Ffion	1967	Welsh	N	Education	Married	Gwen (mother)

Notes:

[a] Paternal grandparent (interviewed in relation to their son's children).

[b] Interviewed as maternal grandparents but also have grandchildren via sons.

born in 1931 and so was 86 at the time of interview. Penny, the youngest grandparent interviewed qua grandparent, was born in 1959 (aged 59 at time of interview). We also include, however, Ffion, Gwen's daughter, who we interviewed as a parent but also had a young grandson with another on the way at the time of interview. Ffion was born in 1967 and so was aged 50 at the time of interview. Thirteen lived with their spouse/partner, five lived alone and two lived with other family members: Moira shares her home with her daughter (Bridget) and grandson Cian, and Muriel shares her home with her son (Hywel).

In the following sections we use the longitudinal and interview data to explore the many ways in which becoming a grandparent appears to influence the level and nature of civic and political engagement.

Grandparenting, work and family obligations

Becoming a grandparent marks the beginning of a new stage in the lifecourse, with numerous implications for their civic and political participation. There are various indications that grandparents are becoming increasingly prominent in the organisation of family life. First, across the developed world, people are living longer than ever before and are therefore more likely to live to see the birth of their grandchildren. Indeed, in the UK, over a quarter of the adult population are grandparent to one or more grandchild(ren), and the majority of 65-year-olds are now grandparents (Wellard 2011). Increased longevity also extends the period of time that individuals experience grandparenthood: it is estimated that the average person now experiences grandparenthood for around a third of their lives (Smith 2005) with grandmothers experiencing an average of seven years longer than grandfathers (Leopold and Skopek 2015).

In addition, the rising number of 'beanpole' families – where many generations coexist but with few members of each generation in a tall, thin family structure (Bengtson et al 1990; Hagestad 2000) – has important implications for grandparenting. On the one hand, with typically fewer grandchildren, grandparents may have more time and resources available to devote to individual grandchildren. On the other hand, so-called 'sandwiched' grandparents (Wellard 2011) may find themselves caring for both their own parents and their grandchildren, leaving less time for any other activities. Little is known about how these family responsibilities interact with various forms of civic engagement, and whether grandparents are more or less involved in civil society than non-grandparents.

Time pressures are likely to be particularly acute for grandparents who are still in paid employment. While most of the grandparents we interviewed were retired, many of them became grandparents while they were still employed. Annie, for example, first became a grandparent when she was 46 years old when she was "mid-career", it was only upon retirement and her daughter's relocation to Wales that she thought more deeply about the grandparent role.

Existing research also suggests that becoming a grandparent can actually trigger retirement – especially for grandmothers (Van Bavel and De Winter 2013). Leaving employment in order to care for grandchildren can help parents (particularly mothers) to return to work (Aassve et al 2012; Arpino et al 2014; Ho 2015; Lumsdaine and Vermeer 2015; Kanji 2018). Where this is the case, it is possible that grandparenting might be associated with an increased capacity for civic and political engagement.

Civic and political participation among grandparents and non-grandparents

Particular retirement activities – such as volunteering in the local community – are thought to embody notions of active and 'successful' ageing (Ahern and Hendryx 2008). While there is little evidence available on the relationship between grandparenthood and participation of this sort in the UK, data from other European countries indicates that having grandchildren increases the likelihood of getting involved in the local community in multiple ways (Arpino and Bordone 2017). However, it seems that having regular childcare responsibilities can disrupt this trend – Arpino and Bordone (2017) found that grandmothers were less likely to volunteer or participate in educational or political organisations if they had regular childcare responsibilities. That there is no similar pattern for grandfathers is intriguing, especially as some research suggests a rise in the proportion of men who take active involvement in their grandchildren's lives, challenging the stereotype of the passive and inactive grandfather. There is evidence that 'grandfathering' conflicts with other activities pursued in the course of active ageing (Mann et al 2016). Given that grandfathers are much more likely to engage in caring behaviour only when they have a partner (compared to grandmothers, who are likely to engage in caring behaviour regardless of whether or not they have a partner to share caring responsibilities with) (Hank and Buber 2009), they may well have more opportunity to engage in both. For a more detailed discussion on gender and grandparenting see Tarrant's (Tarrant

Table 7.2: Associational membership by retirement and grandparent status

	Non-retired	Retired	Non-grandparents	Grandparents
Environmental	2%	3%	4%	2%
Sport	18%	13%	14%	13%
School/ parent–teacher association	7%	1%	1%	1%
Scouts/Guides	2%	1%	1%	1%
Residents'/ tenants'	3%	4%	5%	4%
Community	4%	6%	7%	6%
Professional	7%	2%	3%	2%
Religious/ church	13%	19%	18%	19%
Working men's	5%	8%	7%	9%
Women's Institute	1%	4%	3%	4%
Women's	1%	2%	2%	2%
Pensioners	1%	6%	5%	6%

2018; Tarrant and Hughes 2019) work on grandparents, masculinities and caring, and Muddiman et al 2020 (Chapter 6).

We explored the interests of grandparents and non-grandparents through their memberships of various associations. Membership of a particular organisation conveys a particular interest or value given to the cause of that particular group. As can be seen by the list of organisations in Table 7.2, these interests are broad and various. Some are concerned with local issues (such as community), while others are concerned with wider societal issues (such as the environment). Some appear to centre on specific activities (such as sport or residents' associations), whereas others are more general and related to particular habits or characteristics of the individual (faith- or worship-based). Some categories of membership are related to particular stages of the lifecourse, for example professional memberships or retirement groups. Additionally, as we have seen in the previous chapter, while some memberships might be long-term or even lifelong commitments, others may be more episodic and related to lifecourse stages. For instance, involvement with children and young people's groups is very likely to be most prominent among 'active' parents or grandparents.

We might hypothesise that within the retired group, those with grandchildren are less likely to be involved with organisations than their peers without grandchildren, given the time pressures that active involvement in their grandchildren's lives may have; that is, grandchildren may deplete the free time of grandparents. However, the picture painted by the proportions shown in Table 7.2 show a mixed picture. While grandparents are significantly less likely to be involved in environmental, sport, residents' and professional associations, they are more likely to be members of working men's clubs or the Women's Institute. This heightened interest in these associations, traditionally associated with older generations, may have something to do with the transition into grandparenthood. As Kaufman and Elder state: 'This transition may convey meanings of "later life" that recast the self-concept and may influence self-perceptions of age status and age identity' (2003: 270). It may be that grandparents are more likely to join these groups because these groups represent what they believe to be appropriate associations for grandparents to be part of.

Civic and pre-political participation

As with membership and involvement in associations, time may be an important resource dictating the extent to which individuals can or cannot participate in formal forms of civic participation. The figures in Table 7.3 confirm this in terms of formal instances of volunteering. Respondents were asked if they had volunteered in the last 12 months, with those who had retired (and therefore had more time) indicating that they had volunteered more than those who had not yet retired. Similarly, those without grandchildren indicated that they volunteered more than those with grandchildren, suggesting that involvement with grandchildren may be taking up 'free time' that could otherwise be used for this formal type of civic participation. What these data mask, however, is the intensity of the volunteering, or indeed the type of volunteering that is being undertaken.

Table 7.3: Volunteering and charitable giving by retirement and grandparent status

	Non-retired	Retired	Non-grandparents	Grandparents
Donated to charity (last 12 months)	73%	81%	82%	81%
Volunteered (last 12 months)	21%	23%	25%	22%

The amount of time that grandparents are able to dedicate to voluntary or civic activities may also be influenced by the domestic division of labour, with grandmothers typically taking on more caring responsibilities for grandchildren when compared to grandfathers. This is evident in our interview data. For example, Ian is involved in a male voice choir which meets once or twice a week, and also sings and plays guitar in his church choir on Sundays. He is a school governor and sits on the appeals panel, and is part of a German society that meets once a fortnight. Conversely, Ian's wife, Beryl, who was also retired, had significant 'sandwiched' caring responsibilities for both her grandchildren and her own mother who was 94 at the time of interview. She was supportive of Ian's many hobbies, joking that "It gets him out of my hair", and spoke about getting "dragged in" to help out with Ian's choir events. Taking into consideration time spent together as a couple – going to the gym twice a week, for example, and being involved together in a charity that arranges pilgrimage trips – this seemed to leave little time for Beryl to pursue her own hobbies and leisure activities.

Family routes into volunteering

It was common for the grandparents we interviewed to talk about getting involved with voluntary activities via the family. Rita become involved with her local Meithrin (Welsh language preschool) while looking after her grandsons, and ended up "running it" with her husband for six years, finding a way to make it work despite the fact that neither of them were able to speak Welsh:

> 'We ran the Meithrin for six years ... I don't speak Welsh, but they didn't have anybody to do it, so I said I'd do it if the mums would help out with story time, and it worked really well ... The boys came to that, too, so it was good. So, yeah ... I've been really lucky doing everything I like doing.' (Rita)

For Veronica, "it started with the kids"; she joined the parent–teacher association (PTA) with her husband and would volunteer to do reading practice in the classroom. Her voluntary activities paused when she returned to work full-time as the children got older, but as soon as she began to reduce her hours to part-time, she returned to the school to volunteer reading practice again, and began helping out with a toddler's group at church. Now in her 80s, Veronica is still very actively involved:

'I still do that now, I love it. That's my bag [pointing excitedly] I'm sorting out for toddlers, sorting the money out and everything. I did that on a Wednesday afternoon and then a few years later I gave up Mondays, and went back to the local school doing reading with the kids again. I still do that now as well, I go every Monday … Now, we've got four toddler groups now that run at church in the week, Tuesday, Wednesday and Thursday mornings, and Wednesday afternoons. I don't do all of them, unless somebody is ill or on holiday, or we have to swap around. All the groups have got their own leaders. I mean, I've got to go on Wednesday because it's parties next week, the Christmas parties with Santa, and presents, and goodness knows what else … I shall be there all day Wednesday, that'll be fun.' (Veronica)

Veronica is one of the grandparents we interviewed who was living over an hour away from her teenage grandchildren, with another set of grandchildren living abroad. She particularly loves looking after the "screaming twos", telling us "I think they're adorable at that age". She has fond memories of her own children and grandchildren at this young age, and her voluntary work seemed to help her connect with happy memories of family time spent together. She also enjoyed "chatting to the mums" and the social element of getting out and meeting people via volunteering. It is possible that this social contact made up, in some ways, for the fact that neither of her two sons lived close enough for such regular contact.

From a slightly different perspective, Victor started volunteering at his local library after an intervention from his daughter: "My daughter volunteered me last year. She thought I needed to do something." The council had closed the library and it had reopened as a charity endeavour. Victor was happy that he had begun volunteering and said that he found it interesting. He agreed with his daughter that he needed to get out and do something, and his account suggests that working in the library rekindled his desire to "put some back in" to the community in retirement.

Volunteering was so central to some of the grandparents that we interviewed that it became part of family identity. Shelly, a self-confessed animal lover, was perhaps the most committed and enthusiastic grandparent that we interviewed when it came to her volunteering. She had been volunteering for an animal charity for more than ten years, and both of her daughters and various grandchildren were now also involved – volunteering was presented as an important part of family life:

> 'Because, like, it is fun and you, like, meet loads of people and you know you can have a great time as well as helping the animals and that. And then Tara joined, and then her son done a little bit and Jay is there, that's the son of my other daughter ... Yeah, so they've all come through ... I worked my way up, like she's a key volunteer [daughter, Tara], so is my other daughter, so am I and we worked our way up through our badges like different levels so we can actually open up shops, shut shops down now.' (Shelly)

Even when she is not volunteering at the local charity shop, Shelly said that she was "thinking about what you can do the next day to help bring more money in to the shop", and on a recent holiday she was keen what to know what was happening in her absence and called her grandson Jay regularly to check in and ask about the running of the shop – "How much did we do today? Did you do this, did you do that?!" (Shelly). Shelly describes the atmosphere in the shop as "like you're one family ... a very happy, friendly environment", and she enjoys talking to older people who might be feeling lonely: "Volunteering is good in that way, you know ... you can reach out to other people and give them that quality of life as well."

Informal volunteering

Grandparents in our study also spoke about instances of 'informal' civic engagement – practices that they wouldn't necessarily categorise in terms of volunteering, but that nonetheless indicate a desire to support and help others who aren't friends or family members. On the day of his interview, Ray had just made a cake for "the old dear downstairs" who was in her 90s and couldn't get out and about, this seemed like a regular arrangement: "Yeah that's my little bit, she moans a bit, mind, and a lot of people don't like her, but I can see that she is a very lonely, married twice, both husbands gone." Similarly, Winnie kept watch over one of her neighbours who doesn't have any children: "Her memory is going so I ring her on a Sunday just to keep an eye on her." Winnie's neighbour was also invited over to the Christmas dinner that she shared with her son and his family every year. These little acts of generosity and inclusiveness might not figure on formal measures of volunteering, but are arguably part of the welfare function identified by Foley and

Edwards (1998). It may also be the case that helping others who are considered to be more infirm helps grandparents to feel younger and more active in comparison.

In Winnie's case, her interview also indicated that she didn't necessarily feel as though she was a 'volunteer' if she was spending her time doing something that she enjoyed. As a keen writer, she prepared the newsletter for the housing association where she lived: "Oh yes, I'm counted as a volunteer because I do the newsletter."

Charitable giving

The longitudinal survey data indicates that there is little difference in a donation made to charity in the last 12 months between those with and without grandchildren in the retired group. Similar to the lack of difference between these individuals in their religious or church membership, this may indicate that the differences between those with and without grandchildren are arranged around differing levels of time available, rather than differing interests or values.

Although there is little indication that grandparents are more charitable than non-grandparents, there is some indication that the type of charitable giving could be influenced by family ties. Muriel was prompted to "give to asthma" because her daughter suffers from the condition, alongside her other regular donations to the Heart Foundation and a school. Gwen organises coffee mornings to raise money for Macmillan nurses, remembering how good they were to her husband when he was very ill. She also donates to Cancer Research, as a cause close to her heart, and the local hospice.

Supporting grandchildren's interests and personal development

In addition to their civic engagement activities such as volunteering, becoming a grandparent is likely to have significant – if harder to identify – implications for the development of their grandchildren's dispositions and skills. Grandparenting can be an important vehicle for the intergenerational transmission of civic 'virtues'. It is clear from our interview data that a key part of grandparents' obligations towards their children was to nurture their talents and support their interests. This support could be practical (such as giving lifts to various activities) or financial (for example, Roger buying his grandson a new drum kit). It could also take the form of emotional support and encouragement, for example going to watch the school play or music recital. Both

Moira and Rita, for instance, were heavily involved in supporting their grandsons' sporting efforts. Moira's grandson has sports practice almost every day of the week, requiring careful coordination between Moira and Bridget over lifts and preparing meals around his schedule. Winnie was delighted that her granddaughter shared her love of music and had helped her to learn the piano, while Gwen was very proud of her rugby-playing grandsons and nephews and always tried to go and see them play.

In some instances, a by-product or side effect of this grandparental support might be regarded as somewhat civic – local youth sports teams and school bands might not survive and prosper without the financial and practical support of parents and grandparents, and the morale-boosting effect of having an audience or proud spectators – especially for grandparents who may have more time to attend than parents, if they are retired. While it might be overstating things to argue that supporting your grandchildren's interests is, in itself, a civically minded act, sports and the arts, in particular, might be regarded as public goods, and family support for some children may enable other children without the same levels of support to participate.

Rita's involvement with her grandson's learning at school provides an interesting lens through which to understand her dual commitments to volunteering her time and helping out her family. She had taken a particular interest in her grandson's educational development when it became clear that his dyslexia was holding him back. She was already volunteering to help with reading skills at the school – and argued to be assigned to her grandson so that she could focus on him:

> '[I]t was beginning to cause him a lot of problems, so we went to school to speak to the head teacher. She said, "Well, unfortunately he's very bright so he won't get any help" and I said, "Well, I come here to help children every day with their reading, so why can't somebody help him?" She said, "Well, we don't get volunteers". I said, "Well, I'll volunteer", so she said "Yeah, but you're his grandmother." And I said, "Well, I know that, but, you know, he needs help." And it was a really difficult time for him, but the teacher actually agreed, and she said, "If Stuart agrees then you can come here." The rest is history. He just flew after that, because I helped him with his writing, only one morning a week.' (Rita)

This is an example of overlapping commitments and allegiances – Rita is a committed volunteer to the school but also perceives that her grandson needs her special attention, and so negotiates in order to fulfil both of these priorities, using her voluntary work to date as a kind of leverage.

Grandparents might also be seen to be acting civically when they teach their grandchildren certain values and perspectives. When asked, "What do you think is the most important thing that you've taught your children and grandchildren?", many focused on civic virtues such as kindness, generosity and open-mindedness:

> 'I suppose it's about tolerating and respecting other people and to take a wider view of things than the kind of immediate little world and to be welcoming to people from other countries.' (Annie)

> 'I suppose, to be kind – I suppose that was a very big value, to be kind and generous I guess to other people, I hope. You don't know how that comes out but, I hope, that's what we tried to do.' (Gillian)

> 'Well, just to think that there are people worse off than us … You see people now relying on food banks and things and it does get me down mind, I wish I could change it. Sam is good with things like that and, you know, we do try our best … they do think about other people, not always "what's in it for me" which is good.' (Gwen)

Annie had also taken her granddaughter to the charity shop where she volunteers so that she could see what it was like 'behind the scenes' even though she was too young to become a volunteer herself. In this sense, it might be argued that the everyday actions of grandparents might help to sow seeds of civic virtue among their grandchildren. Indeed, having grandchildren may in fact act as a motivation for role modelling certain civic virtues – providing grandparents with an opportunity to extend their nurturing role beyond the confines of family.

Religious faith was central to many of our grandparents' accounts of their civic engagement. Of the 20 grandparents we interviewed, only Annie did not identify at all with a religious faith. All of the grandparents were members of Roman Catholic, Methodist or Baptist churches, the Church in Wales or other non-conformist denominations of the Christian faith. It was important to many of these grandparents that their grandchildren shared their faith. For Gillian and Winnie, it was the most important thing that they sought to pass down through the family, and Victor viewed it as his "job to see that they get the same faith". Although Victor felt a strong responsibility to pass down his faith, he wasn't sure whether he had done "a good job with it", explaining of his daughter Steph's family "they don't practise at all so that's very disappointing". His other three children and their families did share his faith, and while they didn't always worship together, in part because they didn't always meet up at weekends, he did make sure that when visiting his two sons further afield, that they attended mass together as a family. Winnie was also determined to pass down "a love of Jesus" and the practice of prayer to her grandchildren. While she could no longer attend church due to mobility issues, she prayed with her family whenever they visited, and she was delighted that one of her grandsons was working for a Christian organisation. Gillian was also hopeful that her grandchildren would absorb the family faith through shared activities and discussions, but was also alive to the possibility that they may choose their own paths in the future.

Religious faith and attendance had prompted other forms of civic engagement among the grandparents we interviewed. Colleen had been involved with the Union of Catholic Mothers in her church and had helped with flower arranging and had organised various events over the years. When asked how she got involved, she explained: "I just wanted to, I think and my husband did as well. We just felt part of the community and we wanted to do it and help. We had a lot of friends … all our age with children." For Colleen, then, helping at church seemed to be tied up in her sense of community and was closely linked to her social life. She, too, lamented the fact that all of the children were grown up and "hardly go to the church now", meaning that it was "not like it used to be", despite the fact that her daughter was very involved in her local church. For Bonnie, church had become a bit of a lifeline. She described it as "a big part of my life" because church was the only place close enough to her home that she could drive to on her scooter independently. She remembers taking all of her grandchildren to church when their parents were working, and is pleased that three of them are now church servers. Despite Bonnie's ill health she participates in church fundraising efforts and the family attend fairs, afternoon teas and other charity events linked to the church to support the work that they do.

Church was also a huge part of Gillian's life – her whole family was deeply involved, with her son and daughter taking leading roles in the organisation of their non-traditional community congregation. Gillian and her husband had relocated to be closer to their children and grandchildren, and "from day one" since their move "the church has always been important". With her family, Gillian had created a "ministry", collecting furniture and other goods for people in need. With her husband Vinnie, Gillian had also taken a lead on church pastoral support. As part of this commitment to their church community, Gillian and her husband had also hosted Alpha[1] courses at their home. While they had had a strong faith beforehand, their move seemed to have intensified their commitment to church, meaning that, alongside family, it was their top priority. In this sense, it seems that Gillian's relationship with her children and grandchildren had galvanised her faith and her desire to help others through the church.

Interestingly, some of the grandparents that we interviewed, including Gillian, were deliberately scaling back their involvement with their respective churches in order to make way for the next generation. Gillian no longer hosts Alpha courses at her house – "we're much too old now [laughter]" – and has shifted to a mentoring role: "I see my role [now] more as helping and releasing younger people, handing on the baton I suppose … because things have had to expand."

Political participation

The informal and formal types of civic participation described thus far in this chapter can be thought of as pre-political, although their relationship to political forms of participation are not necessarily straightforwardly causal (Ekman and Amnå 2012). Along with formal political participation measures, we also examine interest in politics in this section as we know that this particular type of interest can be directly linked to formal participation (Robison 2017), as well as wider civic participation (Putnam 2000). Table 7.4 shows that those who have retired are more likely to be interested in politics, to affiliate with a particular party,[2] and to be a member of a political party. Not included in Table 7.4 is trade union membership, which Ekman and Amnå consider to be a distinctly political form of associational membership. Unsurprisingly, the non-retired were much more likely to be a member of a trade union than those were retired, although membership was generally low (at 4 per cent and 0.6 per cent, respectively).

Although grandparents were significantly less likely that non-grandparents to indicate an interest in politics, levels of party affiliation and party membership were comparable between the two groups. Among the grandparents that we interviewed for the ITCV study, levels

Table 7.4: Political participation by retirement and grandparent status

	Non-retired	Retired	Non-grandparents	Grandparents
At all interested in politics	75%	82%	84%	81%
Affiliates with a particular political party	56%	68%	69%	67%
Member of a political party	2%	2%	2%	2%

of political interest were higher than we might expect than for the general population (this is unsurprising given the sampling procedure we used). The interview data also allow us to go beyond voting and political membership rates to consider less conventional measures of political engagement.

While many of the grandparents in our study emphasised the importance of voting (no matter what) as an important right that has been fought for, some were disillusioned with the contemporary selection of political advocates. This sense of weariness with the political arena was echoed by other grandparents who reported becoming less politically engaged over time. Bonnie described her frustrated attempts to change local parking arrangements to accommodate her mobility issues and had become resigned: "Yeah, well, I've just given up. They're not going to do anything now … I won't bother again now, I don't think. You just cope with what you've got." Bonnie expressed consternation that she might have passed a "let it go" mentality on to her daughter and was concerned that this might lead her grandchildren to shy away from political and local issues too: "That's not a very good thing I taught her … she's obviously teaching the children the same way." A lack of investment in formal political processes did not necessarily indicate that grandparents were apolitical, though – many expressed views on current affairs, social issues and articulated a connection to, and concern for, their local community. Moira, for example, often watched the news with her grandson Cian, sparking conversations about welfare, poverty and healthcare provision. "We don't talk about, you wouldn't think it was politics, because you might bring something up talking about it after you've seen something on the news, and you will air your views then." Even Veronica, who emphasised "I'm not a political animal" and told us that all of the political parties wound her up, had strong views about the European Union (EU) Referendum. Indeed, the desire to pass on political values to children and grandchildren seemed to be an important motivator for the continued involvement of some of the grandparents in our study.

The grandparents in our study who had been politically engaged prior to retirement and grandparenthood were also keen to pass down a sense of political engagement to their children and grandchildren. Penny took a particularly active role in encouraging her children and grandchildren to vote:

> 'I am always on my soapbox preaching to my children you must vote because … the eldest grandson now, he didn't want to go and vote and I was saying, "You must vote, Tanner, it's important." … So, yeah, he did actually go and vote and I said, "You've done it once now, it's easy after that." And you've got to vote, whatever happens in your life you must vote, I think.' (Penny)

Penny didn't necessarily expect her grandchildren to vote in the same way that she did, but felt that it is important to "take an interest", to "believe in something" and to "fight some cause". For Penny this meant supporting the underdog and not just acting in self-interest. Victor held similarly strong views about voting, making the effort to go to the polling station and spoil his ballot if he didn't support any of the candidates. He explained that his parents instilled the importance of voting into him, and that he sees it as part of his role to pass on this value to his children and grandchildren. In addition, Victor regularly wrote to his Member of Parliament (MP) about a range of issues, triggered by an initial letter to Margaret Thatcher in the 1980s: "I can't remember the subject now … I wrote to Margaret Thatcher and they just sent the standard reply back, and so … I thought, well, I'll go to my MP and I started then asking what the procedure was." While Victor had been the first in his family to write to politicians, his daughters had followed his lead and would contact local representatives, particularly about educational issues. Victor had also encouraged his teenage grandchildren to get involved:

> 'I encourage them to do simple things like the size of crisp packets in the EU … just to get them into the motion of writing, so, yeah … they're downgrading the size, well they're doing it to everything now with chocolate didn't they? So writing to the EU Commission to find out why this is happening, just to get involved in it.' (Victor)

For these grandparents, it seems important to role model political engagement and to encourage their involvement as they come of age. While non-grandparents might also seek to encourage younger generations to engage with politics, it is unlikely that this would take the same shape as the exchanges between grandparents and grandchildren.

Political discussion within the family

Victor invited political debate with family members despite having different views, especially on the EU Referendum. He described how the family all "carry on" around the dinner table: "We always argue politics, every time I vote Conservative." Victor's grandchildren were often present during these debates, and while they were "still learning" they listen to the conversation, "pick little snippets up" and ask questions. Victor wanted to show them "don't be afraid to challenge things" and to set an example of standing up for what you believe in. Victor's account suggests that although family political discussions were sometimes heated, they were a source of pride and brought the family closer together:

> 'When we have arguments they get quite heated sometimes as arguments do, only for a bit, short time, and I, straightaway then I say to them "I'm proud of you because you've got a point of view" and I feel proud of it then because they feel so strongly about something. I think that's good.' (Victor)

Other grandparents were more didactic in their approach to political discussions with their grandchildren. Rita describes an encounter with her grandson prompted by an upcoming general election, in which she hoped to steer him away from supporting Jeremy Corbyn:

> 'I said, "So, Stuart, what do you think?" He said to me, "Nana", he said, "Who're you going to vote for in the election?" and I said "I don't know, I really don't know, it's just so hard this time … Who would you vote for?" He said "I think it would have to be Corbyn" [laughter] I was like mmm, I said, "Really, why?" He said "Well, I think he's more for young people." I said "I think you're being swayed by what you've seen on television, and I think really, if it was me I'd be looking at more what he's likely to do and what his beliefs are really." So, he said, "Oh, why?" I said, "Well, when I was growing up," I said, "I would've

thought he was more like these people who went on bomb marches and things like that" and he said, "Really, why do you say that? … Because he looks scruffy?" And I said, "No, not necessarily that," I said, "but it's just I'd be worried about his values." So, he said, "Oh, you're going to vote for Theresa May are you?" I said, "I'm not too sure about that", I said, "but she is a more stable person you know? She's got different values, maybe I will maybe I won't … I'll wait and see how it pans out." So, coming up to polling day we were talking again, and I said "So, how're you feeling about it now?" And he said. "Well, I don't really know," he said, "I don't know if I'd vote for anybody" [laughter]. I said, "That's an easy way out," I said, "You can't not vote," but, I think he'd changed his mind a little bit and looked into things. I said, "Always remember when you're voting that … you take them for what they are when they're speaking to you, but they're not always quite the same." You know, I've said this to them many times when they were growing up … it's not always what you see is what you're going to get, so always remember that and think about it more carefully. So, whether he did or he didn't, we didn't finish the conversation, but I didn't vote for Jeremy Corbyn [laughter].' (Rita)

For other families, there was a sense of shared family identity when it came to politics. Annie, for example, said, "We tend to agree about all those sorts of things … it's sort of fairly predictable really." Similarly, Gwen said that while her family didn't talk about politics "all the time … they all know and they all feel the same". Gwen explained that she had always been passionate about politics and had marched against Margaret Thatcher many years ago, and described herself as "just as bad now" in terms of being politically engaged. She was glad that her political nature had "rubbed off on" younger family members and was particularly pleased that her grandson was studying politics at university.

Running through some grandparents' accounts of their levels of political engagement was a concern for the future and the lives that their grandchildren and great-grandchildren would be able to lead. This was particularly an issue during the time of the referendum to leave the EU in 2016. Victor, who voted Leave was hopeful that his children and grandchildren would eventually see that leaving the EU was for the best: "I've voted Brexit so hopefully they'll be saved any— they'll be saying to their grandkids, 'If it wasn't for your grandfather and the people like you we'd be in a right mess – look at Europe now', and that's what I voted for. I honestly believe that that's what'll happen, yeah." Conversely, Gwen was deeply concerned about "the way the country is going now", and was concerned about the eventual consequences of the EU Referendum: "I do fear a bit what the future holds now for my grandchildren and great-grandchildren. It's so up in the air." This comment from Gwen suggests that being a grandparent may sustain or galvanise engagement with political issues linked to a forward-looking concern for the future circumstances of younger family members.

The literature on intergenerational transmission nearly always focuses on what gets passed 'down' from older to younger generations. However, there is some evidence in our data that grandchildren influence grandparents' political attitudes and practices. Winnie's grandson Toby was frustrated that he wasn't old enough to vote in the EU Referendum:

> '[H]e was annoyed because he hadn't got a vote for the referendum. I mean, I didn't feel strongly about the referendum. But he did. So I mean, he's far more political than I am ... I voted the way he told me to ... I mean, we don't talk much about politics really. It's only Toby that likes. It was the referendum. He felt strongly enough, he felt strongly he should have been able to vote.' (Winnie)

Grandchildren also seemed to be invaluable in helping their grandparents to keep up with new technology. Winnie described how her 12-year-old granddaughter fixed her Wi-Fi connection, exclaiming, "I mean, the children know far more than the parents." Likewise, Gwen, who had her own laptop and tablet, said, "They've taught me nearly everything I know about it ... they're keeping me up to date." Given the now well-established online means for political participation, the role of grandchildren in facilitating their grandparents' digital literacy may be important in enabling new forms of political engagement. Many of those grandparents who had embraced technology in order to keep up with the busy lives of their grandchildren had also used their skills to sign e-petitions and find out about various political issues. This seemed to be especially important for those with mobility issues, like Winnie, who frequently signed online petitions and used the internet as a window onto the outside world.

Conclusion

This chapter sought to explore how grandparenthood interacts with participation in civil society. Using nationally representative survey data we have demonstrated how patterns of engagement differ or otherwise from retired grandparents' contemporaries. Although the quantitative data showed relatively small differences between associational membership, it is important to bear in mind the often very small proportions of people who generally participate in these activities. While the literature indicates that grandparenthood may trigger retirement, and potentially increase individuals' capacity for participation in civil society, this action may be purposeful; those who take entry into grandparenthood as a motivation to take retirement may be doing so specifically to look after their new grandchildren. Indeed, the quantitative data suggests that time pressures do exist for grandparents, with a smaller proportion reporting volunteering despite similar levels of membership and charitable giving.

The quantitative data mask much of the nuance in and underlying individuals' civic participation that makes direct comparison between grandparent and non-grandparent groups somewhat shallow. However, the rich data drawn from the in-depth interviews with a range of grandparents offer further insight into these participation practices. Using the lens of volunteering practices, we see that grandparents may be differently motivated to volunteer, when they do, with practices directly inspired and influenced by their grandchildren. What emerges from the data is a sense of the importance of shared family identity, intergenerational solidarity and a responsibility felt by the grandparents to pass on civic values as well as behaviours. This intergenerational transmission of values can be seen as operating both directly and indirectly via parents to grandchildren, with instances of both seen in the data. Examples of direct transmission, particularly around discussion of politics with grandchildren, demonstrates that this 'transmission' can operate in both directions; discussion can stimulate the cultivation of civic values across the generations, highlighting the open and holistic nature of some family dynamics.

Overall, our chapter positions grandparenthood as important to the motivations underlying grandparents' participation in civil society. The role of grandparent is positioned as one of responsibility, enacted through the direct participation in certain types of behaviour. While we have seen that grandparents feel a responsibility in shaping the younger generation's civic values and participation, they also demonstrated an openness, suggesting a co-creation and negotiation of shared family values. As well as quelling authoritarian notions of grandparenthood, the stereotypical image of the frail, inactive grandparent is also quashed by our data. Grandparents provide important contributions to civil society, not only through their direct participation, but also through their important role of both enabling and inspiring younger generations to participate.

Notes

[1] Alpha courses consist of a series of interactive sessions designed to explore the Christian faith: https://alpha.org.
[2] Respondents were asked if they supported a particular party and whether they felt closest to a particular party. The figures in Table 7.4 are an amalgamation of these two variables.

References

Aassve, A., Arpino, B. and Goisis, A. (2012) 'Grandparenting and mothers' labour force participation: a comparative analysis using the Generations and Gender Survey', *Demographic Research*, 27(3): 53–8.

Ahern, M.M. and Hendryx, M. (2008) 'Community participation and the emergence of late-life depressive symptoms: difference between women and men', *Journal of Women's Health*, 17(9): 1463–70.

Arpino, B. and Bordone, V. (2017) 'Regular provision of grandchild care and participation in social activities', *Review of Economics of the Household*, 15(1): 135–74.

Arpino, B., Pronzato, C.D. and Tavares, L.P. (2014) 'The effect of grandparental support on mothers' labour market participation: an instrumental variable approach', *European Journal of Population*, 30(4): 369–90.

Bengtson, V.L., Rosenthal, C.J. and Burton, L.M. (1990) 'Families and aging: diversity and heterogeneity', in R. Binstock and L. George (eds) *Handbook of Aging and the Social Sciences* (3rd edn), New York: Academic Press, pp 263–87.

Ekman, J. and Amnå, E. (2012) 'Political participation and civic engagement: towards a new typology', *Human Affairs*, 22(3): 283–300.

Foley, M.W. and Edwards, B. (1998) 'Beyond Tocqueville: civil society and social capital in comparative perspective', *American Behavioral Scientist*, 42(1): 5–20.

Hagestad, G.O. (2000) 'Adults' intergenerational relationships', in *Generations and Gender Programme: Exploring Future Research and Data Collection Options*, New York: United Nations, pp 125–43.

Hank, K. and Buber, I. (2009) 'Grandparents caring for their grandchildren: findings from the 2004 Survey of Health, Ageing, and Retirement in Europe', *Journal of Family Issues*, 30(1): 53–73.

Ho, C. (2015) 'Grandchildren care, intergenerational transfers, and grandparents' labour supply', *Review of Economics of the Household*, 13(2): 359–84.

Janelli, L.M. and Sorge, L. (2002) 'Portrayal of grandparents in children's storybooks: a recent review', *Gerontology and Geriatrics Education*, 22(2): 69–88.

Kanji, S. (2018) 'Grandparent care: a key factor in mothers' labour force participation in the UK', *Journal of Social Policy*, 47(3): 523–42.

Kaufman, G. and Elder, G.H. Jr (2003) 'Grandparenting and age identity', *Journal of Aging Studies*, 17(3): 269–82.

Leopold, T. and Skopek, J. (2015) 'The demography of grandparenthood: an international profile', *Social Forces*, 94(2): 801–32.

Lumsdaine, R.L. and Vermeer, S.J.C. (2015) 'Retirement timing of women and the role of care responsibilities for grandchildren', *Demography*, 52(2): 433–54.

Mann, R., Tarrant, A. and Leeson, G.W. (2016) 'Grandfatherhood: shifting masculinities in later life', *Sociology*, 50(3): 594–610.

Margolis, R. (2016) 'The changing demography of grandparenthood', *Journal of Marriage and Family*, 78(3): 610–22.

Muddiman, E., Taylor, C., Power, S. and Moles, K. (2019) 'Young people, family relationships and civic participation', *Journal of Civil Society*, 15(1): 82–98.

Muddiman, E., Power, S. and Taylor, C. (2020) *Civil Society and the Family*, Bristol: Policy Press.

Putnam, R.D. (2000) *Bowling Alone: The Collapse and Revival of American Community*, New York: Simon & Schuster.

Robison, J. (2017) 'The social rewards of engagement: appealing to social motivations to stimulate political interest at high and low levels of external efficacy', *Political Studies*, 65(1): 24–41.

Smith, P.K. (2005) 'Grandparents and grandchildren', *The Psychologist*, 18(11): 684–7.

Tarrant, A. (2018) 'Care in an age of austerity: men's care responsibilities in low-income families', *Ethics and Social Welfare*, 12(1): 34–48.

Tarrant, A. and Hughes, K. (2019) 'Qualitative secondary analysis: building longitudinal samples to understand men's generational identities in low income contexts', *Sociology*, 53(3): 538–53.

University of Essex, Institute for Social and Economic Research (2018) 'Understanding society: waves 1–8, 2009–2017 and harmonised BHPS: waves 1–18, 1991–2009', [data collection] (11th edn), UK Data Service. SN: 6614. Available from: http://doi.org/10.5255/UKDA-SN-6614-12.

Van Bavel, J. and De Winter, T. (2013) 'Becoming a grandparent and early retirement in Europe', *European Sociological Review*, 29(6): 1295–1308.

Wellard, S. (2011) *Doing It All? Grandparents, Childcare and Employment: An Analysis of British Social Attitudes Survey Data from 1998 and 2009*, London: Grandparents Plus. Available from: https://www.grandparentsplus.org.uk/report/doing-it-all-grandparents-childcare-and-employment/.

8

Retiring into civil society

Laura Jones, Jesse Heley and Sophie Yarker

This chapter explores the role played by volunteering in the lifecourse transition from paid work to retirement. As life expectancy rises, the increasing proportion of over-50s in the UK population is challenging the persistent negative stereotypes that signal both older age and retirement as a withdrawal from active life. Many people are now retiring with good levels of health, education and disposable incomes, as well as having outlooks and expectations regarding this phase of life that are different from their predecessors. In this context, volunteering has been promoted in public policy discourse since the early 1990s as a desirable pathway into retirement, which can bring well-being benefits to the individual as well as allowing them to continue contributing to social and economic life.

Despite the promotion of volunteering, various surveys have found that volunteering rates decline post-retirement for both men and women. However, such surveys, although telling us much about broader trends in civil society participation across age cohorts, are arguably limited in their ability to capture the complexity of a great many older lives these days as they negotiate multiple demands on their time and resources. This chapter seeks to go some way towards fleshing out this complexity by drawing on recent work in human geography on the relational geographies of ageing, which foregrounds the concepts of linked lives and non-linearity in life transitions. Drawing on detailed interviews with older volunteers across a number of organisations in mid-Wales, we consider how decision-making in the retirement transition is narrated by these individuals through reference to their relations and connections with other people, places, organisations and events throughout the lifecourse.

Retirement transitions

As discussed by Ian Rees Jones and colleagues (2010), there have been dramatic changes in the perceptions and experiences of the retirement process from the early 1990s onwards. This has been linked in part to a movement away from mandatory retirement ages, as well as greater flexibility on retirement age for some workers across a range of economic sectors (Rees Jones et al 2010). Focusing on the UK context, Blaikie (1992) noted the growing 'fragmentation' associated with retirement as an increasingly less consolidated phase of the lifecourse, while Higgs et al – writing a decade later – talk about the growing recognition of 'multiple pathways'(2003: 765) into (early) retirement.

The literature more broadly shows how the decision to 'finally' exit the labour force can be related to a combination of push and pull factors: with economic-industrial restructuring and technological advances having 'pushed' many manual workers towards redundancy or early retirement since the 1980s (Davis Smith and Gay 2005), and so, too, poor health and disability, particularly among individuals from lower social classes (Phillipson and Smith 2005); whereas those 'pulled' towards early retirement are more likely to be in higher income occupations and able to exit employment in receipt of generous pension provision (Banks and Smith 2006). Personality and lifestyle factors clearly play a significant role, too, in retirement decision-making, as do family and caring responsibilities (see Van Bavel and De Winter 2013). At the same time, shifts in UK government policy have sought to 'pull' older workers towards remaining in the workforce for longer, in response to an ageing population and associated pensions demands on the public purse (McNair et al 2004; Foster 2018).

While the latter policy discourse might be seen to be feeding into negative portrayals of the older population as a financial burden on wider society, the increasing proportion of over-50s in the UK population is challenging negative stereotypes of both older age and of retirement as a phase of life associated with social redundancy. Increasing diversity within the over-50s age group means that many people are retiring into their 'third age' with increasingly good levels of health and physical fitness, as well as being in receipt of generous private or occupational pensions. There are, therefore, different attitudes and expectations regarding retirement in comparison to previous generations (Higgs et al 2003). As Davis Smith and Gay describe: 'retirement is seen as a multifaceted stage in the life cycle with opportunities to use free time in ways that please the individual' (2005: 24).

Set in this context, volunteering has been identified as a productive way of negotiating the transition from paid work to retirement; providing a means for older people to stay mentally and physically active, as well as offering time structure and social contact, and the opportunity to make a (further) valuable contribution to society (Davis Smith and Gay 2005). The well-being benefits of different types of voluntary participation had been attested to by older volunteers themselves in a number of studies (for recent examples, see Bernard et al 2014; Guell et al 2016). This characterisation of volunteering in the retirement transition as an individual and social 'good' has furthermore been reproduced within a neoliberal discourse of 'active ageing' promoted by governments across Europe (Walker 2008; Laliberte Rudman 2015; Jones and Heley 2016). This policy agenda seeks to promote individual responsibility for ageing 'well' or ageing 'productively' so as to remain a net contributor to family, community and economic life. However, as critical scholars have argued, normative assumptions of 'successful ageing' can overlook inequality and structural barriers to activity (Kojola and Moen 2016).

And yet – despite increasing numbers of the newly retired over-50s seemingly in possession of the health, time and financial resources necessary to undertake voluntary activity – evidence indicates that an individual's involvement in voluntary activity falls after retirement age. Matters are further complicated by reported variations in the levels and types of volunteering between different classes, as well the role of volunteering in maintaining social hierarchies (Whittaker and Holland-Smith 2014). More fundamentally, there are significant variations in how surveys define and account for voluntary activities; particularly so in respect to those which are more informal in nature (see Hustinx et al 2010). For example, some of these issues are discussed elsewhere in this volume in terms of caregiving roles often undertaken by grandparents (Chapter 7 of this volume; see also Hank and Buber 2009). Implicit in all this is the understanding that different settings attract and compel different people to volunteer their time, experience and expertise in a variety of ways.

These trends have been similarly noted by Davis Smith and Gay (2005) in their study of volunteering in the retirement transition. They advocated utilising life histories as a way of offering greater insight into the lifeworlds of older people and understanding some of the barriers and motivations surrounding this decision. In this chapter, we look to build upon and extend this work through engagement with geographical literatures calling for relational studies of age and the lifecourse (Hopkins and Pain 2007). These have variously sought to challenge the individualism often inherent in biographical approaches and look to better situate older people within the social and political relations that connect them with others over time and space.

Lifecourse, transitions and relationality

Lifecourse theory (Elder 1994, 1995) is a well-established concept across a range of disciplines including social gerontology, sociology and cultural studies (as outlined in Chapter 1). Within geography, a number of important collections have deployed the concept in ways that draw attention to the importance of time and place within individual biographies (Katz and Monk 1993; Teather 1999). A parallel and interconnected strand of work on the geographies of ageing has similarly drawn attention to the importance of place, space and time in the lives of older people (see Skinner et al 2014 for a recent overview).[1]

The lifecourse approach has subsequently been built upon and developed within geography through engagement with broader theoretical currents within the discipline, including emotion and embodiment (Anderson and Smith 2001), as well as relational thinking (Jones 2009). As regards the latter, calls for a 'relational understanding of age' have sought to 'complicate the ways in which we understand the relations between personal and social time-spaces' (Hörschelmann 2011: 378). One the one hand, this has focused on notions of intergenerationality and age relationality, exploring interactions between ages and generations geographically (Hopkins and Pain 2007). On the other hand, a second and arguably more pertinent current of work for this study has applied relational thinking to lifecourse transitions, helping us, as Skinner et al note, 'to grapple with questions regarding the unpredictability and precariousness of life, linked lives, and diverse and non-linear life pathways for older adults' (2014: 784; and see Hopkins and Pain 2007; Hörschelmann 2011; Schwanen et al 2012).

Unpacking this quote somewhat, a more relational understanding of the lifecourse has drawn attention, first, to the ways in which important events or transitions within one's own lifecourse such as retirement are 'taken in relation to the life trajectories, needs and understandings of others' including children, family members, spouses and significant others', as well as bearing the influence of past events and encounters (Hörschelmann 2011: 379; see also Elder 1994; Jarvis 2005). Second, the notion of a 'life transition' also needs to be critically reassessed in light of this complexity. Following Hörschelmann (2011) we should look to avoid all-too-common assumptions that people move through life stages in a linear fashion, and that the choices, possibilities and responses in individual lives can be straightforwardly categorised on a timeline. As such, studying life transitions should recognise the possibility for 'diverse outcomes, reversals, returns and reinventions' (Hörschelmann 2011: 379).

Applying this conceptual framing to a qualitative study of older volunteers across a number of organisations in rural mid-Wales, this chapter aims to examine how the transition to retirement – and specifically the choice to undertake voluntary activity as part of this process – is often a relational achievement; with such decisions being the result of interconnections between multiple lifecourses, past and present, as well as 'social institutions, expectations, structures and changes' (Hörschelmann 2011: 378). How this study was undertaken, its aims and methods is outlined in the following section.

Introducing our methods

As we have seen in Chapter 6, a significant number of studies of volunteering have employed quantitative analyses as a basis for identifying broader trends and motivations for volunteering in different sectors and across different scales. At a more local and individual level, qualitative approaches are also required which illuminate those 'complex, embedded relationships between setting, motivations, attitudes about sociopolitical participation, and personal and community experience and identification' (Stewart and Weinstein 1997: 809). In the vein of the latter, this study draws upon in-depth interviews and observations undertaken in five organisations where older people (aged 50 and above) constitute an important component of their volunteer base. In light of that expressed requirement to develop more relational understandings of volunteer spaces, this process involved talking not only with older volunteers, but also with other individuals who inhabit and manage these spaces. Participant observation was also undertaken with several of the organisations over the course of several months in order to more fully understand the situated context of engagements.

The organisations we worked with included: the National Botanic Garden of Wales (NBGW), a village shop run as a community enterprise (CS), a volunteer-run town museum (TM), and local branches of the University of the Third Age (U3A) and Royal British Legion (RBL). These were selected on the basis of them being sited in mid-Wales and, following initial scoping conversations, indicated that they were highly dependent on older volunteers. They furthermore provide interesting variations in the size of their volunteer workforce and organisational structures. Here an expressed purpose of the study was to provide feedback on the experiences of this volunteer base to these organisations as a basis for developing their own policy and provision.

This chapter draws on 27 interviews carried out with individuals or small groups of volunteers across these organisations, thereby comprising 34 older people in total (12 male, 22 female). The large majority of interviewees would be characterised as being in their 'third age' between the ages of 60 and 75, although several members of the U3A were in their 80s. The recruitment process was such that interviewees were self-selecting, and often part of friendship networks within those organisations they volunteered for. In adopting a 'snowballing' technique we therefore accept an inherent level of bias and make no grand claims regarding the ability of our findings to represent the ambitions and experiences of older volunteers within our host organisations – much less about the nature of 'grey volunteering' more broadly.

Considering those individuals who took part in the research, it is the case that they were largely 'white' and (outwardly) 'middle class' in terms of their occupational backgrounds. Moreover, the broadly rural context of our host organisations also impacted upon our demographic; with the shop, museum and (to a lesser extent) botanic garden all being situated within village and small-town locations. In the case of the shop and museum in particular, it is clear that these spaces were deeply embedded within wider social and institutional forms in these localities, and a significant number of participants highlighted the importance of community in geographical terms as well as in respect to shared interests. And yet, those expectations concerning, motivations for, and experiences of, volunteering explored during the fieldwork were variable and highly subjective, belying any straightforward associations with residential or occupational biographies. Echoing findings from Hardill and Baines' study of volunteering in later life in the English East Midlands (2009), these individualised explanations centred on reactions to milestone events, including retirement or a major change in family circumstances. What Hardill and Baines refer to as **getting-by narratives**, these variously reflect a desire to embrace new opportunities, but also those feelings of loss and tension that accompany stepping away from formal employment (Hardill and Baines 2009: 43).

The interviews focused more broadly on experiences of volunteering in older age and in rural place. Interviews were thematically coded, and analysed using NVivo CAQDAS software. The coding categories used were focused on issues relevant to our research questions and shaped by theory, and were refined through a process of rereading the interviews. For the purpose of this chapter, we focus on narratives surrounding the retirement transition and the decision to volunteer, or continue volunteering, at this time; considering how individuals talk about and make sense of this time in their lives relationally through reference to aspects of their own lifecourse and the lifecourses of those connected to them. Findings are presented in the following section structured around three key themes that emerged through an interpretive process of analysis.

Volunteering and the transition to retirement

Reading narratives of retirement from a relational perspective, three main themes emerged: first, the increasingly blurred boundaries of work and retirement experienced by many older people who move into retirement in hesitant, partial, uncertain and sometimes non-linear ways by undertaking varying combinations of paid work and unpaid voluntary activity. Second, the decision-making surrounding this transition process is shaped by a goodly number of interrelated factors and motivations including: personal preferences, health, finances, family, place, biography, and caring roles and responsibilities. Third, the experience of volunteering is frequently made sense of through reference to working lives and the cultures and norms associated with paid employment. However, not all aspects of this comparison are desirable. Thus, an increasing professionalisation within civil society is in some cases placing unwanted pressure and burdens onto volunteers.

Blurred boundaries of work and retirement

By virtue of the project design, all of our interviewees were currently volunteering for one or more civil society groups or organisations[2] and identified themselves as retired to some degree. This indicates at the outset that, for many, retirement was not a clearly defined state of being where all forms of work ceased. In this sense, retirement was not experienced as a cliff-edge event, but a more gradual phase of adjustment, experimentation and negotiation that involves exploring new forms of identity and meaning not necessarily tied to career or occupational status. As part of this process of exploration, many of our interviewees had experienced a more hesitant and/or partial movement from paid employment to voluntary forms of participation as a part of the retirement transition. The following quotation, for example, captures some of the uncertainty felt by different individuals at a time in the lifecourse where norms and expectations of behaviour are less clearly defined:

> 'Well, I just, because I had a lot of things in my life, but then I just had gaps, so it just seemed like a lot of time to fill and I just felt like, I just needed to be doing more because I was debating whether to get another job or not. Because I'm quite secure financially, because I've had quite good jobs, I don't have to work anymore. But as I say I am on a budget, so.' (Female, 60s, NBGW)

A number of the individuals we interviewed had chosen to transition to retirement more gradually by lessening their paid employment over time, either by going part-time or by undertaking freelance forms of work such as consultancy, giving private music lessons or, as in the following quotation, taking on project work linked to an academic institution:

> 'The other day I got a call from someone I'd worked with saying, "would you like to go in on a tender with us for a project up in North Wales", and although both Charlie and I both said ... I mean, he's younger than me, but he's sort of said "I'm retired now", but when someone actually contacts you and says would you be interested in doing a bit ... So in a way, in theory I'm totally retired but ...' (Female, 70s, CS)

This partial process of retirement allowed our participants the time and flexibility to begin to engage both physically and intellectually with other interests and activities, including taking on voluntary roles and responsibilities. This chimes with the findings from Kojola and Moen's (2016) study of the boomer cohort in the US, for whom standard pathways for work and retirement are being transformed in relation to processes of economic, cultural and political change. They note how, for many members of this cohort, the traditional and irreversible, 'lock-step move' from employee to retiree is no longer desirable. Instead, the notion of 'phasing out to retirement' is recognised as an appealing trajectory for many, in terms of scaling back by taking on part-time or less demanding work roles. However, as Kojola and Moen (2016) note, while for some this phasing-out is a choice, for other older individuals it may be out of financial necessity as they cannot afford to stop working completely. Many of the individuals within our own study, it should be noted, were in a relatively comfortable financial position and this is perhaps reflected in the avenues of volunteering they had chosen to engage in. The NBGW, for example, was characterised by one of our research participants as a manifestation of "ever so nice middle-class volunteering". Indeed, the majority of volunteers we interviewed through this organisation had maintained professional careers including teachers, managers and local government employees. They had therefore been in possession of the resources necessary to exercise a degree of choice about when and how they retired, as following quote describes:

Respondent: A couple of years later I finished at the university. The project came to an end and I thought I don't really actually need to work. I'm sorry. I've got three pensions coming which I've worked very hard for.
Interviewer: Can I ask, what age you were at that point? If you don't mind?
Respondent: I was 57, 58 I think. Yeah, 58. So I was looking for something. So I started getting involved here …
                                    (Male, 60s, NBGW)

For others, however, there had been no option for 'phasing out'. In these cases, the timing of retirement was forced upon them, to an extent, by different circumstances. These included redundancy, the need to give up work to undertake caring roles for family members (notably elderly parents and grandchildren), and ill health. One participant, for example, had been forced to give up her paid employment due to chronic pain associated with a disability. Describing her current situation as "semi-retired", she saw volunteering as a way of continuing to use her skills and experience in the interim as she sought to eventually return to a less physically demanding job role through retraining. However, she noted how the flexibility encountered through voluntary work (part-time hours, shorter shifts) – which was enabling for someone with her particular disability – was missing from the labour market more broadly. Another female participant had started volunteering at NGBW following a number of lifecourse transitions occurring in a relatively short period of time. She underwent a divorce as well as taking early retirement to look after her elderly mother. However, following her mother's death she decided to begin volunteering in order to regain forms of social contact:

'I'd worked freelance for a long time and I found that working freelance because I worked from home it was fine when I was married but then when I was divorced living on my own, it was a bit quiet, I like to get out and about, so I found that again when I was volunteering. Because I packed my job in and at the time when I was home after my mother [passed away], the week was just stretching out, even though I do lots of exercises and go walking and doing this that and the other with groups. Still need that contact with people.' (Female, NGBW, 60s)

Her enjoyment of working alongside other volunteers and "doing something really different from work" led to the decision to return to the workforce in a part-time role as a volunteer coordinator for the charity Oxfam. In both cases, the move from work to volunteering was not understood by the older person themselves as one-directional and this chimes with Hörschelmann's (2011) problematisation of lifecourse transitions as a linear progression, instead recognising the possibility for forms of return and reinvention.

Relational motivations

There is a comprehensive literature addressing what motivates people to volunteer. This includes the large-scale studies outlined in the previous chapter, based on the self-reported motivations of volunteers themselves, ranging from the self-interested to the altruistic (see Davis Smith 1998). People in reality are more complex than this type of continuum can readily capture and most volunteers will usually cite a mix of motives. Here we focus on what we identify as being the more relational aspects of this decision-making process; that is, the ways in which other people, places and institutions, both now and in the past, appeared to play an active role in the accounts given by our interviewees as to why they decided to volunteer in the transition to retirement.

In this way, we draw attention to the importance of linked lives across the lifecourse for how the retirement transition is negotiated and experienced. On the one hand, this includes taking into account the current situation and the needs and wishes of family, friends and neighbours. Several interviewees noted that their decisions about when, where and how much to volunteer were made in relation to other caregiving commitments both actual and potential:

'I don't know what will happen within the family; my mother's problems can pop up, anything within an hour sort of thing, and I support my daughter who's working and the grandchildren as well. It's the balance of having something outside of the family, because you can get overwhelmed with all of that but not too much. And doing enough to be useful.' (Female, 60s, TM)

In this circumstance, and in a sentiment echoed by a number of interviewees, one respondent referred to themselves as a "sandwich generation" who – due to social and economic shifts – had found themselves in the situation of caring for both grandchildren and their own elderly parents. As indicated in an earlier quotation, caregiving for the latter had forced at least one of our interviewees to take early retirement. Another interviewee described how he and his wife were travelling from mid-Wales to Cardiff for three days every week during the first couple of years of his retirement in order to care for their granddaughter. A more formalised form of volunteering for a local museum had therefore come about after several years of being "retired" once the grandchild had started school and this intensive phase of informal caregiving was over.

As one interviewee put it simply, when asked how you go about deciding how to spend your time in retirement, "You ask your wife first, or your partner first." For several of our interviewees the transition to retirement had been a shared experience and, for some, a negotiation of working out how to spend time together and apart. The decision to volunteer by one interviewee, and her subsequent enjoyment of doing so, had directly influenced the retirement transition of her husband and his discovery of new ways of being:

'Well, I volunteered first because he was still at work and then I think he felt that he was missing out because I was going, "I'm off to the Garden now." He'd say, "Oh, are you?" So he actually ended up leaving work. He worked it out financially. He was no better off staying until he was 65. So he decided to leave at 60 and retired. Then we took up beekeeping together and doing the volunteering and stuff. So his life changed completely, because he never had any hobbies. He just worked. He didn't really do anything.' (Female, 60s, NBGW)

While taking into account these contemporary relations, many of our respondents also reflected back on their lifecourse, drawing attention to the formative influence of family when they were growing up and how this had influenced their decision to volunteer in later life. In particular – and a reflection of the social structures and gender norms in which many of this age cohort will have grown up – many invoked their father as being a particularly influential figure in their accounts through their politics, values and behaviours. Grandparents and the occasional mother were also mentioned. This could be in terms of the direct and indirect passing on of interests and values such as care for the natural world through, for instance, going on long country walks together, while in several accounts the example of their father's voluntary activities was presented as a strong influence on their own participation:

Respondent: Yes, that's another thing when I was young as well, so my dad used to be, well, he's with the Samaritans and then he used to go to [a] small swimming pool and on a Thursday night they had people with physical disabilities. So my dad used to do that, and I ended up helping out with that.

Interviewer: You dad was quite social, civically minded then, if he worked for himself and he was doing things like that?

Respondent: Yes, he enjoyed all of that, must be in the blood.

(Female, 60s, NBGW)

For some this perhaps represented a burden or 'sense of duty' to maintain a family legacy of involvement in public life:

Respondent: I'm more academic but I do it, I mean I do it out of sense of duty.

Interviewer: Do you?

Respondent: Because I come from a family, several generations have been involved in public life.

(Female, 80s, U3A)

Not all accounts of childhood were necessarily happy, however, nor all fathers positive role models. One interviewee described growing up in an abusive household and while this was not directly linked to the decision to volunteer (something she had done throughout her life and continued into retirement at NGBW), it was nevertheless discussed as a factor in her ability to be an effective and empathetic volunteer with a family support charity. Another respondent described how his own left-leaning values have been formatively shaped in opposition to those of his domineering father:

Respondent: My father would rant and rave about such things. Socialism, communism, and I, from quite an early age, thought "this is rubbish". So I default to kind of left of centre political ethic

Interviewer: Almost a reaction against his views?

Respondent: So I've always been a bit left ... so those things developed fairly early on ... I've always had this kind of sense of communities working together really.

(Male, 60s, CS)

The complex intertwining of family relations, life experiences, ethics and values are hinted at in the following quotation, which draws attention to feelings of guilt felt at not been able to help his family out of poverty growing up, which is then related to a sense of wanting to help alleviate conditions of social deprivation encountered more widely in society after leaving the military:

'I guess it was a mix of feeling a little bit guilty that I had not helped my family and I wanted to make amends through to seeing lots of deprivation that I had been sheltered from in the Military. And I thought "Oh my god, we need to do something about this", through to personal I don't know, wanting to change things a bit even though you knew you couldn't change a lot. You just wanted to have a go.' (Male, 70s, NGBW)

In their study, Davis Smith and Gay (2005) noted the entwining of family and religious influences as an 'ethical legacy' that motivated many people to undertake voluntary 'good works' outside the confines of a conventional religious setting. Religion was not something we directly asked about during our interviews – and only a handful of interviewees chose to invoke their faith as bearing a direct influence on their voluntary participation ("I suppose being a committed Christian I always look outside of myself and what can I do for other people") – although voluntary involvement in church-based activities was mentioned by a greater number. In contrast, many more of our respondents discussed secular values around environmental care and conservation; particularly those volunteering at the NBGW where such values are obviously aligned with the ethos of the organisation itself. In some cases, these involved an intergenerational ethic of wishing to preserve the environment for future generations, including their own grandchildren.

Living in a rural area or community – either now or throughout the lifecourse – was also strongly referenced in this regard. Relations and experiences in place were associated with fostering a shared outlook and sense of cultural norms and values that was also linked to a sense of heightened community engagement (Winterton and Warburton 2012). Indeed, the success of the community café enterprise was attributed by one volunteer to its particular rural location – between the towns of Aberystwyth and Machynlleth – and the type of residents this has been attracting since the back-to-the-land movements of the 1960s. Here she included herself among eco-minded professionals, with the community ethos, time and knowledge resources to contribute towards the project:

Respondent: There was a lot of that in the '70s ethos and saving the planet and, you know, against Greenham Common, we were against nuclear power, we were against, you know, missiles and all of that. I did demonstrations and stuff, anti-apartheid, all that stuff when I was at university. So, I moved to Wales and I did this all this off-grid stuff, and there is quite a lot of that around the Dyfi Valley. Renewable energy is one of the main, or has been one of the main, employers actually around here.

Interviewer: Yes, it's interesting isn't it, a pocket for that kind of alternative thinking ...

Respondent: A real serious pocket. I mean, I know because I've been involved since the beginning and a lot my friends are involved or were, but there's a lot of really educated people, engineers, you know, a surprising number for such a rural environment ... there's an awful lot of very progressive kind of green leaning people here ... So, this kind of project I think people would be instantly sympathetic to it, I do think that's one of the reasons why it's been so successful – it's had lots of support.

(Female, 70s, CS)

For those involved in projects such as the community café, which involved writing business plans and proposals to secure funding followed by ongoing administration, volunteering could often seem like 'work'. In this final section of findings, we reflect on how retirement was understood within the narratives of our interviewees through its relations – its similarities and differences – to what went before.

Relating volunteering to work

Interviewees were mixed in terms of the extent to which their chosen volunteering trajectory seemed to directly build upon and relate to their work careers. For some respondents, volunteering had seemingly become a way of continuing said career into retirement. This was not necessarily in terms of occupying the same role or even in the same sector, but by allowing them to use the skills and experience developed through a lifetime of work. This seemed most true of volunteers who had occupied high-ranking positions in their working lives and perhaps spoke to a desire to maintain a sense of status and identity tied to this, particularly through trustee or committee roles:

> 'It was really the first I'd heard of U3A and we were hooked. That's my husband and I. We both still belong to Flintshire and I was chairman of Flintshire within a year, I'm that sort of person. I happen to like organisation and I like to … if I see something being done, but not being done as well as … I'm cocky enough to think I could do it. So, you know, I like to do it, so I did three years as chairman of Flintshire, then I did three years as the network chairman.' (Female, 70s, U3A)

A number of our interviewees – including retired teachers, administrators and civil servants – described how they were volunteering in roles and undertaking tasks not completely dissimilar to those carried out in their professional lives. Whether this was always the preferred choice of the volunteer is debatable, with a former teacher describing how he had "foolishly" mentioned his proficiency with computers only to be "handed the role of IT coordinator" for the organisation in question. At the same time, others expressed the desire to do "something completely different". In particular, a number of people who had been employed in predominantly office-based jobs had purposefully chosen to volunteer at NBGW in gardening roles that allowed them to be outside and physically active. A similar desire to distance themselves from their prior responsibilities was evident among interviewees who had worked in emotionally intensive jobs such as social work or nursing, who described a deliberate choice to do something "less heavy" in their retirement.

While some tasks can be similar to those undertaken in working life, volunteers commented on the different ways of working they had experienced in their various organisations. For example, a small team volunteered together in the library at NBGW and discussed why they enjoyed working in a different way as compared to their busy professional lives as teachers or, in one case, as a professional librarian:

Respondent 1:   I think it's a very important point actually because all of us held responsible jobs and I certainly was in charge of a number of people, as you were in your job, and it's nice not to do that now because there's nobody in charge here now, the way it's structured. We all work together and that's very nice.

Respondent 2:   It's a relaxing atmosphere.

Respondent 1:   But it's a liberating way of working, there's nobody telling us what to do, we're not telling each other what to do, we wouldn't dream of doing that.

Respondent 2:   Well, I wouldn't.

Respondent 1:   We work together as a team, it's nice, it's great. (Female & Female, 60s, NBGW)

Here our interviewees drew attention to the different working culture encountered as a volunteer in contrast to their experiences as a paid employee. This included working in a less hierarchical and more collegiate way, as well as engaging without the responsibility of managing other people. Other differences mentioned across our interviews included the lower levels of pressure and stress associated with volunteering. At the same time, some aspects of volunteering were favourably compared with work. These included having specific tasks that could be achieved through their volunteering, thereby instilling a sense of usefulness and purpose.

Quality of commitment was one area where interviewees noticeably differed in how they talked about the comparison between volunteering and work, and the expectations associated with each. For some, volunteering had become too much 'like work' in terms of the demands it was placing on them; particularly so where it had ceased to be a discrete or bounded activity within the temporal structure of the retirees week and instead, in the words of the next interviewee, had become "all-encompassing":

> 'Sometimes the museum definitely feels like work. The volunteering I do in [other place], it's for a set period of time and I know that I go every Wednesday and when I'm not there I don't think about it. Whereas the museum here is all-encompassing, really, in the sense that I do try not to be sitting at my computer all day every day. So I make a point of trying to do some work in the garden and also just reading the paper and emailing my friends and those sorts of things.' (Female, 70s, TM)

In this way, volunteering had started to become a burden, taking time away from other pleasurable activities and impacting on personal relationships with friends and family. As another interviewee similarly described:

Interviewer: Sometimes you can end up talking about these things as if it's is your job?

Respondent: Yes, well, I'm sure my husband thinks that and yes, sometimes I feel thoroughly guilty and I beat myself up about it and then I think, well, hang on a minute, I'm a volunteer, I'm doing my best and I want to help people as much as I can, but sometimes I'm going to have to say, "No, I'm sorry, I can't do that." (Female, 70s, U3A)

The work-like nature of volunteering was particularly evident in an organisation such as the town museum, which is reliant on a volunteer committee of individuals who undertake the administrative and statutory requirements of running the museum – including managing a larger pool of volunteers. This two-tiered system allowed other individuals to 'just' be a volunteer (see McAllum 2018), an identity they perceived as desirable without any of the additional demands and professionalism associated with committee roles: "I'm just someone who turns up to do a shift at the museum as part of the rota that's drawn up" (Female, 60s, TM).

The museum was formerly run by the local authority but had been threatened with closure, as the impacts of austerity since the global financial crisis of 2008 have forced branches of local government to seek to divest themselves of such financially unprofitable assets. This speaks to wider neoliberal trends involving the devolution of direct service provision in areas of health, welfare and education to non-profit organisations. Such shifts in responsibility are argued to have contributed towards the blurring of boundaries between non-profit, government and corporate sectors (Baines 2010). A consequence of this has been the increasing encroachment of discourses of professionalism 'as an operational discipline or a series of behavioural prescriptions' into volunteer roles and identities (Ganesh and McAllum 2012: 155), where organisational expectations of volunteer practices are often based on specific work norms such as efficiency, fairness or promptness (McAllum 2018).

The desirability of this trajectory for volunteers is subject to debate. On the one hand, it can provide opportunities for training and sector-specific knowledge acquisition, as well as volunteers potentially wielding more power and responsibility for their actions. At the same time, studies have documented volunteers' dissatisfaction with rigid organisational practices, bureaucracy and unreasonable tasks that make volunteering 'better organized but too much like paid work' with negative consequences for volunteer retention (Paine et al 2010: 101). Within our study this was not necessarily a topic directly engaged with by many of our interviewees, although references – as in previous quotations – to increasing and largely undesirable bureaucratic and administrative burdens were fairly common. However, for one interviewee professionalism and voluntarism were discussed and reconciled as compatible social systems (McAllum 2018), particularly in terms of commitment that volunteering was perceived to entail:

Respondent: And as a volunteer it's the same as working. You give a commitment and if you give the commitment, you're expected— if you say I am going to do one day a week or one day a month or whatever, you're expected to do that in the same way as when you turn up for work at nine o'clock. And therefore, that's how you should treat it. On the other hand there are occasions— you know, you're talking to people in my sort of age group and, you know, you do have family issues, you do have medical issues and so on. But you know there's no point in saying, okay, I'll give you a day a week and then don't even tell them you're not coming in. So, it's a commitment.

Interviewer: And there's a certain level of professionalism it sounds like from what you're saying?

Respondent: Indeed, there is a big level of professionalism and it's probably trite to say it but the more you put in, the more you get out. But you have to look after yourself.

(Male, 70s, NBGW)

Here there was a clear sense that volunteering was not something to be taken on lightly in the retirement transition; rather it should be understood as a serious undertaking requiring a realistic assessment of one's ability to commit time and energy in relation to the myriad other demands and relationships associated with complex older lives.

Conclusion

Retirement, as one of our interviewees described it, is "a phase in your development … it's the opportunity to do things that I haven't had the chance to do". Retirement, for those in possession of the necessary resources, can be a time in life to explore different ways of being and relating in the world away from the structures and identities associated with working life, including engaging in voluntary forms of participation. On the other hand, volunteering in the retirement transition can also provide a sense of continuation and continuity between different phases of the lifecourse by allowing the skills, experience and knowledge acquired through working lives (here recognising both paid and domestic labour) to be applied in different institutional contexts.

Decisions about when and how to retire are not made in isolation and this chapter has therefore sought to draw attention to the relational elements of this process, foregrounding notions of linked lives as well as drawing attention to the often more hesitant, partial and non-linear nature of some transitions (Hörschelmann 2011). This includes recognising how the desire and the choice to volunteer may be constrained and even overridden by lives and their associated demands. As a volunteer organiser at NBGW related:

> 'I've been doing this for three years and literally we've had probably about 150 volunteers that have gone through. Some of them obviously change because they're my age group and sometimes older. They've got grandchildren. They've got elderly parents sometimes or they've got sick husbands. So we have lost quite a few people. Not that

they've not wanted to be here, but they've had other things that have happened in their lives.' (Female, 60s, NBGW)

Given the complex and differentiated lives of many older people, it would seemingly be advisable for voluntary organisations to offer a degree of flexibility in their working practices in order to better accommodate and to retain the volunteers upon whom they are often heavily reliant. However, such organisational flexibility may be incompatible with drives towards professionalism and professionalisation witnessed within the voluntary sector, often hedged around required legal frameworks and codes of conduct. This presents a tension that requires further research and policy consideration.

Finally, it is worth noting that the experiences related by our interviewees were spatially contingent; shaped in part by the rural environment and communities of mid-Wales in which some were long-term residents and other more recent in-migrants. At the same time, these experiences are also temporally contingent (Skinner et al 2014) and facilitated in part by the generous pension provision enjoyed by this particular generation of recent retirees that has allowed many the choice of taking early or partial retirement. The experience of retirement transition is likely to be very different for future generations of older people, with this uncertainty recognised by our interviewees:

'We're a golden generation because we've had everything on a plate really, we had the best of the National Health, we had the best in terms of pensions ... but my children, for example, I don't know what it will be like when they retire. Will they have to take on part-time jobs to earn money to keep them going?' (Male, 60s, TM).

Notes

[1] This includes attention to the challenges (and opportunities) faced by older adults living in rural environments and communities (Joseph and Cloutier-Fisher 2005; Chalmers and Joseph 2006; Jones and Heley 2016).

[2] For some, this was a continuation of volunteering they had done throughout their lives, both formally and informally, and whether continuously or intermittently around other lifecourse events such as having children. For others, volunteering was a response to the time freed up by retirement and not something they had previously participated in. In this way, we recognise the threefold typology of lifelong, serial and trigger volunteers developed by Davis Smith and Gay (2005) and are mindful of the ways in which an individual's volunteering history can impact their experience of

retirement transition. However, this is an aspect we choose not to examine further in this chapter.

References

Anderson, K. and Smith, S. (2001) 'Editorial: emotional geographies', *Transactions of the Institute of British Ge-ographers*, 26(1): 7–10.

Baines, D. (2010) 'Neoliberal restructuring, activism/participation, and social unionism in the nonprofit social services', *Nonprofit and Voluntary Sector Quarterly*, 39(1): 10–28.

Banks, J. and Smith, S. (2006) 'Retirement in the UK', *Oxford Review of Economic Policy*, 22(1): 40–56.

Bernard, M., Rickett, M., Amigoni, D., Munro, L., Murray, M. and Rezzano, J. (2014) 'Ages and stages: the place of theatre in the lives of older people', *Ageing & Society*, 35(6): 1–27.

Blaikie, A. (1992) 'Whither the third age? Implications for gerontology', *Generations Review*, 2(1): 2–4.

Chalmers, A.I. and Joseph, A.E. (2006) 'Rural change and the production of otherness: the elderly in New Zealand', in P. Cloke, T. Marsden and P. Mooney (eds) *Handbook of Rural Studies*, London: Sage, pp 388–400.

Davis Smith, J. (1998) *The 1997 National Survey of Volunteering*, London: Institute for Volunteering Research.

Davis Smith, J. and Gay, P. (2005) *Active Ageing in Active Communities: Volunteering and the Transition to Retirement*, Bristol: Policy Press.

Elder, G.H. Jr (1994) 'Time, human agency, and social change: perspectives on the life course', *Social Psychology Quarterly*, 57(1): 4–15.

Elder, G.H. Jr (1995) 'The life course paradigm: social change and individual development', in P. Moen, G.H. Elder Jr and K. Lüscher (eds) *Examining Lives in Context*, Washington, DC: American Psychological Association, pp 101–39.

Foster, L. (2018) 'Active ageing, pensions and retirement in the UK', *Journal of Population Ageing*, 11(2): 117–32.

Ganesh, S. and McAllum, K. (2012) 'Volunteering and professionalization: trends in tension?', *Management Communication Quarterly*, 26(1): 152–8.

Guell, C., Shefer, G., Griffin, S. and Ogilvie, D. (2016) '"Keeping your body and mind active": an ethnographic study of aspirations for healthy ageing', *BMJ Open*, 6(1): e009973. Available from: https://bmjopen.bmj.com/content/6/1/e009973.

Hank, K. and Buber, I. (2009) 'Grandparents caring for their grandchildren: findings from the 2004 Survey of Health, Ageing, and Retirement in Europe', *Journal of Family Issues*, 30(1): 53–73.

Hardill, I. and Baines, S. (2009) 'Active citizenship in later life: older volunteers in a deprived community in England', *Professional Geographer*, 61(1): 36–45.

Higgs, P., Mein, G., Ferrie, J., Hyde, M. and Nazroo, J. (2003) 'Pathways to early retirement: structure and agency in decision-making among British civil servants', *Ageing and Society*, 23(6): 761–78.

Hopkins, P. and Pain, R. (2007) 'Geographies of age: thinking relationally', *Area*, 39(3): 287–94.

Hörschelmann, K. (2011) 'Theorizing life transitions: geographical perspectives', *Area*, 43(4): 378–83.

Hustinx, L., Cnaan, R.A. and Handy, F. (2010) 'Navigating theories of volunteering: a hybrid map for a complex phenomenon', *Journal for the Theory of Social Behaviour*, 40(4): 410–34.

Jarvis, H. (2005) 'Moving to London time: household co-ordination and the infrastructure of everyday life', *Time and Society*, 14(1): 133–54.

Jones, M. (2009) 'Phase space: geography, relational thinking, and beyond', *Progress in Human Geography,* 33(4): 487–506.

Jones, L. and Heley, J. (2016) 'Practices of participation and voluntarism among older people in rural Wales: choice, obligation and constraints to active ageing', *Sociologia Ruralis*, 56(2): 176–96.

Joseph, A.E. and Cloutier-Fisher, D. (2005) 'Ageing in rural communities: vulnerable people in vulnerable places', in G.J. Andrews and D.R. Phillips (eds) *Ageing and Place: Perspectives, Policy, Practice*, Abingdon: Routledge, pp 133–46.

Katz, C. and Monk, J. (eds) (1993) *Full Circles: Geographies of Women over the Life Course*, London: Routledge.

Kojola, E. and Moen, P. (2016) 'No more lock-step retirement: boomers' shifting meanings of work and retirement', *Journal of Aging Studies*, 36: 59–70.

Laliberte Rudman, D. (2015) 'Embodying positive aging and neoliberal rationality: talking about the aging body within narratives of retirement', *Journal of Aging Studies*, 34: 10–20.

McAllum, K. (2018) 'Volunteers as boundary workers: negotiating tensions between volunteerism and professionalism in nonprofit organizations', *Management Communication Quarterly*, 32(4): 534–64.

McNair, S., Flynn, M., Owen, L., Humphreys, C. and Woodfield, S. (2004) *Changing Work in Later Life: A Study of Job Transitions*, Guildford: University of Surrey, Centre for Research into the Older Workforce. Available from: https://www.researchgate.net/publication/268373251_Changing_Work_in_Later_Life_A_Study_of_Job_Transitions.

Paine, A.E., Ockenden, N. and Stuart, J. (2010) 'Volunteers in hybrid organizations: A marginalized majority?', in D. Billis (ed) *Hybrid Organizations and the Third Sector: Challenges for Practice, Theory and Policy*, Basingstoke: Palgrave Macmillan, pp 93–113.

Phillipson, C. and Smith, A. (2005) 'Extending working life: a review of the research literature', Research Report No. 299, London: Department for Work and Pensions. Available from: https://www.keele.ac.uk/csg/downloads/researchreports/Extending working life.pdf.

Rees Jones, I., Leontowitsch, M. and Higgs, P. (2010) 'The experience of retirement in second modernity: generational habitus among retired senior managers', *Sociology*, 44(1): 103–20.

Schwanen, T., Hardill, I. and Lucas, S. (2012) 'Spatialities of ageing: the co-construction and co-evolution of old age and space', *Geoforum*, 43(6): 1291–5.

Skinner, M.W., Cloutier, D. and Andrews, G.J. (2014) 'Geographies of ageing: progress and possibilities after two decades of change', *Progress in Human Geography*, 39(6): 776–99.

Stewart, E. and Weinstein, R.S. (1997) 'Volunteer Participation in Context: Motivations and Political Efficacy Within Three AIDS Organizations', *American Journal of Community Psychology,* 25(6): 809–37.

Teather, E.K. (ed.) (1999) *Embodied Geographies: Spaces, Bodies and Rites of Passage*, New York: Routledge.

Van Bavel, J. and De Winter, T. (2013) 'Becoming a grandparent and early retirement in Europe', *European Sociological Review*, 29(6): 1295–1308.

Walker, A. (2008) 'Commentary: The emergence and application of active aging in Europe', *Journal of Aging & Social Policy*, 21(1): 75–93.

Whittaker, C.G. and Holland-Smith, D. (2014) 'Exposing the dark side: an exploration of the influence social capital has upon parental sports volunteers', *Sport, Education and Society*, 21(3): 356–73.

Winterton, R. and Warburton, J. (2012) 'Ageing in the bush: the role of rural places in maintaining identity for long term rural residents and retirement migrants in north-east Victoria, Australia', *Journal of Rural Studies*, 28(4): 329–37.

9

Leaving a legacy for civil society

Rhian Powell

Historically, charitable bequest giving has been perceived as an act performed only by the wealthiest in society. In recent years, however, charitable organisations have become more aware of the fundraising potential of legacy gifts from 'ordinary' people (Remember a Charity 2019). This has led to an increase in the advertising of legacy bequests and the benefits of these gifts, no matter how small, to charitable organisations. To reflect its increased emphasis, the number of charitable bequests gifted per year has been slowly increasing. The legacy monitoring company Smee & Ford (2019) report that prior to 2012 charitable bequests were lower than 6 per cent; since then this percentage has been consistently higher than 6 per cent. In 2018, 6.3 per cent of the population left a bequest in a will. Currently, charitable bequests are worth around £3 billion to the sector annually. With many charitable organisations facing funding cuts, the income raised through bequests can be vital for the survival of some charities. Philanthropy, and in particular legacy bequests, are seen as 'a vital income stream for civil society' (HM Government 2018: 74).

Drawing on semi-structured interviews with 22 people willing to discuss their ideas about what they would like to do with their assets after they pass away, this chapter will explore the factors considered by the interviewees when deciding whether or not to leave a legacy gift to charity in their will. Decisions about whether to leave a gift to a charity are complex and multifaceted, involving the consideration of multiple different factors. Deciding how to distribute an inheritance requires the testator to confront and prioritise multiple potentially competing moral, social and political beliefs as they try to decide which members of future generations need and deserve the money most. Existing research has shown that charitable organisations are often perceived as being secondary to the needs of the family (see Wiepking 2012; James 2015; Routley and Sargeant 2015). While this is true to an extent, I argue that the unique circumstances of each family mean that the story is more complex than this.

This chapter will have four parts. The first part will provide an outline of the research project from which the data are drawn. The second will discuss the uncertainties of charitable bequest giving. The third will explore participants' reasons for wanting to leave a legacy bequest, and the final part will discuss reasons given by participants that hinder their desire to leave a legacy bequest. This research shows that decisions to leave a charitable bequest are complex and require the donor to balance several potentially competing obligations – particularly between the family, civil society and the state. When participants think about their inheritance, considerations about these competing institutions are strongly connected and consequently how participants think about one will affect their views on the others. For this reason, it is impossible to only discuss participants' attitudes towards civil society without also considering their attitudes towards family and the state.

Introducing our data

This chapter will draw upon data collected for a research project which explores the social significance of people's inheritance decision-making. The research explores the dilemmas that arise when people think about leaving an inheritance. It is about how testators seek to balance competing rights and obligations between the family, charitable organisations and the state. In Wales, as with the rest of the UK, the inheritance legal system is one of testamentary freedom; this is a non-restrictive system that allows individuals the freedom to decide how they want their assets to be distributed after they have passed away. This system can be contrasted with more restrictive systems, like that of France, where people are required to leave a certain portion of their estate to family. In Wales, there is no obligation to leave money to family members and as a result a person could, in theory, decide to leave their entire estate to charity. In practice, however, this is rare, and leaving a bequest to family is still normal in the UK (Routley and Sergeant 2015). Those who do decide to leave a charitable bequest often leave a smaller amount to charity than they do to their family (Rowlingson and McKay 2005). This voluntaristic system allows for the ways in which people seek to balance potentially competing claims between the family and civil society to be explored.

Data were collected through semi-structured, in-depth interviews with 22 people aged 58 and over who were willing to discuss how they intended to distribute their assets when they pass away. The interviews were all carried out in the homes of participants, located in South

Wales. A more detailed profile of each of the research participants is provided in Table 9.1.

Many of the married participants were interviewed jointly with the intention of witnessing the negotiation process that occurs between couples when they try to decide together how they would like to distribute their assets. The youngest participant in the research was 54, while the oldest were in their 80s. Younger participants were less certain about their decisions and usually had expectations to change them in the future, whereas older participants, or those with terminal illness, spoke with more certainty in their decisions. Participants were intentionally recruited through community organisations, which meant that the sample includes a disproportionate amount of people who have been actively engaged in different forms of civil society throughout their lifetimes. The reason for this decision was because it was anticipated that the dilemmas of balancing different obligations were more likely to be present in the accounts of these people.

The act of writing a will was often prompted by particular lifecourse events. Several participants mentioned they had decided to write their first will following the birth of their first child, others mentioned the writing of the will had been prompted by marriage or divorce. A death in the family or an event which prompted consideration of their mortality was given as a reason for writing a will by a few participants. Mr and Mrs Lewis were due to go on holiday when two planes collided on the runway in Tenerife, killing several hundred people. Although they were not directly involved in the crash the incident made them want to write their first wills – despite only being in their 30s at the time. Although this was one of the more extreme examples, several participants mentioned similar life-changing events that triggered their desire to write a will.

All of the participants interviewed planned to leave a gift in their will to at least one family member. Around one third of the interviewed participants had already included a charitable bequest in their will, a further third intended to leave a charitable bequest in their will but had not yet made provision for the gift. The remaining third had no intention of leaving a charitable bequest.

Uncertain decisions

A gift in a will is distinctive from other forms of lifetime giving because it is planned far in advance of the transaction occurring. As a result of this, participants' decisions about what to do with their assets after they pass away were very rarely concrete. Despite having documented

Table 9.1: Profile of interviewees

Name	Gender	Age	Occupation before retirement	Marital status	Number of children
Ms Driscoll	F	80	Schoolteacher	Single, never married	0
Mr Johnson	M	68	Project manager in the construction industry	Widowed; lives with current partner	0
Mr Roberts	M	74	Demographer	Married	3
Mrs Roberts	F	72	Social worker	Married	3
Mr Lewis	M	72	University lecturer	Married	3
Mrs Lewis	F	77	NHS administrator	Married	3
Mrs Thomas	F	75	Matron at Roman Catholic boarding school	Married	2
Mr Thomas	M	72	Headmaster at Roman Catholic boarding school	Married	2
Mrs Harris	F	67	Teaching English to foreign adults	Married, second marriage	2 (+2)
Mr Harris	M	67	Civil engineer	Married, second marriage	2 (+2)
Mrs Wood	F	68	Adult learning – university	Married	3
Mr Wood	M	71	Government	Married	3
Mr Phillips	M	75	Chemist	Married	3
Mrs Phillips	F	71	Supply Teacher	Married	3
Mr Lloyd	M	58	Freelance consultant to third-sector organisations (not retired)	Married	0
Mrs Evans	F	76	Specialist typist	Married	3
Ms Wright	F	78	Civil servant – job centre	Divorced	3
Mrs Griffiths	F	77	Teacher	Married	3
Mr Griffiths	M	80s	Headteacher	Married	3
Mrs Walker	F	80s	Chemist	Widowed	0
Mrs Davies	F	54	Ran clubs teaching French and Spanish to children; full-time carer for husband	Married	0
Mr Davies	M	72	Sales and marketing director and landlord	Married	0

their wishes in their wills, the majority of the participants mentioned their decisions were still ongoing as their situations, thoughts and relationships continued to change. Decisions were often dynamic, fluid and highly uncertain, as participants continued to negotiate and renegotiate their decisions with themselves and also with the people around them.

Participants regularly mentioned the uncertain nature of death being one of the biggest problems when making their decisions, because they did not know how to plan for something when they did not know when it was going to happen or what their situation would be when they passed away. As Mrs Harris said, "I don't know what my life expectancy is, it's hard you know … I could go out and get run over by a bus tomorrow." This required participants to continuously re-evaluate their relationships with their family, civil society and the state to decide what course of action they would like to take.

The majority of participants had wills which they considered to be out of date, having written them sometimes decades before. What is interesting about this is that often people's intentions did not match up with the realities of what they had included in their wills. Many people felt they had moved on from the point at which they had written their wills and wanted their wills to reflect their new realities. Some of the participants no longer felt affinities to the charities that were included in their wills and wanted to replace certain charities with ones they felt were more reflective of their current situation. Mr Johnson, for example, had written his original will with his wife who has since passed away. After meeting his new partner, Mr Johnson decided to include her in his will. However, he still wanted to keep the same charities that he had chosen with his wife as a way to honour her and the decisions they had made together. This meant, though, that Mr Johnson was no longer able to remember why they had chosen certain charities and acknowledged that his own decisions might be different from the ones he had made a long time ago, "strange decisions … decisions are a funny thing" he laughed. This account was similar for several of the participants, particularly those who had not updated their wills for a long time.

An interesting theme that emerged during the interviews was the conflict that can exist between married couples when they attempt to have both of their, sometimes competing, wishes recognised in their joint wills. There were several examples in the interviews of tensions between marital couples as they tried to convince their partner that the assets should be distributed in a particular way. The next excerpt is from the interview with Mr and Mrs Roberts. Mr Roberts had a very negative opinion of charitable organisations after being an executor of a neighbour's will. As a result of his experience dealing with the neighbour's chosen charities, he decided that he never wanted any of his money to be left to a charitable organisation. His wife, however, had been ill at the time when the dispute between Mr Roberts and the charitable organisations had occurred and consequently he had kept the details of the dispute private from her so as not to cause her additional stress. This meant that she did not have the same negative attitude towards charitable organisations as her husband and would like to leave a gift to a charitable organisation:

Mrs Roberts:	Well, I mean, I think I would like to just leave them a sum, not a lot of course.
Mr Roberts:	Well, you haven't done.
Mrs Roberts:	No, I haven't done, but you keep saying we have to rewrite our wills.
Mr Roberts:	I'm quite happy with the way our wills are at the moment.
Mrs Roberts:	Well, I would probably trust you, I'd just tell you I want to leave this …
Mr Roberts:	I mean, you know, if you really want to leave to charities in your will then you're going to have to change your will.
Mrs Roberts:	I know … I could write a letter.
Mr Roberts:	But that's not a will. If you wrote a letter saying you'd like me to do this, I'd simply ignore it.
Mrs Roberts:	No, you wouldn't.
Mr Roberts:	I'd be legally entitled to.
Mrs Roberts:	But you wouldn't.
Mr Roberts:	Of course I would.
Mrs Roberts:	No, you wouldn't.

This conversation shows that the decision-making process is rarely straightforward and can involve many complex negotiations between different actors. When participants had conflicting views about who they would like to inherit, the order in which they would pass away became very important for the outcome. Several participants, particularly those with terminal illnesses which meant they were likely to pass away first, were aware of how their partner would not have to follow their wishes once they had passed away. The presence of a terminal illness meant these participants felt they were lacking agency when it came to their inheritance decisions. They could make suggestions about what they would like to happen but whether or not their wishes would be respected was up to their partner. This becomes even more problematic in complex or blended families, particularly where there are remarriages and stepchildren. Controlling where the money goes becomes much harder to achieve. As the data presented earlier have demonstrated, the need to make decisions jointly meant there were several instances where participants were unable to reach agreement on their conflicting ideas. Inability to reach an agreement almost always resulted in the wills not being changed.

Participants' ambivalence towards their inheritance planning was another prominent theme throughout this research. The following sections will discuss the reasons people gave for wanting and not wanting to leave a legacy for civil society. It is important to note that very few of the participants held concrete views and were often in two minds about leaving a charitable bequest. Participants who planned to leave a charitable bequest gave reasons that made them hesitate in making their decision and some participants who had no intentions of leaving a bequest gave reasons as to why they would consider leaving a bequest.

Reasons for leaving a charitable bequest

"Making a difference" and "doing good"

Respondents mentioned they wanted to leave a charitable bequest to make a difference to the world. Often when people leave a bequest in their will, the value of the gift is much larger than they would usually give in a monthly donation. Respondents felt this was an important reason as to why they wanted to give in their wills, rather than just giving during their lifetimes. A larger sum of money, they felt, could enable them to contribute towards something that could make a real difference.

When discussing why they had chosen the particular charities, the participants spoke about how it was very important to give money to an organisation they felt could use their money to make a difference. For money to make a difference, participants wanted the money to be allocated for a specific purpose rather than being lost in the everyday expenses of the charity. As Mr Johnson explained when talking about his charitable choices, which were all small/medium-sized charities:

> 'Two of those are local charities … The only worry I've got with some of these you see is that it's like throwing a stone

into a pond almost ... there are some ripples but after about ten seconds its disappeared and some of the big charities just mop up money like there's no tomorrow.'

Participants felt their gift was more likely to be visible and meaningful if it was given to charity that did not receive as much funding from other sources. This often meant that they preferred smaller charities, local charities and charities they felt would spend their money wisely. As Mrs Davies explained: "I think we would both rather leave it to local charities, small and maybe local, where you know the money is being spent and you know they haven't got loads of officials and staff members, big offices and so on."

It was important to participants that they chose charities they felt would use their money for good. Mrs Davies mentioned that it was important to her that her money was used to "do good". She explained: "I think you just want to try to do as much good with it as you possibly can, so you help people on their way really." Her husband, Mr Davies, agreed with his wife, stating later in the interview that, "It would be a dereliction of duty not to put [our money] to a place where it could go to good use." Mr and Mrs Davies were undecided on which charities they would like to leave a bequest to. Like Mr Johnson, they didn't have any children, which meant that leaving a gift to a charitable organisation was a more important consideration for them.

When explaining why they had chosen particular charities, many of the participants focused on the good the charity did and how giving to that charity could help to make the world a better place. Examples of this are:

> 'There are so many charities and they do so much good stuff. The Marine Conservation Society I feel very strongly about because they affect the whole world.' (Mrs Roberts)

> 'We are curing cancer, we are getting success rates, yes, but certain kinds of cancer, the more standard ones. A lot of the other ones are still at high levels.' (Mr Johnson)

> 'It's absolutely brilliant. It's touched so many people's lives, it really is brilliant. When they go out on those bikes than they're the same as everybody else.' (Mrs Wood)

Titmuss's (1970) study on the gift relationship can be useful for making sense of this data. The central premise of Titmuss's (1970) work *The Gift*

Relationship: From Human Blood to Social Policy is that blood donors give blood because of an altruistic motivation to help others. This is at odds with anthropological theories of gift giving which tend to portray gifts as being based on self-interest and reciprocity (Malinowski 1922; Mauss 1990).Titmuss argues the unique circumstances of blood donation, that recipients are unknown to one another, means they are unable to respond to the social expectation of reciprocation but they are willing to give blood regardless, out of an altruistic desire to help others.

Life events, personal experiences and passions

For Routley and Sargeant (2015) the reasons people had for selecting particular charities were because they 'connected to significant life events, personal experiences and passions' (2015: 876). According to Routley and Sargeant (2015), wills are therefore a way for many participants to capture what they feel are the important aspects of their life and also to make a statement about how they would like to be remembered after they have passed away. These reasons for wanting to leave a charitable bequest are echoed in this research. This section will explore the presence of these themes in this research but will also add a fourth reason which is that of circumstance – the point in time a person made their will had a significant impact on the person's decision-making.

Mrs Walker does not have any children and her husband passed away several years ago. She intended to split her money between her niece and two charities – St Fagan's National Museum of Wales and a patchwork society based in North Wales. Mrs Walker spoke extensively about her family's relationship with St Fagan's National Museum and how it was therefore important for her to leave money to them in her will. She shared happy memories about attending the museum as a child with her family:

> 'My father used to bring us up in the car from Swansea, I should say at least once a year. We used to love coming, we used to buy loaves and Mother used to cut the loaves … they also sold butter and a very delicious Caerphilly blue cheese and we used to adore this stuff. Dad and Mum used to have a beer and we'd have a cold drink of some sort or another and we used to love that.'

She also explained that her aunt, with whom she had a close relationship, had planned to leave *all* her money to St Fagan's Museum of Wales. However, as Mrs Walker and her brother had cared for their aunt in her old age, they asked her to include them in the will so she would leave one third of her estate to each. Mrs Walker felt that because of this, leaving some of her own money to St Fagan's Museum was the right thing to do. After explaining the connections St Fagan's Museum had to her family, Mrs Walker said: "The other, the patchwork group, well, that's *my* interest." When explaining this, Mrs Walker put a great deal of emphasis on the word 'my'. Mrs Walker's account demonstrates two of Routley and Sargeant's reasons for leaving a charitable bequest – personal experiences and passions. Her account shows how people might use their charitable bequests as a way of balancing their competing obligations towards their families and themselves. By including both, and giving equal amounts of money to each, Mrs Walker was making a statement about what is important to her and how she used her will as a way of saying thank you to things that were important to her throughout her life.

Many of the participants interviewed selected charities that were important to their families in some way. Mr Harris planned to leave a small cash amount to a charity in his will; however, he was torn between deciding on the charitable organisation that had supported his brother or the charitable organisation that was currently supporting him. He only planned to leave the money to one charity. He explained: "My brother died of motor-neurone disease, so I spent 25 years working with sufferers of that. Now I have Parkinson's, so my loyalties are split. But either of those would be good. Cancer won't get much I'm afraid, or animal charities." Although Mr Harris was unsure whether he wanted to give to a charity that had supported his brother or one that had supported him, he was quick to discount "cancer" and "animal charities", which he had no personal connection to. Having a personal connection to the charities made it easier for many of the participants to justify their decision to themselves as well as their families.

For many of the participants, the decision to leave a charitable bequest was situational. That is, the point in their lives at which they wrote their will influenced what charities and family members were included in their wills. These autobiographical factors are important because so many of the participants had written their wills many years ago and had not updated them since. Many of the participants were aware that if they rewrote their wills now, their charitable choices would be different. We have already seen an example of this earlier, when Mr Johnson explained that his decisions were "strange decisions ... decisions are a funny thing". The circumstantial nature of the decision-making can also be seen in a conversation between Mr and Mrs Wood:

Mrs Wood:	Well, I was very ill about 20 years ago with an autoimmune disease called Lupus. I'm quite well at the moment.
Mr Wood:	At the time you were involved in …
Mrs Wood:	Oh, yes! I worked for Lupus South Wales. Trying to raise funds for Lupus. I just thought it's really nice to put some money into research because little is known about it really.
Mr Wood:	But you don't do that anymore …
Mrs Wood:	No.
Mr Wood:	Well, perhaps that's another reason for revisiting the will.

This account shows that different charities can be important to people at different stages of their lives. The participants might have been involved with many different charities during their lifetimes; however, the charities that made it into the will were the charities that person was involved with at the point of writing the will. This suggests there is an element of chance in the way people determine which charity to leave a charitable bequest to. This idea of chance can be seen when Mrs Lewis explained: "I could have given it to the Eve charity, which is about cancer. There are loads of other things I could have given it to but, erm … I just happened to land on those."

The number of available charities means that participants often need to adopt ways of deciding which charities they should leave a charitable bequest to. The data presented here suggest that people often use their emotional attachment to a charity to decide whether they would like to leave the charity a bequest. The emotive reasons the participants in this research had for selecting their chosen charities are: wanting to make a difference; having a personal connection to the charity; and circumstances. This emotional attachment was expressed clearly in an interview with Ms Driscoll, who, when asked why she wanted to leave a bequest to her chosen charities but not to other charities she supported, explained: "Well, I just emotionally don't feel like doing it. I mean, I don't think I have a specific reason, it's just a feeling which I suppose is based on some things."

Reasons for *not* leaving a charitable bequest

Family comes first

Although there are no restrictions in UK inheritance law stipulating that inheritance *must* be left to family, it remains a firmly rooted social norm and consequently the largest barrier to charitable bequest giving is the family (Wiepking et al 2012). This idea that family acts as a barrier to charitable giving is popular among third-sector research into legacy giving (Wiepking 2012; James 2015; Routley and Sargeant 2015). According to Wade-Benzoni, the discrepancy between gifting to charity and gifting to family shows that people tend to 'demonstrate more altruism towards future generations than towards needy contemporaries' (2006: 247). As James, explains the idea that 'family comes first' actualises into 'family comes first and only' (2015: 75).

This idea that family should come first was reflected in the attitudes of the participants. *All* participants, including those who are childless, wanted to leave most of the assets to their family. None of the participants planned to leave all of their inheritance to charitable causes. Ideas of who counts as family, for inheritance purposes, were consistent with those in Finch and Mason's (2000: 30) study of inheritance and family relationships. Participants mostly adopted a narrow definition of family which included spouses and children. In a few cases this also extended to grandchildren. Participants without children were required to be more creative about who they counted as family. This often required them to branch out to nieces and nephews, cousins and second cousins.

When explaining why they wanted to leave all or most of their money to their family rather than leaving a bequest to a charitable organisation, many of the participants mentioned they felt that leaving money to family was the "right thing to do" because they had made the decision to have children and so ensuring their children were looked after was seen as being their responsibility. As Mrs Griffiths stated: "when you die, the wealth cascades down through the generations and I think whatever money is there ... you've always used your money to support your family and if it's enough to support the family further then I think it should be left to the family first". As with all of the participants who had children of their own, Mrs Griffiths and Mr Griffiths had adult children. This suggests that despite the age of the children, the parents still felt they had an obligation towards them. Ms Wright was also of the view that her children should receive the inheritance money rather than a charitable organisation because as she stated: "I feel that in my case rather than give to an outside charity, my charity begins at home." One of Ms Wright's three daughters had cerebral palsy and it was therefore very important to Ms Wright to ensure that her daughter had enough money throughout her lifetime to meet all her needs. Ms Wright spoke passionately throughout the interview about how it was very important for her that her family never went without. She had lived very frugally to make sure that her children and grandchildren lived as comfortably as possible. It was therefore very important to Ms Wright that her money passed to family rather than to any outside sources.

Four male participants, who were planning to leave money to family, recognised that their children no longer needed their financial support and stated they would be happy for *all* the money to go to charity. However their wives would not allow for that to happen. This conflict over different ideas can be seen in this excerpt from the conversation between Mr Thomas and Mrs Thomas:

Mr Thomas: You could give it all to the dogs ... I mean it is actually a very questionable assumption of our sort of people but it's not one that we're going to question. It's very questionable, our kids have already had a fair number of benefits from being our kids and we intend to perpetuate that ... it's totally immoral.

Mrs Thomas: It's not that we are not willing to gift something to one or two charities or something like this, I'm sure we will, but the main thing will go to our children.

Mr Thomas: It is a bit, it's a level which is ridiculous. I mean [daughter] and [son-in-law] don't need it now, but they'll get it.

Mr and Mrs Thomas explained that they have been putting off rewriting their out-of-date wills because they did not trust their son, who currently lives with them and suffers from severe mental illness, to spend the money they left him wisely. They were already concerned about the relationship between their son and daughter and were very aware of the potential for their money to perpetuate this conflict. Due to the potential their money had to perpetuate family conflicts, they spoke about their decision as if it was burdensome. Mr Thomas repeatedly mentioned the idea of leaving all the money to various charities throughout the interview; however, each time he did Mrs Thomas would make it clear that she wanted to leave most of the money to their children. This conflict suggests that decisions about leaving inheritance to family aren't as straightforward as they originally seem and the norm of giving to family is questioned by several of the participants, although this didn't alter any of their ways of doing things.

In their research on what inheritance practices can tell us about complex family relationships, Finch and Mason (2000: 30) found that in families where there had been divorce and remarriage, people would try to ensure that money did not 'pass out of the family'. For many people this meant bequeathing to blood relatives only. This research, however, suggests the concept of preventing money from 'passing out of the family' can also be extended to bequests to charitable organisations. Several participants commented that money bequeathed to charity was money taken away from family, implying that family have an entitlement to the ownership of assets. When talking about how much they planned to bequeath to their chosen charities, Mr Wood commented: "The other thing is that if you left £10,000 to a charity, each individual child would have effectively lost £3,000 from whatever their inheritance would be." What this tells us is that for Mr Wood, leaving his inheritance to his children is the default position; any other bequests would be a deduction from their amount. Several participants felt it was particularly important to prevent wealth they had inherited from another family member from 'passing out of the family'. This was an important matter for Mr Johnson. Mr Johnson does not have children or any close family and was planning on leaving a large portion of his estate to charities. Mr Johnson, however, felt that at least some of his money should go to his deceased wife's family because he had inherited some of this money from other family members and this was a fair thing to do. He explained:

> 'We thought, yes, give them some because there should be some— because some of it is inherited wealth, it is from … well, my parents died a long time ago but some of it was mine, but then some of it came from [wife's] parents because she was an only child as well, so it's kind of through the family side, so we didn't want to chuck it all away.'

Keeping money in the family was seen as the normal course that inherited money should take, whereas money passed outside of the family was seen as being "chucked away".

"I've done enough in my lifetime"

For some participants death was the wrong stage of the lifecourse for charitable giving to occur. The participants who felt this way were people who had been more actively engaged in civil society throughout their lives: they either volunteered their time to charitable organisations or worked in the third sector. For these few participants, giving to charity was seen as something that should only be done when you are alive and anything that was left when you passed away should be transferred to family. Mrs Walker had worked as a scientific researcher for a charitable organisation for many years, she said: "No, I think I have worked for the benefit of the community for most of my life, most of my working life so I see no reason to support any charity that has a social aspect, you know, like the hospital or what have you." Mrs Wood also supported this view:

> 'I feel, I've always … I give regularly to certain charities and I do a lot of informal charity work, not a lot, but I do as much as I can and, yeah, I think, well, it's up to your children to decide what to do with it. Leave it to your children rather than a cat's home, it's as simple as that. As far as I'm concerned it belongs to my children and then their children.'

Mr and Mrs Wood were firmly of the view that charitable giving was something that you should only do during your lifetime and family should take priority when you passed away. They believed, however, that they had passed on the correct charitable values to their children which meant their children would continue their legacy of charitable giving. For them, ensuring they had passed on these values to their children was more important than leaving a charitable bequest in their will.

Trust and control

A reason given by many participants about why they were concerned to leave a charitable gift was that they were unable to control how the money would be spent after they had passed away. It was therefore very important for participants that they were able to trust the charitable organisation they were leaving a bequest to. This was mentioned by participants who weren't planning to leave a charitable bequest as well as those who were. Consistently with other research into charitable bequests (Sargeant et al 2006; Pharoah and Harrow 2009; Routley 2011; Routley and Sargeant 2015), trust in the charitable organisation was regularly mentioned as a reason why they had chosen that particular organisation over other similar organisations. As Ms Driscoll said: "It's trouble enough to control things while you're here, you certainly can't control anything when you're not here." It was very important for Ms Driscoll that her money was spent in a way that she intended it to be and consequently she had put conditions on several of her charitable gifts to ensure this. Ms Driscoll wanted to leave money to the Alzheimer's Society and Cancer Research UK; however, she only wanted the money to be spent on research and not "on things other than research". She explained: "I'm not saying these things are not valuable, but they don't appeal to me, should I say, and it is my money …". Most of the other participants leaving charitable bequests had decided against putting conditions on their gifts because they had chosen charities that they hoped would spend the money wisely. As Mr Harris explained: "If you like the charity, they're going to spend it wisely aren't they, or you think they are. So, I wouldn't stipulate what they need to spend it on." This was despite his view that the "big dogs at the top get too much in salary".

Concerns about how their money would be spent by the charitable organisation was a primary reason for many of the participants not wanting to leave a charitable bequest. Many of the comments made by participants about inefficient spending by charities were unprompted. Examples of this are:

> 'You do hear about charities mishandling money, everyone's got stories about charities mishandling money. You'd hope most of it would go to the charity and they wouldn't take half of it in unnecessary fees.' (Mrs Harris)

> 'If they're going to handle the money, I don't want it handled by a fool. I want somebody who will look after it, invest it wisely and do the right thing … they should be paid a salary but there are limits.' (Mr Davies)

Mostly decisions about whether a charity spent their money "wisely" were based on how frequently they were contacted by a charity and whether there had been any media attention relating to the charities' spending practices. As Ms Wright explained when discussing her decision to not leave a legacy gift to a charitable organisation:

> '[T]hey were ringing me asking me to up my subscription and again I stopped it in the end; they won't allow me to give what I was prepared to give. They really are quite intrusive and aggressive in raising funds. It puts me right off. All these foreign water aids, you've got all these corrupt governments. I even feel suspicious of the doctors who go out and do the

cataract ops; I give reluctantly but it has to be prised out of me … I end up getting a whole raft of things asking to leave money. I just ignore them. It does annoy me. What annoys me is they'll send you half a dozen Christmas cards, why don't they save that money? Save the postage? I mean I had through the post once an umbrella … an umbrella!'

Similarly, participants spoke highly of charities that didn't send them large amounts of correspondence and used that as a reason for wanting to leave that charity a bequest. When explaining why she would like to leave a charitable bequest to one charity, Mrs Roberts commented:

'[T]hey never pester either. They send you a report twice a year. They never ever go on and they're just an amazing, amazing charity in my opinion, they have such a specific target. You know they spend a very small proportion on admin and fundraising, it all goes towards what they're trying to do.'

Conclusion

This chapter has shown how people consider their relationship with charities when planning their inheritance. In the same way that will-writing can be triggered by certain lifecourse events, lifecourse events can impact how a person chooses to distribute their assets. Whether or not certain lifecourse events occur will affect how they write their will. The data presented in this chapter show the complex relationship that exists between families and charities, and how a participant thinks about one will affect their thinking about the other. Although most participants saw family as being in tension with charities, some of the participants saw family as being positioned within civil society (Power et al 2018). As Ms Wright explained: "I feel that in my case rather than give to an outside charity, my charity begins at home."

References

Finch, J. and Mason, J. (2000) *Passing On: Kinship and Inheritance in England*, Abingdon: Routledge.

HM Government (2018) *Civil Society Strategy: Building a Future That Works For Everyone*, London: Cabinet Office. Available from: https://www.gov.uk/government/publications/civil-society-strategy-building-a-future-that-works-for-everyone.

James, R.N. III (2015) 'The family tribute in charitable bequest giving: an experimental test of the effect of reminders on giving intentions', *Nonprofit Management and Leadership*, 26(1): 73–89.

Malinowski, B. (1922) *Argonauts of the western Pacific: an account of native enterprise and adventure in the archipelagoes of Melanesian New Guinea*, London: G. Routledge & Sons.

Mauss, M. (1990) *The Gift: The Form and reason for exchange in archaic societies*, London and New York: Routledge.

Pharoah, C. and Harrow, J. (2009) 'Charitable legacies in an environment of change', *The Smith Institute*. Available from: http://smith-institute. org.uk/book/charitable-legacies-in-an-environment-of-change/.

Power, S., Muddiman, E., Moles, K. and Taylor, C. (2018) 'Civil society: bringing the family back in', *Journal of Civil Society*, 14(3): 193–206.

Remember a Charity (2019) *Strategic Priorities 2019–2021*, London: Remember a Charity. Available from: https://cdn. rememberacharity.org.uk/app/uploads/2013/12/Remember-A-Charity-Strategic-Report-2019.pdf.

Routley, C. (2011) 'Leaving a charitable legacy: social influence, the self and symbolic immortality', PhD thesis, Bristol Business School, University of the West of England.

Routley, C. and Sargeant, A. (2015) 'Leaving a bequest: living on through charitable gifts', *Nonprofit and Voluntary Sector Quarterly*, 44(5): 869–85.

Rowlingson, K. and McKay, S. (2005) *Attitudes to Inheritance in Britain*, Bristol: Policy Press.

Sargeant, A., Ford, J. and West, D. (2006) 'Perceptual determinants of nonprofit giving behaviour', *Journal of Business Research*, 59(2): 155–65.

Smee & Ford (2019) 'Legacy Trends', *Wilmington Charities*, June. Available from: https://go.wilmingtonplc.com/Legacy-Trends-Report-2019_Legacy-Trends-2019.html?&utm_source=exacttarget&utm_medium=email&utm_campaign=Legacy+Trends+2019+rep ort+-+gen+prospects.

Titmuss, R. (1970) *The Gift Relationship: From human blood to social policy*, Oxford: Alden & Mowbray Ltd.

Wade-Benzoni, K.A. (2006) 'Legacies, immortality and the future: the psychology of intergenerational altruism', in A. Tenbrunsel (ed) *Ethics in Groups: Research on Managing Groups and Teams, Volume 8*, Bingley: Emerald, pp 247–70.

Wiepking, P., Scaife, W. and McDonald, K. (2012) 'Motives and barriers to bequest giving', *Journal of Consumer Behaviour*, 11(1): 56–66.

10

Civil society through the lifecourse

Sally Power

The chapters in this book have all sought to throw light on how engagement with civil society is associated with different phases and events of the lifecourse. This concluding chapter summarises the principal findings of each chapter, identifies cross-cutting issues and reflects on the merits and challenges of the lifecourse approach. It concludes by briefly considering the implications of these findings for those policy makers and civil society organisations which are concerned to foster civil and political participation.

Principal findings

As noted in Chapter 1, Gilleard and Higgs (2016: 302) identify two approaches within lifecourse sociology – one which focuses on the stratification *of* the lifecourse and that concentrates on different 'stages' and how these produce particular obligations and opportunities, and another that concentrates on stratification *over* the lifecourse and how events and institutions shape biographies. We need, and this book has highlighted the importance of, both approaches if we are to understand changing patterns of civil and political participation. In the first empirical chapter of this book (Chapter 2), Chris Taylor uses longitudinal data from one of the British birth cohort studies (the 1958 National Cohort Development Study) to try to grasp *both* dimensions of the lifecourse approach. His analysis of the changing levels of civic participation within the cohort from the age of 16 until they were 55 years old reveals a complex picture of change and continuity – although, as he acknowledges, the disadvantage of using a single cohort like this is that it is not possible to separate the effects of the lifecourse from wider structural changes over time – a well-known methodological challenge of any longitudinal study of civic participation, particularly as there have been some major changes in civic participation over recent times.

Taylor's analysis shows how different stages of the lifecourse – family formation, child-rearing and employment – have implications for civic engagement as measured in terms of trade union membership, volunteering and voting. However, he also shows how important *prior* civic participation is for later civic participation. In this connection, social class background appears to have an important role in determining initial levels of civic participation over the lifecourse, particularly in terms of formal volunteering. Furthermore, while changes to socio-economic circumstances, such as social mobility, can have an impact, early adult life influences appear to be more important in shaping later civic participation. The role of education and the intergenerational transmission of civic behaviours and attitudes, particularly during childhood, would seem to be an important component of this.

The importance of institutional belonging at different phases of the lifecourse for shaping civic engagement is clearly evident in the following chapters that concentrate on young people – and on how going to school and/or university contributes to civil and political participation. Sally Power's analysis of survey data from nearly 1,000 14-year-old school students (Chapter 3) challenges the largely negative media portrayals of young people as being selfishly, rather than civically, minded. She finds that while levels of associational membership are relatively high, levels of charitable activity and volunteering are extraordinarily high – engaged in by the overwhelming majority of young people and far more frequently than by older people. It is difficult to make age-based comparisons in terms of levels of political participation simply because the young people in the survey are too young to vote. However, a significant minority have undertaken some kind of politically oriented activity, in particular signing petitions for a wide variety of campaigns. Overall, the young people are motivated to get involved in order to improve things and help people, rather than for more instrumental reasons. These data paint a picture of a post-millennial generation that is actively engaged with a strong sense of social responsibility. While this might give policy makers and the voluntary sector reasons to be optimistic about the future of civil society, there are reasons to be doubtful about the potential of some forms of engagement for future civic and political participation. For example, in relation to associative activity, the overwhelming majority of club memberships related to sports – and school sports in particular – which is not a strong predictor of future political participation. Similarly, the high levels of volunteering and charitable activity can be at least partly explained by school-sponsored activities. The 'mainstreaming' of charities in schools and the *requirement* that school students participate in volunteering may act as much as a deterrent as an encouragement for future levels of participation. The young people were deeply ambivalent about the virtues of volunteering and charities – and not entirely convinced that their contributions were of benefit to either themselves or others.

The variable impact of educational institutions on civil and political engagement is evident in the chapter by Ceryn Evans, Esther Muddiman and Chris Taylor (Chapter 4). Drawing on interviews with more than 30 graduates, they explore the extent to which citizens 'graduate' into civil society as a result of their educational and social experiences while at university. The different narratives of those who had studied arts- or science-oriented subjects show that the notion that education straightforwardly leads to the formation of socially liberal attitudes and values and high levels of political and social participation is problematic. The curricula or disciplinary culture of certain university departments seem to be more influential in this regard than others. However, there is evidence that the social networks and friendships developed at university are important for providing spaces for fostering social attitudes and cultivating interest in civic activities. This would appear to transcend the disciplinary distinctions. Of course, it should be noted that in many cases the university 'experience' simply confirms or reinforces prior attitudes. Nevertheless, for some students it is also clear that this period of emergent adulthood is important in leading to divergent trajectories of civic engagement

As Chris Taylor noted in his analysis of longitudinal data (Chapter 2), while there are clear trends across the NCDS cohort over time, the levels of civic engagement fluctuate widely. He concurs that there is little evidence that levels of formal volunteering, for example, are a particularly stable and continuous activity for most participants. Family formation and child-rearing would appear to have an effect. It is these effects that were explored in more detail in Chapters 5, which focuses on parenthood and, again in Chapter 7, which examines the relationship between grandparenthood and civic engagement.

Esther Muddiman's chapter (Chapter 5) throws light on the double-edged nature of family life for civic engagement. It is widely recognised that parenthood reduces the time available to individuals to engage with current affairs or political issues beyond the family home – especially in the initial stages of caring for very young children. However, she shows how particular kinds of civic engagement might be maintained or adapted to accommodate family life, and how parenthood itself might even trigger *new* forms of civic engagement. So, while parenthood might limit some forms of civic engagement, it sparks or prompts others. Drawing on Hogg (2016), Muddiman identifies two patterns of civic engagement among her parent interviewees. For some, civic engagement is a core part of their identity and remains constant throughout their life. For others, engagement is episodic and triggered or halted by particular stages or events in the lifecourse. Parents in the former category gave accounts of long-standing involvement with various civic activities and political movements throughout their youth and prior to becoming a parent. These were activities that they largely maintained after parenthood – and while these parents spoke of the tensions between their civic and their family duties, they often reconciled this through reframing civic activities as family activities. For others, though, parenthood acted as a trigger for civic engagement. These parents had no prior engagement, but having children made them more aware of community issues and local activities concerning their children's welfare. Her interviews also suggest that parenthood can bring about a subtle reorientation towards civil society – a shift in mindset prompted by bringing new life into the world. Parents spoke about experiencing a greater sense of responsibility and described how their attention was drawn to environmental issues, in particular. Shifting attitudes and practices towards environmental issues were not the only change in mindset described by parents. In numerous instances, parents described learning from their children, prompting them to expand their understandings, re-evaluate tacitly held beliefs and reflect on the social changes that had taken place since their own childhood.

The next four chapters all focus on civil and political participation in later life. The complex relationship between growing old and civil participation, in this case volunteering, is underscored by Martijn J.A. Hogerbrugge (Chapter 6) in his detailed analysis of data from England's 'Helping Out' survey. Most research on volunteering has mainly looked at the differences between volunteers and non-volunteers. While this simple distinction does give an indication of the incidence of volunteering and how it varies by age, he argues that it tells only part of the story. It ignores variations in, for example, the number of times and hours people volunteer and their diverse motivations. When these variables are considered, it is clear that older volunteers are far from a homogenous group.

Overall Hogerbrugge's analysis confirms other research on the impact of background characteristics of respondents on volunteering. However, he is also able to reveal that some characteristics, like marital status, education and religious background, have a bearing not only on whether or not someone volunteers, but on the number of times and hours spent volunteering. This indicates that those who volunteer most frequently are not necessarily those who also volunteer for the most hours. Time is mentioned as one of the barriers to volunteering – along with health issues. It is worth noting that among the 50–70-year-olds, one of the most commonly mentioned barriers is the perceived bureaucracy within volunteering organisations. There are also some interesting age-related variations in the type or organisation and nature of volunteering activities. For example, volunteers aged 75 and over are mainly volunteering for organisations the benefit the elderly. Another age-related variation is the proportion of volunteers working for religious organisations; starting from age 60, each successive age group is more likely to have a larger proportion of volunteers working for this type of organisation.

Lifecourse events that are likely to have an impact on the extent to which older people can volunteer are grandparenthood and retirement. The complex interplay between family responsibility, retirement and civic engagement for grandparents is explored by Jennifer May Hampton and Esther Muddiman (Chapter 7) using a combination of panel data from the 'Understanding Society' survey and interview data with grandparents. There are various indications that grandparents are becoming increasingly prominent in the organisation of family life – and particularly when they are 'sandwiched' between generations – providing both childcare for grandchildren and support for ageing parents. They show that levels of civic participation, and especially volunteering, vary according to the grandparent's employment status. It would appear that time pressures are likely to be particularly acute for those grandparents who are still in paid work – although becoming a grandparent may in itself accelerate retirement – especially for grandmothers. In addition to their own engagement in civil society, though, grandparents play an important part in the intergenerational transmission of what might be seen as 'civic virtues'.

Retirement (with or without grandchildren) potentially enables older people to undertake a wide range of civic and political activities. This is explored by Laura Jones, Jesse Heley and Sophie Yarker (Chapter 8), who focus on the relationship between retirement and volunteering through exploring the 'volunteering careers' of retirees who 'work' in a range of different kinds of organisations. Three main themes emerge from their research. First, they reveal that there is an increasingly blurred boundary between work and retirement, with many older people undertaking varying combinations of paid work and unpaid voluntary activity. Second, the decisions about the transition were contingent on a wide range of interrelated factors, such as health, finances and family. Third, their interviewees' experience of volunteering reflected their experiences of paid employment. Jones et al express concern that the increasing professionalisation within civil society is in some cases placing unwanted pressure and burdens onto volunteers.

This brings us to the final empirical chapter (Chapter 9). The anticipation of death – the final stage of the lifecourse – is the motivation for writing wills, the subject of the final chapter. Rhian Powell's interviews with older people show how decisions to leave a charitable bequest are complex and require the donor to balance a number of potentially competing obligations – particularly between the family, civil society and the state. When participants think about their inheritance, considerations about these competing institutions are strongly connected. She finds that the act of writing a will is, in itself, often prompted by particular lifecourse events – such as the birth of a child, or marriage or divorce. Those who were intending to make a charitable bequest in their will were keen to 'make a difference' after their death and tended to identify charities with which they had particular loyalties. However, others were far more ambivalent about the virtues of charities. Somewhat contrary to expectations, some interviewees felt that their own charitable work during their lifetime – either in the form of donations or volunteering – meant that it was time for them to privilege their family after their death.

Reflecting on the lifecourse approach

The extent to which civic engagement is triggered or hampered by stages of the lifecourse (such as going to school or going to university) or lifecourse events and transitions (such as becoming a parent, a grandparent or retirement), and the various ways in which the focus and nature of civil and political participation change as one gets older, shows the usefulness of a lifecourse perspective.

Despite the different sources of data and divergent foci of the chapters in this book, there are some common themes emerging from applying the lifecourse approach. The first of these is **the complexity of the association** between the lifecourse and civic engagement. The chapters certainly demonstrate that a simple division of individuals into those who are civically engaged and those who are not is untenable. It is not only that the intensity of civic engagement varies across the lifecourse – the research reported here also reveals that the nature of activity changes as people grow older. Parents appear to be more engaged with educational and community organisations that support parents and children (Chapter 5). Those in employment are, unsurprisingly, more likely to be members of trade unions (Chapters 2 and 6). Older people are more engaged with voluntary sector organisations that support the elderly (Chapter 6). It is also worth noting that the apparent congruence between the lifecourse stage of the volunteer or donor and the intended beneficiaries of their time and money suggests that the simple conventional classification of 'altruistic' versus 'selfless' motivations for civic engagement is also too simplistic.

The second emerging theme is **the unevenness of engagement**. It is clear from the statistical analyses of longitudinal and cross-sectional data that the level of civil and political participation varies across cohorts (Chapter 6) and within cohorts (Chapters 2, 5 and 6). Variations between individuals will reflect a complex combination of prior experience, disposition, level of resources, constraint and opportunity. Clearly factors such as social class, ethnicity and geography have a bearing here. However, emphasising patterns and demographic factors associated with phases or particular life events is not to underplay the extent to which there are divergent trajectories of civic engagement throughout the lifecourse. The qualitative and survey data indicate that there are some individuals – while at school (Chapter 3), at university (Chapter 4), after parenthood (Chapter 5) and grandparenthood (Chapter 7) – who are far more active in civil society then others. To this extent, Hogg's distinction between two patterns of engagement is useful: those for whom civic engagement is a core part of their identity and remains (relatively) constant throughout their life, and others, for whom engagement is episodic and triggered or halted by particular stages or events in the lifecourse.

A further theme is **the interrelatedness of the lifecourse** with broader social change. At various points, authors in this book have expressed frustration that their data do not enable them to disentangle a lifecourse effect from broader social change. However, it is difficult to see how this could ever be achieved because the lifecourse is embedded within the wider social landscape and is itself shaped by these broader social changes. Thus, delayed entry into employment reflects the raising of the school-leaving age and massification of higher education. Delayed retirement reflects changes in the age at which the state pension can be taken, itself a result of the increased longevity. Changing levels of trade union membership are as much about deindustrialisation as about personal change and labour market entry. Weighing up the relative importance of generational differences, lifecourse imperatives and shifts in the wider society for civic engagement could never be a case of 'either/or'. Nowhere is this clearer than in relation to religious belonging. Hogerbrugge is surely correct in his speculation about the strong association between religious belief and civic engagement among older people. While he acknowledges that the cross-sectional nature of the data he analyses makes it impossible to determine whether this association is due to a cohort or age effect, he speculates that *both* effects are likely to be important. We know from a large number of studies that older generations are more religious than younger generations (Voas 2010). However, it is also likely that individuals become more religious as they get increasingly closer to death and they engage in what is sometimes rather cynically referred to as 'cramming for the finals'.

The extent of the interrelatedness between the individual lifecourse and broader social change is also evident in the claims of those who argue that the division of the lifecourse into distinct phases is no longer viable. For instance, Brückner and Mayer (2005) speculate whether the individualisation of late modernity has made the lifecourse far less standardised than it was hitherto. There is some justification for this criticism in Jones et al's chapter on volunteering in retirement (Chapter 8) which highlights the difficulty of dividing older people into 'employed' and 'retired', the variability of the age at which they retire and the permeability of the boundary between work and non-work in their volunteering. However, other chapters indicate the enduring significance of stratification within the lifecourse – particularly its institutionalised stages (Chapters 3 and 4). Thus, our young people's civic engagement is heavily promoted and channelled by their school, and while our graduates' levels of civic and political engagement appears partly determined by their preschool orientations and experiences, this is not true for all. For some, their time at university marks the start of their civic engagement.

Implications for policy

Finally, it is worth considering what the implications of the findings reported in this book are for those who are keen to foster greater levels of civil and political participation. First, it should be noted the impact of targeted policy levers is likely to be relatively limited. As discussed earlier, the chapters in this book have revealed the way in which the lifecourse phases and events that foster or hinder civic engagement are shaped by broader social, economic and cultural trends over which policy makers have only limited control. It should also be noted that the future of civil society may not be as bleak as some social commentators and academics have predicted. Nevertheless, this does not mean that there are not some steps that might be taken to enhance the conditions that foster civic engagement and reduce the circumstances that hinder civic engagement.

The relationship between civil society and government policy is, of course, contested. Civil society is frequently upheld by politicians in the UK as the 'solution' to a range of problems. For example, in 2010, the then-prime minister, David Cameron, launched the 'Big Society' – an initiative designed to foster 'a new culture of voluntarism, philanthropy and social action' (Cameron 2010). The development of the Big Society would 'depend on the daily decisions of millions of people – on them giving their time, effort, even money to causes around them'. In 2017, in her speech to the Charity Commission, his successor, Theresa May, launched the 'Shared Society' and endorsed the importance of 'our great movement of charities and social enterprises' in 'helping to meet some of the greatest social challenges of our time' (May 2017).

While various voluntary associations appreciate the recognition of their contribution, some commentators (such as Levitas 2012) have argued that this kind of political promotion of civil society is an ideologically and economically driven attempt to reduce public welfare in a climate of 'austerity'. The use of civil society organisations to 'plug the holes' in a diminished welfare system may lead to disillusionment on the part of volunteers and charitable fundraisers and donors.

There is already some evidence of this disillusionment in research presented in this book. For example, it is undeniable that young people's current levels of civil and political engagement appear to be high (Chapter 3). However, their attitudes towards civil society display deep ambivalence. Particularly notable is the dominant perception that charities are 'just big businesses' and that volunteering is 'a way for governments to get people to work for free'. These negative attitudes, and their implications for young people's future civic engagement, may lead one to be cautious about *compelling* young people to volunteer or fundraise for charities while they are at school. Other research (see, for instance, Šerek 2017) has also indicated that the increasing professionalisation of civil society organisations is putting young people off getting involved. It would appear, then, that policy makers need to ensure that voluntary work remains voluntary.

The negative effects of blurring the boundary between work and volunteering are also evident in the chapters that look at the motivations for civic engagement in later life. Concerns about liability and bureaucratic demands appear to act as a disincentive for older potential volunteers (Chapter 6) – although, of course, some of these bureaucratic demands have been put in place in order to safeguard vulnerable individuals from abusive volunteers. And while it is understandable that voluntary organisations want to recruit highly skilled volunteers who can draw on their own work experience, it is also important that volunteers do not just feel that their volunteering is simply a continuation of their working life – something that was expressed by retirees (Chapter 8)

Similarly, those charged with developing policies within charities need to be mindful about the negative implications of the corporatisation of charities. As we saw in Chapter 9, many older people are reluctant to bequeath money to charities because they felt it would simply be absorbed into the organisation. Their lack of confidence in charities may have also been influenced by a range of scandals related to the persistent 'pestering' of the elderly for donations and allegations of sexual misconduct by overseas aid charities. Charities clearly have some work to do to rebuild trust.

In addition to rebuilding trust, the findings of this book show that individuals experience a range of barriers to civic engagement that civil society organisations and policy makers might be able to reduce. The most frequently cited barrier is lack of time (Chapters 5, 7 and 8). It is difficult to see how this can be easily addressed through policy interventions – although some organisations, such as the UK's National Council for Voluntary Organisations (NCVO) are trying to address this through promoting 'family volunteering' that may be helpful for time-pressed parents and grandparents. In addition, policy makers might want to find more ways to reward employers who enable their staff make a civic contribution.

The importance of higher education in fostering civil and political engagement should also be embraced. The research presented here suggests that is it not just going to university that makes a difference, but the kind of subjects that are studied. If, as Evans et al (Chapter 4) argue, disciplinary specialisms in the arts, humanities and social sciences are more likely to foster particular kinds of civic-mindedness, they do have an important role to play in maintaining a vibrant civil society. Perhaps policy makers (at government and university level) might think of creative ways to ensure that the virtues of these disciplines are experienced by those studying STEM subjects – to which universities are becoming increasingly geared. It would indeed be unfortunate if Nussbaum's (2010: 2) prediction comes to pass whereby we 'will soon be producing generations of useful machines, rather than complete citizens who can think for themselves, criticise tradition, and understand the significance of another person's sufferings and achievements'.

References

Brückner, H. and Mayer, K.U. (2005) 'De-standardization of the life course: what it might mean? And if it means anything, whether it actually took place?', *Advances in Life Course Research*, 9: 27–53.

Cameron, D. (2010) 'Transcript of speech by the Prime Minister on the Big Society, 19 July 2010'. Available from: https://www.gov.uk/government/speeches/big-society-speech.

Gilleard, C. and Higgs, P. (2016) 'Connecting life span development with the sociology of the life course: a new direction', *Sociology*, 50(2): 301–15.

Hogg, E. (2016) 'Constant, serial and trigger volunteers: volunteering across the lifecourse and into older age', *Voluntary Sector Review*, 7(2): 169–90.

Levitas, R. (2012) 'The just's umbrella: austerity and the Big Society in Coalition policy and beyond', *Critical Social Policy*, 32(3): 320–42.

May, T. (2017) 'The shared society: Prime Minister's speech at the Charity Commission annual meeting', 9 January. Available from: https://www.gov.uk/government/speeches/the-shared-society-prime-ministers-speech-at-the-charity-commission-annual-meeting.

Nussbaum, M.C. (2010) *Not for Profit: Why Democracy Needs the Humanities*, Princeton, NJ: Princeton University Press.

Šerek, J. (2017) 'What's the matter with civil society? The declining effect of civic involvement on civic identity among Czech adolescents', *Youth and Society*, 49(7): 879–901.

Voas, D. (2010) 'Explaining change over time in religious involvement', in S. Collins-Mayo and P. Dandelion (eds) *Religion and Youth*, Aldershot: Ashgate, pp 25–32.

Index

Note: page numbers in *italic* type refer to figures; those in **bold** type refer to tables.

www.ingramcontent.com/pod-product-compliance
Lightning Source LLC
Chambersburg PA
CBHW070923030426
42336CB00014BA/2518